The
Obama Doctrine

The
Obama Doctrine

Socialism, Corruption and Economic Collapse

Frans Waterlander

ISBN: 978-1463641139

To all freedom- and democracy-loving people of the world

Freedom is never more than one generation away from extinction. We didn't pass it to our children in the bloodstream. It must be fought for, protected, and handed on for them to do the same, or one day we will spend our sunset years telling our children and our children's children what it was once like in the United States where men were free.

\- Ronald Reagan

CONTENTS

4. SPENDING, DEFICITS AND NATIONAL DEBT 79

5. BAILOUT AND STIMULUS – CHOOSING WINNERS AND LOSERS ----------------------------- 117

9. ILLEGAL IMMIGRATION AND OPEN BORDERS 199

10. NATIONAL SECURITY ---------------------------- 209

11. FOREIGN POLICY---------------------------------- 232

Preface

When I was two year old, my country of birth, the Netherlands, was liberated from Hitler's Nazi tyranny. Altogether, hundreds of millions of people in Europe were liberated, thanks in great part to the heroic efforts and sacrifices of the American people. For that I am forever grateful.

After the war, Dutch society became more and more weighted down by an oppressive socialist system, resulting in a stagnant economy, chronically high unemployment and a low standard of living. For the first 34 years of my life, I experienced this Western European-style, post-WWII socialism. Laws, regulations and corruption grew at an alarming rate. The cradle-to-the-grave, womb-to-the-tomb straightjacket mentality of the Welfare State didn't appeal to me at all.

The more I learned about the United States of America, the more it looked like Ronald Reagan's "shining city upon a hill whose beacon light guides freedom-loving people everywhere", a land of promise, freedom and opportunity. After I visited the U.S. in the sixties and seventies, I knew I wanted to live there. While working in the Netherlands as a sales engineer, I was offered a job in California to support European customers. I grabbed the opportunity with both hands and moved my family to the U.S.

This country welcomed us with open arms and offered plenty of opportunities. But over the years I became more and more concerned. At times it seemed that America had lost its way. There were lows and highs, for sure. Carter's lack of leadership was troubling, to say the least. Reagan gave me hope, particularly because he spoke out against the tyranny and threats from the Soviet Union. After all, Soviet missiles in Eastern Germany were only minutes away from my relatives and friends in the Netherlands. Then we got Clinton's debauchery, his finger pointing at "that lady" and making a laughing stock of the American presidency. George W. Bush got mixed reviews from me and an F in terms of keeping our fiscal house in order.

And then there was Obama and all hell broke loose.

He turned the decades-old battle between conservatism and liberalism into a race toward unadulterated socialism and economic collapse. I got really concerned and started to follow the news more closely, researched issues and made notes for myself. My notes about issues and concerns kept growing to the point where they could fill a book, and they did. The title of the book, I'm afraid, speaks for itself.

We need to educate ourselves, decide what kind of a country we want to live in, and speak out. We need to take action. And we need to vote. We just cannot allow this once-great county to continue on the road to damnation. May my writings help to open our eyes, set us in motion, turn this country around and reconstruct our "shining city upon a hill"!

Frans Waterlander, July 2011.

Introduction

Like never before, we face clear choices: conservative principles of individual freedom and prosperity or the Left's radical agenda of ever-increasing power and reach of the government, income redistribution and loss of our freedoms. We need to stop the mad march to destruction, we also need to rebuild our society and undo decades of mismanagement, corruption and decay. And the road to recovery will be difficult and long.

The threats to our wellbeing are varied and numerous, but they all arise from the struggle between the two opposing and mutually exclusive principles of conservatism and liberalism. For clarity's sake, I have divided this book into chapters addressing each of the key issues as I see them. They are not in any particular order, except for chapter 1 and 2, which describe the nature of the battle we are engaged in and the culture of the radical Left.

Chapter 1: The Battle between Conservatism and Liberalism

Our nation is under siege; we are engaged in a battle of historic proportions, a battle between conservatism and liberalism. Each and every day, powerful forces push us farther and farther into the direction of socialism, corruption and economic collapse.

Chapter 2: The Obama Culture

Obama, the most radical and corrupt president ever, has surrounded himself with Liberals, Progressives, Radicals and outright Socialists, at least one Communist and sympathizers with Maoism and Marxism. He pushes through his socialist agenda, using propaganda, scare tactics, empty promises and bribes. He violates our laws and wields absolute power and Congress fails to rein him in. Our democracy is in danger of becoming a lawless dictatorship.

Chapter 3: The Economy

Our economy is being hammered by high unemployment, out-of-control spending, government interference, disastrous energy policies, a lack of affordable energy, an obsession with the environment, devastating health care reform and illegal immigration. A weak recovery may turn into a double-dip recession or even a full-blown depression, but Obama continues his anti-free-market, anti-business policies on the road to economic collapse.

Chapter 4: Spending, Deficits and the National Debt

The Left is spending money we don't have to push through their radical, socialist agenda. Taxpayer money is wasted like there is no tomorrow. Deficits and debt are increasing rapidly to disastrous levels. Serious attempts to rein in our spending are dismissed with contempt. We are heading for economic collapse and burdening future generations with crushing debts.

Chapter 5: Bailouts and Stimulus – Choosing Winners and Losers

Obama made up "The Worst Financial Crisis since the Great Depression" to create an atmosphere of crisis and fear and push through the single biggest waste of taxpayer money in the history of the world: the nearly-trillion-dollar so-called "Stimulus Bill". Winners and losers do not emerge as a result of free-market forces, but are arbitrarily chosen by the Obama Regime.

Chapter 6: Energy

The Left's devastating energy policies choke off the supply of oil, drive up the price of energy and strangle our economy. The thought of having sufficient energy to support our economy and making us independent from foreign energy sources as much and as fast as possible, appears alien to Obama and many others on the Left.

Chapter 7: Obsession with the Environment

Despite ample proof to the contrary, the Left continues the hysterical claim that human activity causes "catastrophic, global warming" or "climate change" and wastes our tax money on unproven and non-competitive so-called "renewable energy." Never mind that science shows that solar activity, planetary interactions and natural processes cause global temperature variations.

Chapter 8: Health Care

Our world-class health care system is under siege. The Left forces ObamaCare down our throats using scare tactics, gross exaggerations of issues with our current system and the number of truly uninsurable people, bribes and a myriad of false claims about the advantages of ObamaCare. Never mind that universal or socialized health care hasn't worked anywhere else it has been tried.

Chapter 9: Illegal Immigration

Illegal border crossings, drug running and crime are rampant at the U.S.-Mexico border, but Washington claims things are under control and largely ignores the issue for political gains. A partial fence doesn't stop illegal activities. State laws to protect American citizens are attacked by the federal government. "Comprehensive immigration reform" aka "amnesty for illegals" is the slogan of the Left.

Chapter 10: National Security

Our security has been diminished greatly. The military is attacked from within. Our intelligence capabilities are diminished. An apologetic and waffling president has damaged our standing in the world. Our enemies no longer fear us. The biggest threats to our security and peace in the world, an Iran with nuclear weapons and radical Islam, are largely ignored. Obama's so-called outreach to the Muslim world has failed miserably.

Chapter 11: Foreign Policy

The foreign policy of the Obama Administration, if it even deserves that title, appears weak, confused and splintered; not a domain of thoughtful diplomacy, born out of clear visions, but a sad state of affairs. We appease dictators and radical Islam and treat our allies with contempt. We no longer lead and stand up for freedom and human rights.

Definition of Terms

Bush: George W. Bush, the 43rd president of the U.S.

Bush 41: George H.W. Bush, the 41st president of the U.S.

Bush 43: George W. Bush, the 43rd president of the U.S.

Democrat: member of the Democrat Party; it used to mean belief in the political and social equality of all people, but over time Democrat means more and more Left, Liberal, Progressive, Radical, Socialist and Statist.

Dictator: a person exercising absolute power.

Left: having radical views in politics.

Liberal: it used to mean favorable to progress or reform, but has been perverted over time to mean radical.

Maoism: adherence to or reverence for Mao and his teachings of guerrilla warfare and Marxist revolution.

Marxism: it defines life as a struggle between social classes, in contrast to a capitalist society where the capitalist minority dominates and exploits the working class majority; it preaches that around the world, the working class must seize power from the capitalists and place the means of production into collective ownership.

National Debt: the total of all federal debt, as reported by the U.S. Treasury Department. The national debt has a "public debt" component and "government debt" component: Often people, including the White House Office of Management and Budget, mislead us by quoting the "public" component only when talking about the national debt. For instance, on May 1, 2011 the national debt stood at almost 14.3 trillion while the "public" component stood at $9.7 trillion.

Obama Regime: I use this term to describe Obama **and** his entourage in his administration and Congress: Obama, his cabinet, his White House staff, his czars, his advisors, and members of Congress who toe the Obama line.

There are many others in the tank for Obama, who religiously support his radical-Left, socialist agenda. To name a few: the radical base of the Democrat party, the far majority of the mainstream media, many labor unions, radical organizations and entertainers.

So what does it mean when I talk about Obama or the Obama Regime? Very often it is difficult or impossible to make a distinction between Obama's own decisions, actions, inactions, policies, etc. and those of who work for him directly, act in his behalf or support his positions and policies. So I often speak in general terms out of necessity, when I refer to Obama and the Obama Regime without making this distinction.

Progressive: it used to mean favorable to progress, change, improvement or reform, but has been perverted over time to mean radical.

Radical: holding extreme political, economic and social convictions.

Republican: member of the Republican Party; it used to mean belief in the conservative principles of freedom, accountability, the free-market economy, etc., but over time many Republicans have abandoned their conservative principles.

Socialism: it was originally defined as the abolition of private enterprise, nationalization of the means of production and central economic planning, but over time the definition has been broadened to include the extensive re-distribution of wealth through taxation and the institutions of the welfare state.

Tyranny: arbitrary or unrestrained exercise of power; despotic abuse of authority.

1. The Battle between Conservatism and Liberalism

Our nation is under siege; we are engaged in a battle of historic proportions, a battle between conservatism and liberalism. Each and every day, powerful forces push us farther and farther into the direction of Socialism, corruption and economic collapse.

Conservative Guiding Principles

What we need is very different from what we have and what we are going to get if we don't rein in the out-of-control and out-of-touch Obama Regime. The march to Socialism and economic destruction must be stopped. We need to take our county back and restore the values of personal responsibility, the free-market economy system, living within our means and a strong national security. After all, the government works for us, we don't work for them. Standing in stark contrast to the Left's radical agenda, the principles that guide conservatives are:

- Uphold the Constitution, enforce our laws
- Limited size, reach and power of government
- Follow the Constitution and move certain powers away from the federal government to states, local communities and the private sector
- Fiscal integrity and accountability
- Limited government spending, balanced budgets, paying off the debt

- Low taxes
- Limited regulations
- Openness and transparency
- Moral integrity and accountability
- Common sense
- Individual freedom, power, responsibility, accountability and self-reliance
- Respect for human life
- Limited government entitlements and safety nets only for those who truly need them
- Full application of free-market economy system principles
- Full development of our country's energy sources; energy independence
- Nurture a business-friendly environment
- Strong national security; peace through strength
- Strong foreign policy
- Support of our allies
- Opposition to, not appeasement of, evil in the world, dictators and tyrants
- Free-market health care solutions

The Left's Radical Agenda

The Left elements of our society – Democrats, Liberals, Progressives, Radicals, Socialists, Statists, etc. - are driven by a radical ideology which includes:

- America is an evil country
- Blame America, whites and those evil rich people first
- The U.S. is a source of evil in the world and needs to be "fundamentally transformed"

- The U.S. has had an unfair economic advantage at the expense of others and needs to transfer wealth to those others to amend for its past abuses
- Corporations, businesses and profits are evil
- Capitalism is bad, Socialism is good
- Punish achievement, award failure
- Support failing companies with taxpayer dollars; choose winners and losers
- Ordinary people don't know what's good for them, society and the rest of the world, but the Left's elite knows
- Ordinary citizens can't govern themselves
- A from-the-womb-to-the-tomb and from-cradle-to-grave Nanny State with entitlements for the masses
- Hide what ordinary people supposedly can't understand or shouldn't know about; most people are just too stupid to know what's best for them and "the common good"
- Establish a socialist Utopia in America first and then in the world, even if it would destroy our economy, national security and well-being
- Let laws of other countries influence our judicial system
- Pervert good causes like the environment and compassion for others, to promote the radical agenda
- Subsidize the Left's pet projects like solar energy and electric vehicles with taxpayer dollars, rather than letting the free market system drive development and implementation of sound solutions
- Spending taxpayer money is always the best solution for any problem
- Unlimited size, control, power and reach of the government at the expense of individual freedom, respon-

sibility and accountability, ultimately leading to absolute power and control

- The U.S. Constitution isn't really the "law of the land", but a living document that is for the most part outdated and needs to be ignored or tweaked to suit the Left's agenda, without having to go through the outdated amendment process
- Use whatever is necessary to reach your goals, even if it violates the Constitution
- Things like common sense, moral integrity, accountability, respect for human life, fiscal responsibility, balanced budgets and paying of our national debt, will be sacrificed for "the common good"
- Increasing regulations to transfer power and control to the government
- Government control of the economy; health care, energy, transportation, trade, etc.
- Suppress development of our energy resources at the expense of more dependency on foreign countries
- Increase taxation and government spending; expand existing entitlement programs and create new ones
- Fan the flames of racism and other discrimination to expand the liberal voting base
- Encourage illegal immigration and amnesty to expand the liberal voting base
- Sympathy for like-minded regimes in other countries
- Appease and pander to evil in the world, dictators and tyrants
- Support the United Nations as a vehicle to pander to countries and regimes hostile towards the U.S., freedom and free-market economies; ultimately surrender American sovereignty to establish a world government

This ideology invariably leads to corruption, abuse of power, tyranny, loss of freedom, Socialism and economic collapse.

Progressive Double-Speak

One of the radical Left's favorite tactics is the use of Orwellian double-speak to perverse the language, distort the facts and hide their agenda. Here are some examples:

"Freedom of religion" = freedom from religion
"Secular" = hostile towards religion
"Transparency" = secrecy and meetings behind closed doors
"Transforming America" = realizing your radical-Left agenda
"Lobbyist ban" = revolving door for lobbyists
"Post-racial" = playing the race card at every opportunity
"Bipartisan" = strictly partisan
"Reaching across the aisle" = strict partisanship
"Comprehensive immigration reform" = amnesty for illegal aliens
"Path to citizenship" = amnesty for illegal aliens
"Protecting the little guy" = seizing control of private enterprises, nationalization
"Liberal" = Leftist
"Progressive" = Leftist
"Community organizing" = political agitation
"Compassion" = redistribution of wealth
"Economic justice" = redistribution of wealth
"Tax reform to cut spending from the tax code" = tax increase

"Leveling the playing field" = redistribution of wealth, rewarding failure, punishing success

"Social justice" = redistribution of wealth

"Investments" = government spending of our tax dollars

"Contributions" = taxes

"Fair share" = unfair share

"Reproductive rights" = abortion on demand

"Women's right to choose" = abortion on demand

"Pro-choice" = pro-death

"Free choice" = forced union membership

"Fairness Doctrine" = suppression of free speech

"Man-made disaster" = terrorism

"Overseas contingency operation" = War on Terror

"Kinetic military action" = acts of war; launching cruise missiles; using B52's to drop bombs on airfields; shooting airplanes out of the sky; firing missiles at tanks

"Racist" = any Caucasian who disagrees on any issue with any non-Caucasian

"Racial profiling" = law enforcement when non-Caucasians are involved

"Save the planet" = excuse to advance your radical agenda

"Catastrophic, man-made global warming" = naturally occurring climate cycles

"Bio-fuel" = taxpayer subsidized burning of food and driving up prices

"Renewable energy" = taxpayer subsidized flights of fancy

"Crisis" = golden opportunity to advance the radical agenda

"Deficit neutral" = guaranteed to increase the deficit

Bias in the Mainstream Media

Objective journalism is very hard to find these days in America. While 40% of Americans identify themselves as conservative and only 21% as liberal, [1] reporting by the so-called mainstream media is overwhelmingly biased towards the liberal Left. About 88% of the White House press corps votes Democrat. [2]

Most of the so-called mainstream media has become a propaganda machine for the Left's ideology. They were in the tank for Obama during his campaign. They failed to properly vet him as a presidential candidate. They ignored his radical ambitions, his record as the most radical-Left senator ever and his associations with radicals and terrorists like Bill Ayers, the Reverend Jeremiah Wright, Antoin "Tony" Rezko and Raila Odinga, to name just a few.

Most of the mainstream media still are in the tank for Obama and toe the line of President Obama.

In May of 2011, the Associated Press or AP published an article highly critical of Israel's Prime Minister Benjamin Netanyahu's speech to the U.S. Congress. [3] Not only did the article portray this man in unfairly negative terms, it also grossly distorted the deadly reign of radical Muslim terrorist organizations Hamas and al-Qaida. The article stated: "Although Hamas and al-Qaida have killed **hundreds** of people in religious holy wars…" The article was picked up without any correction or footnote by news outlets all over the country and the world. So, let me refresh the so-called mainstream media's short-lived or politically motivated, selective memory: al-Qaida alone has killed thousands and thousands. Remember the first World Trade Center bombing, the U.S. embassy bombings in Kenya and Tanzania, the USS Cole bombing, 9/11, the Bali bombings, the Madrid train bombings, the London subway and bus bombings, etc. etc.?

If you are interested to learn more about the mainstream media bias, I would recommend you explore the website of the Media Research Center at mrc.org.

Attacks on Conservatives and Free Speech

If the natives are getting restless and are not willing to swallow what you try to force down their throats, apply community activist Saul Alinsky's tactics and vilify those who don't agree with you. The Obama Regime and the radical Left openly attack Republicans and private citizens in town hall meetings and at Tea Party rallies and members of Congress who express their concerns about and disagreement with ObamaCare:

Obama, Democrat, claims they "are misinformed" and are "bearing false witness." [4]

Robert Gibbs, Democrat, White House Press Secretary, called their anger "manufactured." [5]

A **DNC** or Democratic National Committee add called them "an angry mob." [6]

Nancy Pelosi, Democrat, Speaker of the House, called them "un-American". She also said that they were "not grassroots, but Astroturf", (meaning organized and paid by others) and were "carrying swastikas and symbols like that" to town hall meetings. [7]

Harry Reid, Democrat, Senate Majority Leader, called them "evil-mongers" that were "using lies, innuendo and rumor to drown out rational debate." [8]

Barney Frank, Democrat, Representative and Chairman of the House Financial Services Committee, responded to a protester with "on what planet do you spend most of your time?" [9]

Brian Baird, Democrat, Representative for the State of Washington, accused protesters of driving people to violence like Timothy McVeight. [10] "What we're seeing right now is close to Brown Shirt tactics," Baird told a local newspaper. "I mean that very seriously." [11]

Baron Hill, Democrat, Representative for Indiana, called them "political terrorists." [12]

Maxine Waters, Democrat, Representative for California, called U.S. Senators not going along with Obama's plans "Neanderthals." [13]

Kathleen Sebelius, Democrat, Health and Human Services Secretary, issued a gag order to health insurance companies, to prevent them from alerting patients that Obama-Care could eliminate important Medicare and other benefits. This gag order was a flagrant violation of the First Amendment's freedom of speech.

Alan Grayson, Democrat, Representative for Florida, said that the Republican health care plan called for people to "not get sick", and if they got sick to "die quickly" and called Republicans "foot-dragging, knuckle-dragging Neanderthals." [14]

Janeane Garofalo, mouthpiece for the ultra-Left said about Tea Party-goers: "It's about hating a black man in the White House. This is racism straight up and is nothing but a bunch of teabagging rednecks. There is no way around that." [15]

The Tucson Massacre

A mentally unstable madman attacked and shot 20 people, six of them fatally, including a 9 year old girl, near Tucson, Arizona. It happened during an outdoor meeting in January 2011 with Democrat Representative Gabrielle Giffords, who was also shot and critically wounded. The Left propaganda- and attack-machine exploited this tragedy with a despicable lack of civility and attacked their opponents and free speech. Conservatives, Republicans and Tea Partiers were accused of being accessories to these horrible murders and renewed attempts were made to suppress free speech. Democracy requires a well-informed citizenry, as expressed by founding father Thomas Jefferson, so suppressing free speech will help the Left push their radical, undemocratic agenda.

Clarence W. Dubnik, Democrat, Sheriff of Pima County, Arizona, heading the investigation of the massacre, blamed Rush Limbaugh and others of engaging in political rhetoric and encouraging violence.

Patrick Leahy, Democrat, senator for Vermont, said "The seething rhetoric has gone too far. The demonizing of opponents, of government, of public service has gone too far." [16]

Paul Krugman, Democrat, columnist, wrote in the New York Times: "And it's the saturation of our political discourse – and especially our airwaves – with eliminationist rhetoric that lies behind the rising tide of violence. Where's that toxic rhetoric coming from? Let's not make a false pretense of balance; it's coming, overwhelmingly, from the right." [17] He then took a swipe at Conservative Congresswoman Michele Bachmann. The same Paul Krugman who "joked" in his New York Times column: "A message to Progressives: By all means, hang senator Joe Lieberman in effigy." [18]

Deborah White, Democrat, radical liberal blogger, blamed conservative Republican Sarah Palin. She wrote: "Palin's political dog whistle in Arizona yields unintended results. Sarah Palin's political career is dead, felled by bullets from the Glock semi-automatic pistol of mentally unbalanced 22-year-old Jared Loughner in Arizona. The shooting of a political leader was an atrocity waiting to happen… a near inevitability since gun-toting Tea Partiers, urged on by Sarah Palin and her sidekicks, stormed congressional town hall meetings in summer 2009." [19]

Leave it to the shameless Left, from down at the bottom to all the way at the top, to spew their hatred against all who don't agree with them, over and over and then take a tragedy and abuse it to push their radical political agenda.

In a renewed attempt to attack free speech, clearly aimed at conservatives, House Representatives **Jim Clyburn**, Democrat, and **Louise Slaughter**, Democrat, have both suggested in the aftermath of the Tucson massacre that it might be a good idea to call for new media standards to guarantee balanced coverage and revisit the so-called Fairness Doctrine. [20]

Steve Cohen, Democrat, Representative for Tennessee, while discussing House bill H.R. 2 to repeal ObamaCare in January of 2011, attacked Republicans and Sarah Palin and compared them to Nazis: "They say it's a government takeover of health care - a big lie, just like Goebbels. You say it enough, you repeat the lie, you repeat the lie, you repeat the lie, and eventually, people believe it. Like blood libel, that's the same kind of thing. The Germans said enough about the Jews and the people believed it, and you had the Holocaust. You tell a lie over and over again. And we've heard it on this floor: government takeover of health care." [21]

Sheila Jackson Lee, Democrat, Representative for Texas, during the same debate accused Republicans that repealing ObamaCare would result in more deaths in the U.S.: "Frankly, I would just say to you, this is about saving lives. Jobs are very important; we created jobs, but even the title of their legislation, H.R. 2, 'job-killing' — this is killing Americans if we take this away, if we repeal this bill." [22]

Arrogance, Contempt, Lies and Plain Stupidity

Yes, it needs to be said: there is an awful lot of arrogance, contempt, lies and stupidity on the Left. There is much of that on the Right and in the Middle too, but in case you didn't already notice, this book is about Socialism, corruption and economic collapse and the Left works on those harder than anybody else in the U.S. Here are some examples of what I mean:

Obama Falsely Accuses the Supreme Court
During his 2010 State of the Union [23] address to Congress, Obama falsely accused the Supreme Court of enabling foreign companies to spend advertising money to influence American elections. The Supreme Court finding that Obama alluded to left all restrictions on foreign influences fully intact. Way to go, Mr. Constitutional Law Expert! Upon later questioning, Obama stated that he stood by his re-

marks and that he would not apologize to the Supreme Court.

Obama Fakes Fiscal Responsibility

During the same address, [24] Obama talked about fiscal responsibility: "Starting in 2011, we are prepared to freeze government spending for three years ... Like any cash-strapped family, we will work within a budget to invest in what we need and sacrifice what we don't. And if I have to enforce this discipline by veto, I will." What is so fiscally responsible about freezing spending at an all-time high, unsustainable level? Five days later he submitted his 2011 spending budget of $3.83 trillion, the biggest in the history of this country and the world, with a staggering $1.3 trillion dollars deficit! Pants on fire, big time!

Not This Administration, That Administration

In February 2010, VP Biden stated that the turnaround in Iraq and upcoming withdrawal of U.S. troops there could be "this administration's biggest accomplishment!" [25] Both he and Obama vigorously opposed the surge and never acknowledged its success. Bush negotiated a schedule for troop withdrawal with the Iraqi government. But now Obama and his collaborators claimed the successes as theirs.

Driving the Car into the Ditch, Eh, Make That Driving it Off the Cliff

In May of 2010 Obama said that Republicans are like bad drivers, who once drove the car into the ditch and now want the keys back. "After they drove the car into the ditch, made it as difficult as possible for us to pull it back, now they want the keys back. No! You can't drive. We don't want to have to go back into the ditch. We just got the car out." [26]

If Republicans drove the car into the ditch, then Obama was driving it off the cliff!

Unemployment Checks and Food Stamps Stimulate the Economy

While almost 15 million Americans were officially out of work, the Obama Regime spouted nonsense and played politics with high unemployment and yet more deficit spending.

In July of 2010 Speaker of the House Nancy Pelosi sang the praises of unemployment insurance checks: "Unemployment benefits are creating jobs faster than practically any other program." [27] In October of 2010 she repeated this, but added Food Stamps as another major tool to grow the U.S. economy and lift us from the recession: "It's the biggest bang for the buck when you do food stamps and unemployment insurance." [28] Food Stamps and unemployment check are better than pay checks to stimulate the economy? This woman is beyond absurd! The mainstream media repeated this Pelosi nonsense faithfully and frequently. Only card-carrying radicals would utter this complete nonsense and hope you swallow it hook, line and sinker.

When Obama took office there were 33 million people on Food Stamps. In early 2011 the number of people on Food Stamps had increased to 47 million. The Obama-Pelosi team should be proud of getting us the "biggest bang for the buck." I don't always agree with Newt Gingrich, but he nailed it when he said in May of 2011 that Obama was a "food stamp president". [29]

Summer of Recovery

While the stimulus hadn't worked at all, the economy was still in the dumps, jobs were scarce, unemployment was persistently so high that longer unemployment benefits were deemed necessary and a double-dip recession looked very possible, Obama and Biden were on what they called the "Summer of Recovery" tour, traveling the country in the summer of 2010 and making speeches to sing the praises of how the economy was recovering and Obama "saved or created" millions of jobs.

The Federal Government Can Do Most Anything

Pete Stark, a liberal Democrat, Representative for California, was known for his absolutely atrocious reactions to people who didn't agree with his policy positions. In the summer of 2010, when asked at a town hall meeting about the limits of government power he said: "I think there are very few constitutional limits that would prevent the federal government from rules that could affect your private life. Now, the basis for that would be, how does it affect other people?" After the questioner asked what possible constitutional limits there were and if ObamaCare could pass constitutional muster, Stark replied: "The federal government yes, can do most anything in this country." The questioner, outraged: "You, sir, and people that think like you are destroying this nation." Stark smirked: "And I guess you're here to save it. And that makes me very uncomfortable." [30]

Oops

A couple of weeks before the 2010 mid-term elections, the Obama Regime accused Republicans and the Chamber of Commerce of accepting donations from Political Action Committees affiliated with foreign companies and thus buying the elections with foreign money. [31] But wait a minute: a) there's nothing illegal about what the Republicans did and b) it turned out that Democrats got more money that way than Republicans.

Punish Your Enemies

One week before the 2010 mid-term elections, in a last-ditch effort to salvage the Democrat majority in the House and Senate, Obama stooped to rabid hate-speech by encouraging Latino voters to vote against Republicans on Election Day: "If Latinos sit out the election instead of saying, "We're gonna *punish our enemies* and we're gonna reward our friends who stand with us on issues that are important to us,' if they don't see that kind of upsurge in voting this election, then I think it's gonna be harder..." [32]

Deception of the American People is just Fine

One week after the 2010 mid-term elections, in which Democrats suffered a defeat of a magnitude not seen since the 1930's - they lost 63 House seats and 6 Senate seats -, Hillary Clinton, Democrat, Secretary of State, stated that Obama's strategy now would be to use a trick to make it look like he'd be moving to the middle, while sticking to his agenda, like Bill Clinton did after the Democrats got thumped in the 1994 mid-terms. [33] Translation: *deception of the American people is justified to push through your radical agenda.*

Pelosi Pays as She Goes

Nancy Pelosi, Democrat, Speaker of the House and arguably the third most powerful person in the world in that position, blatantly lied at her final press conference in January 2011: "Deficit reduction has been a high priority for us. It is our mantra, pay-as-you-go." [34] Since the Democrats took control of Congress in January 2007 and thus controlled the U.S. purse strings, the national debt increased by **$5.1 trillion** over a 4 year period, the largest in the history of the world!

Those Evil, Mean Muslim Haters

Keith Ellison, Democrat, Representative for Minnesota, testified in March 2011 during hearings on Muslim-American radicalization, held by a House Homeland Security Committee, headed by Peter King, Republican, Representative for New York. Ellison, Congress's first Muslim member, broke down while talking about a Muslim-American paramedic, Mohammad Salman Hamdani, who died in rescue efforts during the 9/11 attacks on the World Trade Center. He said: "Mr. Hamdani bravely sacrificed his life to try and help others on 9/11. After the tragedy some people tried to smear his character solely because of his Islamic faith. Some people spread false rumors and speculated that he was in league with the attackers only because he was Muslim. It was only when his remains were identified that these lies were fully exposed." [35]

This portrayal of what happened was in conflict with reality, to say it mildly. Six weeks after the attacks - and well before Hamdani's remains were identified – he was actually praised posthumously with high honors by Congress when the Patriot Act they signed into law included this statement: "Many Arab Americans and Muslim Americans have acted heroically during the attacks on the United States, including Mohammed Salman Hamdani, a 23-year-old New Yorker of Pakistani descent, who is believed to have gone to the World Trade Center to offer rescue assistance and is now missing." [36]

Very, Very , Very Few People Get Intruded Upon

In May 2011 Secretary of Homeland Security Janet Napolitano commented on the controversial issue of getting patted down at the airport: "Well, actually, very, very, very few people get a pat-down." Really? It turned out that on average about 1.8 million people were patted down every month. [37]

America, the Welfare State

America is on a social welfare binge and is well on its way to become a full-fledged socialist society. There are dozens of programs that make up the U.S. welfare system, including: Temporary Assistance for Needy Families; Food Stamps; Supplemental Security Income; Medicaid; Housing Assistance; Earned Income Tax Credit; Special Supplemental Food Program for Women, Infants and Children; General Assistance; School-Based Food Programs; Low-Income Home Energy Assistance Program. The U.S. government website lists 62 different government benefits, grants and financial aids programs!

An analysis by Wyatt Emmerich [38] shows that in 2010 in Mississippi, due to all these so-called social safety net programs, a one-parent family of 3, earning a minimum wage of $14,500 per year ends up with more disposable income than a family of 4, earning $60,000 per year:

Income and Outlay	One-Parent Family of 3	Family of 4
Money earned in year	$14,500	$60,000
Payroll and federal income tax	-$1,225	-$13,034
Childcare cost	-$9,600	-$9,600
State income tax*	-$725	-$3,000
Earned Income Tax Credit (EITC)	$5,020	0
Food Stamps (SNAP)	$6,312	0
National School Lunch Program (NSLP)	$1,800	0
Medicaid and CHIP	$16,500	0
Section 8 Rent Subsidy	$4,350	0
Utility Bill Assistance	$845	0
Total Disposable Income	$37,777	$34,366

*: state income tax for the State of Mississippi; other states would show different but similar results

America, the Nanny State

Due mainly to the Left's decades-long efforts, America has become more and more a from-the-womb-to-the-tomb and from-cradle-to-grave Nanny State with entitlements for the masses. After all, ordinary citizens don't really know what's good for them and can't take care of themselves or their offspring! The power of government over our private lives is alarming.

Honest concern for people's wellbeing have been perverted more and more by outdated, ineffective and unsustainable programs like Social Security, Medicare and Medicaid. But there are a myriad of other programs and proposals for government to intrude on our privacy and ability to make our own decisions and govern our own lives. Ordinary citizens, government believes, can't take care of themselves or their children and need Big Brother to help them every step of the way. You want some examples? Sure, here goes:

The Salt Police
Democrats want to ban salt in any form in the preparation of any food in New York restaurants, allegedly to lower health care cost and save lives. [39]

There Goes Your Happy Meal
The City of San Francisco, a safe haven for illegal immigrants and criminals, wants to ban toys included in McDonald's Happy Meals and other meals of more than 600 calories that lack agreed-upon amounts of fruit and vegetables. [40]

There Goes Your Goldfish
Again the City of San Francisco: this time adding goldfish, guppies and other tropical fish to an existing proposal to ban the sale of pets like cats, dogs, hamsters, mice, rats, guinea pigs, etc. [41] The proposed ban would not restrict the sale of these critters for human consumption, so you can eat them, but you can't keep them.

Big Brother Goes Birther
In February of 2011 the State of Oregon was considering to allow the Oregon College Savings Plan, where savings for college can grow tax-free, to mine birth certificate information so it could contact parents directly to open accounts for their newborns. The state might even kick in $100, of

taxpayer money of course, if parents matched it within the child's first year! [42]

GPS Replaces Common Sense

In February of 2011 the Anaheim, California school district started a pilot program to give GPS devices to seventh-and eighth-grade students with four or more unexcused absences that school year, to remind them they need to get to school in time and track their location several times a day. [43] Why bother to get the parents involved in raising and disciplining their own children when Big Brother can do that much better and with your tax dollars?

2. The Obama Culture

Obama, the most radical and corrupt president ever, has surrounded himself with Liberals, Progressives, Radicals, outright Socialists, at least one Communist, and sympathizers with Maoism and Marxism. He pushes through his socialist agenda, using propaganda, scare tactics, empty promises and bribes. He violates our laws and wields absolute power and Congress fails to rein him in. Our democracy is in danger of becoming a lawless dictatorship.

Obama the Candidate versus Obama the President

During his campaign Obama tried to portray himself to be a moderate, a uniter of the country, not a divider, post-racial, post-partisan, opposed to "business as usual", for decreasing the power of the executive branch, transparent, fiscally responsible, for eliminating "pork", for reducing health insurance costs, etc. He fooled way too many people with these false claims.

Too many voters in the 2008 presidential election gave Obama the advantage of the doubt, in spite of overwhelming evidence of what he really stood for. Before becoming an Illinois state senator, Obama was a so-called "community organizer", a euphemism for political agitator. His voting records as an Illinois and U.S. senator established him as the most radical-Left senator, ever. On top of that, Obama was (and still is) an economic illiterate who lacks leadership, management, business or executive skills and experience. He never managed as much as a hot-dog stand and never in his life had the responsibility to make a profit in any business, large or small.

After careful examination of all the facts, any objective person will have to come to the conclusion that Obama and his Regime are a radical-Left, socialist, politically agitating, racist, partisan, secretive, fiscally irresponsible, wasteful, "business as usual" political machine. Obama's presidency has been marked by many, extremely negative traits: arrogance; condescension; corruption; disdain for the laws of this country and the will of the American people; lack of leadership; incompetence; economic ignorance and mismanagement; bribing members of Congress; denial of our war with radical Islam; pandering to terrorists and our enemies; hostility toward our free-market economy and business; out-of-control spending, deficits and debt. Harsh words for sure, but in my opinion an accurate description of the harsh realities we face.

Obama the Socialist

Is Obama a socialist? The short answer is: yes. Obama is a socialist at heart and a radical-Left one at that. He has surrounded himself with a coterie of Liberals, Progressives, Radicals, outright Socialists, at least one Communist and sympathizers with Maoism and Marxism. Many people are still in denial, but more and more are starting to see Obama for what he really is. In mid-2010, 55% regarded "socialist" an accurate description of Obama [1] and 56% thought he was too liberal.

Socialism means dependency and slavery: the abolition of private enterprise, nationalization of the means of production, central economic planning, extensive redistribution of wealth through taxation and the institutions of the Welfare state. As you can see, Obama represents all that.

After passing disastrous health care reform and nationalizing student loans in March 2010, the U.S. government directly owned or controlled large parts of the labor unions, communication media, banking-, mortgage-, insurance-, financial- and auto industries, health care and student loans. Our Constitution does not allow the government to own or control **any** part of our economy, but the Obama Regime won't let the Constitution stand in the way.

While Obama hasn't succeeded yet in totally transforming the U.S. into a socialist Utopia, he is doing all he can to get there and we must stop him before it is too late. He is targeting manufacturing and energy through the National Energy Tax bill, aka Cap and Trade, aka Cap and Tax. He used the disastrous oil spill in the Gulf of Mexico as an excuse to squeeze the life out of the U.S. oil industry.

Obama's Radical-Left Associations

As Sean Hannity once said: "Obama is a radical, organizing his fellow radicals." And there are many fellow radicals who inspired Obama, who he associated with and who he appointed to positions in his administration. Obama has surrounded himself with Marxist, socialist, communist and Maoist radicals, but the Left is in denial. Their kneejerk reaction to bringing up Obama's connection to radicals is to protest against the idea of "guilt by association". They say that it is unfair to judge people by whom they associate with, that Obama doesn't necessarily share the ideas of his associates and appointees. But that's a flimsy and intellectually dishonest argument. People do seek a connection with and company of those with whom they share values, and claiming otherwise is disingenuous. You are known by who you hang out with. Instead of accusing someone of assuming "guilt *by* association", the Left should acknowledge that there is a principle appropriately called "guilt *of* association".

These are some of the radicals in Obama's life and those he has either nominated for or appointed to positions in his administration:

Frank Marshall Davis
A communist journalist and poet who became Obama's mentor during his high school years in Hawaii and who worked with groups determined "to wipe out white supremacy".

Saul Alinsky
A Chicago-born, self-styled agitator and radical socialist activist and Obama's community organizing mentor.

Reverend Jeremiah Wright
Radical head of the Trinity United Church of Christ. Wright, an African American, was Obama's spiritual mentor for 20 years, baptized him, married him and Michelle and baptized his children. Wright preached black-liberation theology, an inherently radical theology owing its origin to radical black political thinkers. Amongst other things, Wright claimed that Jesus was black and that the U.S. created the AIDS virus to kill blacks. He blamed the 9/11 attacks on America. Obama finally disassociated himself

from Wright when he became too much of a political liability.

Bill Ayers

In the 1960s Bill Ayers co-founded the violent radical-Left organization the Weather Underground. He participated in the bombings of New York City Police Headquarter, the U.S. Capitol building and the Pentagon. Federal charges were dropped due to illegal tactics of FBI agents. After the 9/11 attacks in 2001 Ayers said, "I don't regret setting bombs", "I feel we didn't do enough" and, when asked if he would "do it all again," said "I don't want to discount the possibility". [2]

When asked about Obama's associations with Ayers, Obama's campaign manager David Axelrod said, "Bill Ayers lives in the same neighborhood. Their kids attend the same school. They're certainly friendly, they know each other, as anyone whose kids go to school together." [3] Come again? Obama's children were grade-school age, while the Ayers children were already adults. Obama had a way closer relationship with Ayers. He consulted him about his idea of getting into Chicago politics, launched his political career and first fundraiser from Ayers' Chicago home and worked with Ayers for years on a foundation for charitable work. Obama knew about Ayers' political views and terrorist past, but only disassociated himself from him when he became too much of a liability in his bid for the White House.

Antoin "Tony" Rezko

Chicago political fixer and slum lord, convicted of political corruption and influence peddling, gave Obama his first political contribution, helped finance five of his election runs and was instrumental is his political career. After first denying it, Obama admitted to the key role Rezko played and finally disassociated himself from him when he became too much of a political liability. [4]

Raila Odinga

A radical Leftist politician from the same Kenya tribe as Obama, with well-known communist political roots. Obama had close ties to Odinga. In 2006, then U.S. senator Obama campaigned for Odinga who ran for president of Kenya as a Muslim sympathizer. In order to secure votes from the significant Muslim community in Kenya, Odinga cut a secret deal with them to allow Muslim law to be instituted in part of the country in case Odinga would win the elections. [5]

Carol Browner

Obama's Climate Czar. On her last day in office as head of the EPA, she oversaw the destruction of agency computer files in brazen violation of a federal judge's order requiring the agency to preserve its records. She bragged about her tenure: "One of the things I'm the proudest of at EPA is the work we've done to expand the public's right to know." [6]

Steven Chu

Obama's Energy Secretary. He backs higher gasoline taxes to force people to buy cars that are more fuel efficient and buy homes closer to work. He said: "Somehow we have to figure out how to boost the price of gasoline to the levels in Europe," at a time when gasoline cost less than $3 a gallon in the U.S. and $7 to $9 a gallon in Europe. [7]

John Holdren

Obama's Science Czar. Supports forced abortions and compulsory sterilization by means of implanting sterilizing capsules and spiking water and food with sterilizing chemicals. He also claims that infants are not human beings but will ultimately develop into human beings when given socializing experiences and food during the early years after birth. [8]

Ron Bloom

Obama's Manufacturing Czar. Previous labor union negotiator. Some quotes from this radical: "the free-market is nonsense... the whole point is to game the system", "we kind of agree with Mao that political power comes largely from the barrel of a gun". [9]

Cass Sunstein

Obama's Regulatory Czar. Supports a radical animal rights agenda, including new restrictions on agriculture and hunting. Wants to establish legal 'rights' for livestock, wildlife and pets, which would enable animals to file lawsuits in American courts. [10]

Van Jones

Obama's Green Czar. A self-described radical, *communist* and revolutionary, [11] big admirer of Chairman Mao of China. Mao, the world's biggest mass murderer, was directly responsible for well over 70 million deaths of his own people in peacetime, by means of executions, purges, withholding medical care, torture to death, working to death and deliberate starvation. At a communist summit in Moscow, Mao, with a flippant indifference to human suffering, proposed all-out nuclear war to establish socialist world domination at the cost of one-third or half of the world population! [12] Only after Jones' radical-Left leanings became common knowledge did he resign in September of 2009. He will teach at Princeton University and rejoin the

Center for American Progress, a radical-Left think tank. He also received the NAACP's President's Award for achievements in public service! [13]

Anita Dunn

White House Communications Director. Called Chinese communist leader and mass murderer Mao one of her two favorite political philosophers that she turned to most. [14] Only after her radical-Left leanings became common knowledge did she resign in November of 2009.

Elena Kagan

Obama's radical nominee for Supreme Court judge and subsequently approved. As dean of the Harvard Law School, she banned the military from recruiting at the university, because she didn't agree with her former boss Bill Clinton's "don't ask, don't tell" policy. [15] If she had a problem with that policy, she should have picked a bone with the Bill Clinton Administration, not the military. The Supreme Court ruled against her unanimously in that case.

In the Kagan case, it's important to mention that the Department of Justice thwarted congressional efforts to learn more about nominee Kagan. In June of 2010 members of Congress asked the Department of Justice if and to what extent Kagan might have been involved legally in the Obama health care reform. If she was involved and if she were appointed, she would have to recuse herself if Obama health care reform issues would come before the Supreme Court. The Department of Justice did not provide any information, claiming that they did not understand the term "Obama health care reform". Obama's Department of Justice was intellectually dishonest for political purposes and Congress should have raked them over the coals about it. [16]

Donald Berwick

Administrator of the Centers for Medicare and Medicaid Services. Berwick is an avowed *socialist*. He admires the British universal health care system, *health care rationing* and *income re-distribution*. He included "death panel" provisions in 2011 Medicare regulations, after Congress specifically rejected them in the health care reform legislation. [17]

The Honduras "Coup"

This case deserves special mention, as it displays Obama's sympathies for radical leaders in other countries. Weary of corruption by long-term presidents, Honduras enacted a law in 1981 not allowing reelection of its presidents. Manuel Zelaya, elected president in 2005 as a centrist, veered more and more to the Left, finding a soul mate in Hugo Chavez of Venezuela. When he wanted to rewrite Honduran law to stay in power, perhaps indefinitely, the country's courts, Congress and other institutions agreed to have the military remove Zelaya from the presidency and the country. [18]

Incredibly, Obama joined communist radicals Hugo Chavez and Fidel Castro to condemn Zelaya's removal and call it a "coup", another strong indication of his Left leanings. Apparently it's OK for Obama to meddle in Honduran affairs and side with a Leftist who wants to violate its laws, but it's not OK for him to "meddle in the internal affairs of Iran" when its government brutally suppresses its citizens speaking out and protesting what they see as voter fraud.

Lonnie Rashid Lynn, Jr.

This hip-hop artist, poet and actor goes by the name of Common. He is a Chicago native and happens to be a member of the Reverend Jeremiah Wright's Trinity United Church of Christ. It's a small world indeed! He was invited to perform at a May 2011 celebration of American poetry at the White House, organized for students by Michelle Obama. President Obama was also scheduled to attend. In the past Mr. Lynn's lyrics called for burning President Bush and shooting police officers. His so-called "art" is offensive in other ways, notably for using racially-tinged and misogynist language. [19] He wrote a tribute to a convicted Black Panther cop-killer, Assata Shakur, [20] who escaped from prison and fled to Cuba. He even named his daughter after the convict. Just the man you want to invite to an evening of poetry for students! Very classy! Very presidential!

Reprehensible as this man's language is, it's protected by the First Amendment and his right to speak freely is not the issue here. The issue is the lack of civility and common sense in the White House. The issue is that the President and First Lady should set the tone for civility and they do the opposite.

The Obama Culture of Corruption

The Obama Regime is the most corrupt in American history. Here's a partial list of nominees for positions in the Obama administration, both withdrawn and confirmed, with tax issues, other Democrats with serious tax and credibility issues, briberies to push the Senate health care bill through and some other juicy scandals:

Timothy Geithner

Democrat, confirmed as Secretary of the Treasury under Obama; failed to pay taxes of $34,000 when he worked for the International Monetary Fund. [21] As head of the Federal

Reserve Bank of New York, Geithner oversaw an $85 billion bailout of the AIG insurance company while hiding bailout conditions that were very unfavorable to the taxpayers footing the bill.

Tom Daschle
Democrat, previous long-time senator and senate majority leader; nomination as Obama's Secretary of Health and Human Services was withdrawn because he failed to pay $146,000 in taxes and interest on the free use of a luxury car and chauffeur. [22]

Kathleen Sebelius
Democrat, formerly the governor of Kansas; confirmed as Obama's Secretary of Health and Human Services; failed to pay about $7,000 in taxes and interest stemming from charitable contribution, home mortgage and business expense issues. [23]

Ron Kirk
Democrat, confirmed as U.S. Trade Representative in the Obama administration, owed an estimated $10,000 in back taxes stemming from speaker fees and deduction issues. [24]

Bill Richardson
Democrat, governor of New Mexico; nomination as Obama's Secretary of Commerce was withdrawn because of a pay-to-play scandal. [25]

Nancy Killefer
Democrat; nomination as Obama's "Performance Czar" was withdrawn because of failing to pay taxes on domestic help. [26]

Nancy Pelosi

Democrat, speaker of the U.S. House of Representatives and as such third in line for succession as U.S. president; accused the CIA of routinely lying to Congress, but didn't provide any further explanation or proof; claimed that Americans expressing their concern about ObamaCare were somehow organized by those evil insurance companies. [27]

Charlie Rangel

Democrat, Representative for 40 years and previously Chairman of the House Ways and Means Committee, convicted of multiple ethics violations. Nancy Pelosi clearly failed to "drain the swamp" of ethics violations as she promised during her successful campaign to take over the House in 2006. [28] In February of 2010 Pelosi insisted that she was running the most ethical and honest Congress in history, but at the same time, however, indicated she would not ask Rangel to resign his chairmanship, at least for the time being. Rangel resigned from the committee in March 2010. In November 2010, after a two-year investigation, a bi-partisan House ethics panel convicted Rangel of 11 ethics violations, among them:

- use of congressional staff and letterhead to solicit donations from those doing business before the committee, for a school at a New York City college to be named in his honor
- errors and omissions on his financial disclosure forms
- use of rent-subsidized apartments, including one used as his campaign office
- failure to report hundreds of thousands of dollars of rental income from a Dominican Republic beach villa and pay federal income taxes on it; in 2006 alone, Ran-

gel failed to report $1.3 million in income and pay more than $60,000 income taxes on it.

Rangel was not expulsed from the House, but got a slap on the wrist in the form of censure: a resolution disapproving of his conduct was read by Pelosi while Rangel stood in the House. [29]

Eric Holder

Democrat, Obama's Attorney General, played a key role in the Clinton Justice Department pardon of 16 Puerto Rican terrorists, convicted of bombings, armed robberies and slayings in the U.S. [30] He showed great resistance to uttering the words "radical Islam" when the context was very much appropriate, although he had no difficulty describing America as a "nation of cowards" or calling Bush officials "war criminals." [31]

Barney Frank

Democrat, Massachusetts Representative, Chairman of the House Financial Services Committee. When he was looking to aid OneUnited Bank in the fall of 2009, he urged Maxine Waters, as a colleague on the House Financial Services Committee, to "stay out of it", rather than bring the issues out in the open. [32]

Claire McCaskill

Democrat, Missouri Senator. In March 2011 it came out that for four years she didn't pay property taxes on a turbo-prop airplane, she, her husband and several investors owned privately and owed *$320,000* in back taxes, interest, penalties and fees. [33]

Ken Salazar

Democrat, Interior Secretary. He was the major figure be-hind Obama's drilling moratorium. He *falsified* a federal panel's scientific report by inserting a blanket drilling ban recommendation and presenting it as the scientists' opi-nion. [34] All scientists on the panel came out and stated that they did not favor or recommend a blanket drilling ban. Let me emphasize here: *Salazar lied and committed fraud to advance Obama's anti-oil, anti-free-enterprise agenda.* Salazar should have been fired immediately!

Ben Nelson

Democrat, Nebraska senator. He was bribed with more than *$45 million* of taxpayer money to vote for the Senate health care bill. The bribe became known as the "Corn-husker Kickback". [35]

Mary Landrieu

Democrat, Louisiana senator. She was bribed with *$300 million* of taxpayer money to vote for the Senate health care bill. The bribe became known as the "Louisiana Pur-chase". [36]

Bill Nelson

Democrat, Florida senator. He was bribed with *$5 billion* of taxpayer money to vote for the Senate health care bill. The bribe became known as the "Florida Flim-Flam". [37]

The Sestak Scandal [38] [39]

In February of 2010 Joe Sestak, Democrat, representative for the State of Pennsylvania, confirmed long-time rumors that in the summer of 2009 he had been offered by the White House a high-level job in the Obama administration, if he would not run against senator Arlen Specter in the

Democratic senatorial primaries in Pennsylvania. Sestak didn't want to divulge more, like what position exactly and who had made the offer, but confirmed many times that indeed the offer had been made.

Arlen Specter, a long-time senator from Pennsylvania, started out as a Democrat, but switched to the Republican party in 1965 to further his career, then switched back again to Democrat in 2009 because he said he was "at odds with the Republican philosophy." Translation: Specter did not believe he could be reelected as a Republican, given his liberal views, so why not switch parties and try to salvage your career and the heck with what's best for the country? More importantly, Specter's defection gave Obama a supermajority in the Senate! The dirty little scheme didn't work, because Sestak did run and won the May 2010 Pennsylvania senatorial Democratic primary.

Insiders believed that Rahm Emanuel, the White House Chief of Staff, was involved and that the position might be as high a level as the Secretary or Undersecretary of the Navy, which would make sense given former admiral Sestak's 30 year Navy career.

The White House immediately reacted by saying what Sestak had said in February wasn't true and persistently stonewalled inquiries about the issue. White House press secretary Robert Gibbs was asked repeatedly about this at press briefings, but repeated over and over that he did not have any more information than what was written by the press in the first place. Finally, finally in May 2010 Gibbs admitted that indeed a discussion with Sestak had taken place but that White House lawyers were of the opinion that "***nothing improper***" had taken place. White House lawyers investigating the White House? Nothing improper? Interfering in this manner with an election is *a crime*.

David Axelrod, top political advisor to Obama, also asserted that "nothing improper" had taken place. Then at the end of May 2010 Obama, during a press conference, reiterated that "nothing improper" had happened and that an official response from his administration would be given soon. "Nothing improper" happened but you can't talk about it at a press conference?

The next day the White House released a report saying Obama's chief of staff, Rahm Emanuel, had asked former president Bill Clinton to talk to Sestak about taking an unpaid position on the president's intelligence advisory board, in exchange for staying out of the Senate primary against Specter. It is hard to believe that any ex-president or anybody in the White House would run the risk of discovery over a low-level position such as on an advisory board. It is also hard to believe that Sestak would be interested in such a low-level job to give up his chances for becoming a U.S. senator. Anyway, that doesn't really matter: whether a low- or high-level job, paid or unpaid, such interference with elections is *a crime*.

But wait, there is more! Being a member of Congress, Sestak wasn't even *eligible* to serve on the intelligence advisory board; board members cannot be employed by the federal government. So either the administration was totally incompetent by offering a job that was not even available or there was a cover-up and the White House made a fatal mistake of dreaming up a scenario that wasn't even possible, hoping nobody would notice.

Also, nobody in the White House, not Rahm Emanuel, White House Chief of Staff, not David Axelrod, top political advisor to Obama, not anyone else would make a job offer to a U.S. Representative without Obama's knowledge and approval. So Obama must have been involved in this election fraud, which is an *impeachable offense.*

Sestak said that he only talked about a job offer once, with Bill Clinton, for less than a minute. The report said that discussions – plural! - took place with Sestak in June and July of 2009! After 10 months of cover ups and stonewalling, the White House issues a report that didn't pass the smell test. Change and transparency we all can believe in? Chicago-style thuggery is more like it!

The White House stonewalling didn't stop either. When asked about the White House report's inconsistencies and unanswered questions, Robert Gibbs, White House Press Secretary, kept referring the reporters right back to the report over and over. Several members of Congress asked the White House to release emails and other documents relating to this scandal. The White House refused. Bill Clinton refused to comment as well. Attorney General Eric Holder refused to appoint an independent prosecutor to investigate!

The Romanoff Scandal
Similar scenario of election manipulation and Obama corruption. In September 2009 Jim Messina, Obama's Deputy Chief of Staff, contacted senate candidate Andrew Romanoff from Colorado and told him that an Obama administration job might be available for him, if he would not run for the Democratic nomination against incumbent senator Michael Bennett. Three different positions were suggested. Romanoff declined. [40]

The White House stonewalled this issue for as long as they could, but after the Sestak scandal went critical, they apparently thought it best to offer up a – lame - defense in June of 2010: "No job was ever offered to Mr. Romanoff"! And the White House claimed that Obama didn't know about his people's "interactions" with Romanoff. [41] Riiight! No independent prosecutor here either.

The Meek Scandal [42]

Similar scenario of election manipulation and Obama corruption. Two weeks before the 2010 mid-term election, Bill Clinton tried to persuade Kendrick Meek, African-American Democrat senate candidate for Florida, *to drop out of the race*. The idea was that Meek and the Democrat party could endorse turncoat Charlie Christ for the Senate. Christ was governor of Florida at the time and a Republican in name only. He was running for a Florida senate seat as an Independent, because his chances of winning as a Republican from the strong Republican candidate Marco Rubio, a Latino, were next to zero. So here was the Obama machine trying to unlawfully *influence elections* and ask a Democrat minority candidate to forgo his candidacy, so a white turncoat "Independent" might be able to win from a Republican minority candidate. No doubt Charlie Christ, who as Republican governor was already "in the tank" for Obama, would be a strong ally of Democrats if elected senator. This overture to Meek was made at a time when more than 1,500,000 Floridians had already turned in their voting ballots. One day Bill Clinton's spokesman confirmed Clinton's involvement. The next day Clinton himself denied it.

Voting Machine Fraud [43]

One week before the 2010 mid-term elections, reports surfaced from Nevada, that *suspicious glitches* had been reported by several voters. Democrat Harry Reid's name was *already checked* in the machines when voters went to cast their ballots. As it turned out, the ultra-Left SEIU labor union, fanatical supporters of Obama, was under contract with Clark County, Nevada for their technicians to operate the voting machines. How in heaven's name is it possible for a corrupt, radical labor union to be under contract with government for something as critically important as voting machines?

Obama the Lawless Dictator

Government of the people, by the people, for the people doesn't apply to Obama and his Regime. They treat the will of the American people and those in Congress, who don't agree with them, with utter contempt. Come hell or high water, they push through their radical, socialist agenda through the use of propaganda, scare tactics, empty promises and bribes. While Obama has sworn to live by and enforce our laws and protect Americans, he selectively chooses not to do so.

When the government violates our laws and exercises absolute power - as the Obama Regime is clearly doing – then our country ceases to be a democracy and turns into a lawless dictatorship. Here are some examples:

The Stimulus Bill
The majority of Americans disapproved of the Stimulus Bill, [44] but it got pushed through anyway.

The Health Care Reform Bill
More than 80% of Americans with health insurance and about 70% of Americans in general said that they were satisfied with their health care. [45] Most Americans were against ObamaCare, [46] but it got pushed down our throats anyway.

Failure to Enforce Immigration Laws
Obama doesn't enforce our immigration laws, secure our borders and protect Americans from drugs and violence

spilling over the U.S.-Mexican border. Arizona enacted its own immigration law to do what Obama failed to do. 71% of Arizonans [47] and more than 60% of Americans across the country [48] supported this law, but Obama sued the State of Arizona over it anyway. I go into detail in Chapter 9, Illegal Immigration.

Obama Bypasses Congress to Push Through His Radical "Green" Agenda

Congress didn't buy Obama's argument that his Cap and Trade legislation would fight global warming and rejected it. So, Obama bypassed Congress and took the dictatorial route. In December of 2009 he had his Environmental Protection Agency declared CO_2 - and five other so-called greenhouse gases - dangerous pollutants, which they claimed threatened public health and the environment! [49] CO_2, a non-toxic key building block of about every life form, is a dangerous pollutant? Really? We happen to exhale it and plants, shrubs and trees absorb it to grow. I guess soon enough, the EPA will declare people also to be dangerous pollutants! That would please many on the radical Left fringes, who view people as a scourge of the earth. Oh, and CO_2 also happens to be a key ingredient of about every aspect of human activity: energy, transportation, travel, heating, manufacturing, agriculture, etc. If you want to control about every aspect of human life, regulate CO_2! Big Brother Obama got it all figured out. Who needs Congress if you have the EPA to force your radical, socialist agenda onto those pesky Conservatives?

According to one study, this EPA regulation could kill 1.4 million jobs and cost the economy $141 billion within the first three years and another study found that this regulation could cost job losses of about 500,000 jobs per year starting in 2015. [50]

In January of 2011, the EPA revoked, for the first time in history, a valid clean water permit for a coal mine, claiming unacceptable damage to rivers, wildlife and communities. This made good on Obama's promise to "bankrupt" the coal industry and put a "virtual moratorium" on coal permits. [51] To hell with science and the democratic process! Let's hijack "the environment" to force radical-Left, socialist ideology and evermore governmental control onto the American people!

The Berwick Appointment

In July of 2010 Obama put Donald Berwick in the job of administrator of the Centers for Medicare and Medicaid Services, using a recess appointment during a week-long break for the Independence holiday, bypassing the U.S. Senate confirmation process and skipping public scrutiny. [52] Even the mainstream press, in the tank for the Obama Regime, had foreseen an uphill battle to get Berwick confirmed, because of his radical-Left, socialist stance.

Berwick, an avowed *Socialist*, [53] admires the British single-payer, universal health care system and wants to tailor the U.S. health care system to it. He advocates income redistribution and health care rationing.

Normally, a president may use the recess appointment process in cases where a nominee has been *exhaustively vetted* by Congress, yet chances for Congressional confirmation appear to be slim. So Obama clearly abused the system, hid his true agenda and installed the radical Berwick in a top position with a *yearly budget of $800 billion.* [54] Medicare and Medicaid patients, the elderly and needy, will surely suffer as a result.

So-called "end-of-life" planning was initially included in ObamaCare, but it touched off a political storm over "death panels' and was dropped from the legislation. Obama, unable to achieve his goals through democratic means, used the dictatorial approach and achieved the same goal through regulation. Starting January 1, 2011 new Medicare regulations provided for the government - or more correctly, the taxpayers - to pay for so-called "end-of-life care", including forgoing life-sustaining treatments. [55]

The New Black Panthers Incident [56]

In 2010 Eric Holder's Department of Justice dropped a 2008 lawsuit against members of the New Black Panthers party, who had violated the voters rights act by using coercion, racial slurs, threats of force and intimidation against voters at a Philadelphia polling place. A Department of Justice lawyer involved in this case testified before the Civil Rights Commission, that he was told by the higher-ups in the Justice Department, that no lawsuits where the accusers were white and the accused were black, would be pursued. Obama and Holder refused to perform their duties.

The Defense of Marriage Act

In February of 2011, Obama, in legal and political mumbo jumbo of truly historical proportions, directed his Department of Justice to continue to enforce, but to no longer defend in court the Defense of Marriage Act – the 1996 law that bars federal recognition of same-sex marriages! [57] Obama opined that, while he still did not support same-sex marriages, he felt that the law was unconstitutional. Like everybody else, he's entitled to his own opinions on any subject, including same-sex marriages and whether or not he feels a particular law is constitutional. However, like every other president before him, he has sworn to uphold our laws. He cannot decide to not defend a law. That is willful refusal to perform his duties.

Obama, supposedly a constitutional expert, should know better than anyone, that he must uphold the law and cannot at the same time enforce a law *and* not defend it. If he feels that the law is unconstitutional, he either keeps that to himself as a personal opinion or, if he feels strongly enough about it, proposes to repeal or amend it by democratic means. That's Government 101 stuff: Executive, Legislative and Judicial Branches, and the amendment process!

The Illegal Libyan War

On March 19, 2011 Obama attacked Libya without the required approval from Congress. Since Libya never was an actual or imminent threat to the nation, this was a *violation of the War Powers Act* and an *impeachable* offense.

When asked in 2007 about then-President Bush's authority to possibly bomb suspected nuclear sites in Iran, then-senator and presidential candidate Obama correctly stated that the U.S. president has severe restrictions placed upon him by the War Powers Act. He said in an interview: "The President does not have power under the Constitution to unilaterally authorize a military attack in a situation that does not involve stopping an actual or imminent threat to the nation." [58] Then-senator and -presidential candidate Hillary Clinton correctly stated the same facts. Then-senator and -presidential candidate Biden stated that he would seek to impeach President Bush if he bombed Iran without first obtaining congressional approval.

But now Obama, Biden and Clinton reversed themselves completely on the matter. Let our laws be damned! Obama said: "We cannot stand idly by when a tyrant tells his people that there will be no mercy, and his forces step up their assaults on cities like Benghazi and Misurata, where innocent men and women face brutality and death at the hands of their own government." [59] Note to Mr. Obama, the law expert with acute memory loss: authorizing military attacks without approval from Congress is *a violation of law and an impeachable offense*. Would Obama now impeach himself or Biden and Clinton impeach Obama? The same argument of taking military action against human rights abusers could be made against China, North Korea, Saudi Arabia, Russia, Syria, Yemen, Cuba, etc. So, should we go to war with them as well or more to the point, should Obama go to war with them without congressional approval?

To make matters even worse and even more illegal, Obama failed to obtain congressional approval for his military action in Libya by the legal 60-day deadline of May 20, 2011, another *impeachable* offense. When asked repeatedly about it, his Press Secretary Jay Carney would not say whether Obama would seek congressional approval or if the president would even send a letter to Congress acknowledging the deadline had passed. [60]

Obama showed a complete and utter disregard for our laws. He bypassed Congress and Congress failed to fulfill their duties to the American people. Congress waffled. Congress stalled. Congress did *not* demand that Obama obey the War Powers Act or face impeachment! Congress might as well disband, go home and hand over absolute power to Emperor Obama!

The House finally made a stand against Obama, sort of. [61] They adopted a *non-binding* resolution to *chastise* Obama for not giving a compelling rationale for the war and demanded answers about objectives, costs and impact on the wars in Afghanistan and Iraq. They rejected a measure to outright demand an end to the U.S. involvement in Libya.

The Senate also seemed to kind of wake up from its stupor. It proposed a resolution to express "the sense of the

Senate that Obama should request congressional authorization for continued U.S. military action", forbid U.S. ground forces in Libya and require Obama to answer questions regarding scope, costs and impact on the wars in Afghanistan and Iraq. [62]

And what was the reaction from the White House on both the House and Senate resolutions? They said this: "The White House maintains that it has been in compliance with the War Powers Act and has called the resolutions unhelpful and unnecessary." [63] *In compliance with the War Powers Act?* Doesn't such a blatant lie make your blood boil? They also said that "Obama had the authority to continue the military campaign without congressional approval because U.S. involvement fell short of full-blown hostilities." [64] Somebody should sit our Dictator-in-Chief down and force him to read the War Powers Act: it doesn't differentiate between limited or full-blown military action; it doesn't exempt firing missiles from remotely controlled drones.

Not only is this country going to hell in the proverbial hand basket, it's going there at neck-break speed. We cannot allow a president and Congress to violate our laws and get away with it, lest we become a lawless nation.

Bypassing Congress on the "Disclose Act"

Federal law requires that information about political contributions by contractors bidding for federal government contracts is kept secret from those awarding federal contracts. The obvious reason is to avoid bribery, "pay to play" schemes and other corruption. Awarding contracts should be solely based on merit: the ability to deliver the needed goods or services according to the required time table, at the required quality levels, at competitive prices.

Never mind federal law and common sense! In April of 2011 it became known that Obama was planning to demand from contractors to disclose political contributions as a condition for obtaining federal government contracts. [65] Obama's draft executive order on this issue claimed that this information was needed to ensure that the contracting process "be free from undue influence". His claimed reason for demanding political contribution information was to make sure that contractors followed rules on contribution limitations. So what was behind this suspicious piece of Obama work? To the innocent bystander it might look like Obama acted without thinking about unintended consequences. However, the reality was that he was in full campaign mode for the 2012 presidential election and he was looking for ways to make it easier to reward contractors for their financial support, believing Americans too stupid to catch on. This used to be known in the U.S. as corruption.

Fact was that in July of 2010 the Senate rejected a piece of legislation with similar aims, the "Disclose Act", which Republican Senate Minority Leader Mitch McConnell called "...a cynical effort to muzzle critics of this administration..." [66] So this executive order was clearly meant to circumvent the will of the American people, as represented by the Senate and a despicable abuse of executive branch power under the guise of "transparency".

Obama's Broken Promises

There are too many to list all here and the list is growing and growing. Here are some:
- Uphold the laws of the United States.
- Protect U.S. citizens.
- Transparency.

- Fiscal responsibility.
- No more pork.
- Cut the deficit in half by the end of his first term.
- End the Bush tax cuts for people making more than $250,000.
- Close Guantanamo by January 2010.
- Immigration reform in the first year.
- Allow imported prescription drugs.
- Allow five days of public comment before signing bills.
- Negotiate health care reform in public, televised sessions; during his election campaign, Obama promised on eight separate occasions to conduct all health care reform debates on C-Span.
- Tougher rules against revolving doors for lobbyists and former officials.
- Decrease the power of the executive branch, which according to Obama is a big problem.
- End income tax for seniors making less than $50,000.
- Not raise taxes on anyone making less than $250,000.
- Create a $3,000 tax credit for companies that add jobs.
- Allow penalty-free hardship withdrawals from retirement accounts.
- Reduce the average family's yearly health insurance costs by $2,500; it is estimated that because of Obama-Care the average family's health insurance costs will increase by thousands of dollars per year.
- Democrats often criticized the Bush White House for its use of the presidential signing statement, a means by which the president can reject provisions of a bill he deems unconstitutional, without vetoing the entire legislation. Two days after Obama said he would rein in the use of such declarations, he used it to declare five

provisions of a bill to be unconstitutional and non-binding.

- Be against raising the national debt ceiling.
- Not unilaterally authorize a military attack in a situation that does not involve stopping an actual or imminent threat to the nation.

Obama's Distortions of and Apologies for America

Obama's attitude towards America could easily be mischaracterized as a loser mentality. But it goes much deeper than that. He doesn't believe in American exceptionalism or America being a force for good in the world, so he never talks in those terms. Instead, he repeatedly apologizes for what he sees as great shortcomings of our nation and calls for a "fundamental transformation of America". He bows for dictators, appeases our enemies and throws our allies under the bus. In doing so, Obama has greatly diminished America's standing in the world, emboldened our enemies and weakened our allies.

Obama has said: "We do not consider ourselves a Christian nation or a Jewish nation or a Muslim nation. We consider ourselves a nation of citizens who are bound by ideals and a set of values." [67] Really? Fact is, the U.S. is a nation founded on Judeo-Christian principles. Fact is, about 80% of Americans consider themselves to be Christian. [68]

He also said: "If you actually took the number of Muslim Americans, we'd be one of the largest Muslim countries in the world". Fact is, that, using a high estimate of 7 million Muslims in the U.S., this country ranks 32rd. [69]

His speech in Germany went further than any U.S. president in criticizing his own country's action while standing on foreign soil: "...there have been times where America has shown arrogance and been dismissive, even derisive." [70]

We don't need a president who distorts our nation's founding principles and religious make-up and apologizes to appease the Muslim world or other groups. We need a leader who is proud of our country, our heritage and our values and expresses those clearly. We need a leader who reminds the world of the good this country has done for millions upon millions of people around the globe, bringing freedom and peace, liberating them from the tyranny of the Nazis, Imperial Japan, the Soviet Union and a slew of dictators around the world. We need a leader who speaks from a position of strength, not weakness, when he addresses other nations and in particular the Arab world.

Obama's Culture of Death

People's positions on abortion vary widely and they are entitled to their opinions. However, except for under very specific circumstances like rape, incest, imminent danger to the life of the mother, etc., no well-reasoned person will support the three kinds of horrible abortion described below. Support for those kinds of abortions, ***without conditions or limitations***, is immoral by most people's standards. Most people would strongly support BAIPA laws. Not so Obama and many of his collaborators!

Late-Term Abortions
Unborn babies become viable - able to survive outside the uterus - anywhere between the 21st and 27th week of gesta-

tion. Late-term abortions are defined as occurring when the fetus has become viable. Federal law bans late-term abortions, but state laws vary.

Partial-Birth Abortions

This type of abortion is performed just before the baby is born. When the baby descent into the birth canal and is about to be born, the back of the skull is pierced, the brains are sucked out and the skull is crushed to ease removal of the baby from the mother.

In the Illinois senate, Obama voted against a bill designed to prevent partial-birth abortions. The U.S. Senate passed a similar federal law where a majority of Democrats voted against it with 64% of their votes, while a majority of Republicans voted for it with by 94% of their votes.

Labor-Induced Abortions Where the Baby Survives and is Left to Die

Labor-induced abortion is a form of abortion, where labor is induced at such an early stage of pregnancy that the baby is *very likely* to be stillborn. However, sometimes the baby survives the procedure and is born alive. When this happens, some doctors then provide all the needed medical care to help the baby survive. Some doctors don't provide medical care and *leave the baby to die.* Whatever their position on labor-induced abortions themselves, most reasonable people would consider withholding medical care to infants who survive the procedure as *murder.*

The Born Alive Infant Protection Act or BAIPA

The BAIPA laws require providing prompt and proper care to born-alive babies in order to help them survive.

Obama was the *only* Illinois senator to vote against the Illinois BAIPA law. Jill Stanek, who was intimately involved in the five-year process to get this law passed, lists in her article on this subject 10 excuses Obama gave throughout the years for voting "no" or "present" on the law: [71]

"10. Babies who survive abortions are not protected by the Equal Protection Clause of the Constitution."

"9. A ban to stop aborted babies from being shelved to die would be burdensome to mothers."

"8. Aborting babies alive and letting them die is a doctor's prerogative."

"7. Anyway, doctors don't do that."

"6. Obama apparently read medical charts and saw no proof."

"5. Aborting babies alive and letting them die is a religious issue."

"4. Aborting babies alive and letting them die violates no universal principle."

"3. Introducing legislation to stop live aborted babies from being shelved to die was a political maneuver."

"2. Sinking Born Alive was about outmaneuvering that political maneuver."

"1. Introducing Born Alive was a ploy to overturn Roe v. Wade."

I highly recommend anyone who is concerned about Obama's and the Left's lack of respect for human life, particularly the life of unborn and newly born babies, to read Jill's heart-rending article.

People, including President Obama, who justify murder by neglect of the infant, are *immoral monsters* and people who actually withhold the care are *cold-blooded murderers*. Let me repeat what I just said about Obama, so hopefully it might registers with some die-hard fawners: *Obama's justification of murder by neglect of born-alive infants makes him an immoral monster!*

That callous mind-set should have disqualified Obama for *any* public office, let alone the presidency. The sad fact is that this information was readily available to anyone interested to learn who Obama really was, before voting for him.

The "Czars"

Here's what Obama said in March of 2008: "The biggest problems that we're facing right now have to do with George Bush trying to bring more and more power into the executive branch and not go through Congress at all. And *that's what I intend to reverse when I'm president of the United States*." [72]

Once again Obama has proven that we can't believe what he says. He is not reversing what he claimed to be the trend, he is accelerating it! So, Mr. Obama, why the "shadow cabinet" of 32 "czars" and more in the making? Why so many "czars" with radical-Left and outspoken communist backgrounds?

These "czars" have considerable power, develop policies, make high-level government decisions and yet are not accountable to Congress to maintain checks and balances. Each and every one of these "czars" has responsibilities that are already covered under the job descriptions of Obama's Secretaries, yet they don't report to or are accountable to those Secretaries! For instance, why do we have a Secretary of Labor, Hilda Solis, nominated by Obama, confirmed by the Senate, reporting to Obama and accountable to Congress *and* a Green Jobs Czar, Van Jones, appointed by Obama without Senate approval, not reporting to Hilda Solis, but to Obama directly and not accountable to Congress? Why do we even have Van Jones, an outspoken *communist,* in any position in government?

It should be painfully clear to everyone, that Obama's "czars" are there to circumvent Congress and advance his radical, socialist agenda.

On Claims of Transparency

While running for president, Obama promised, among many others things, to bring transparency to the White House and Washington. That was then. His record started to proof otherwise right after his inauguration. Here are some examples:

EPA May Have Suppressed a Report Skeptical of Global Warming [73]
The Environmental Protection Agency may have suppressed an internal 98-page report, expressing doubt about global warming and the need to regulate carbon dioxide. A staff researcher was chastised for comments, which "do not help the legal or policy case" for the EPA's planned pro-regulation recommendation to the White House. [74]

Administration Admits Bad Recession Forecast [75]
In July 2009 it became clear that previous White House predictions on the economy had very likely been too optimistic. The upcoming midsummer budget update would more than likely include higher unemployment, higher deficits and a slower growth of the economy than was previously assumed in the president's February budget and May update. This could hamper efforts to get ObamaCare and Cap and Trade approved. The budget update, usually done in mid-July, was put off by one month, raising the

suspicion that the White House delayed bad news until after Congress had left for summer recess.

Senator Dodd Admits Adding Bonus Provision to Stimulus Bill [76]

After first denying it, Senator Chris Dodd, Democrat, confessed in March 2009 that he added language to a spending cap provision of the Stimulus Bill, which specifically excluded bonuses in contracts signed before the bill's passage. Dodd claimed that Treasury officials had forced him to modify the language to exclude those bonuses, arguing that otherwise a "flood of lawsuits" would happen.

Health Care Reform Cobbled Together Behind Closed Doors

On the campaign trail Obama said, that the 1993 Bill Clinton effort at health care reform failed mainly because too much was kept behind closed doors and that he would run a presidency marked by transparency. All debate would be open to the public. Yet, ObamaCare health care reform was cobbled together behind closed doors by a few White House and congressional Obamanites.

Obama's Birth Certificate

Even while Obama was campaigning for president, there were questions about where he was born and whether he was qualified to be president. Presidential hopeful Hillary Clinton was one of the first to ask him to release his long-form birth certificate. Many more people, both on the Right and on the Left, started to wonder why it was that first candidate Obama and then President Obama would not release the darned document. Even left-of-center "thrill up my leg" Obama devotee Chris Matthews asked for it in no uncertain terms.

Then in April of 2011 Donald Trump, a possible presidential candidate for 2012, rekindled the controversy and forced Obama to finally produce the long-awaited document. Well, it only took Mr. Transparency about three years.

On Bipartisanship

A central theme of Obama's campaign was that he would end the partisan divide in Washington.

That is not what happened. While Democrats controlled both the House and the Senate, Obama, Nancy Pelosi, Harry Reid and other Democrats in the House and the Senate prevented any Republicans from participating in creating any major legislation like the Stimulus Bill, Cap and Trade and ObamaCare; most Republican amendments were voted down.

But guess what? When Republicans won the 2010 midterm elections by a landslide of truly historic proportions, the Obama Regime looked patently moronic by calling for Republicans to be more accommodating to Democrats and work together! What a bunch of hypocrites!

On Hating the Left

This is not about race issues, which are addressed in the next section. This is about hate. Hate is such a strong word. It has the power to severely damage or even destroy people. It shouldn't be used lightly; accusing someone of hate without over-abundantly clear evidence is a grave injustice.

People who disagree with the Left, and particularly those who disagree with Obama, are often accused of being haters. While not as strong an accusation as being a racist, this one comes very close and makes an honest discussion extremely difficult if not impossible. And I believe that in many cases, that's just what the accusers are after. Often the accusations don't mention hate directly, but imply it, like when Alan Grayson, Democrat, Representative for Florida, said that the Republican health care plan called for sick people to "die quickly". Or they lob accusations at conservatives that they just don't care for the poor, the elderly, the children and a million other groups or causes. Yet the Left is quick to dispense hate towards those that don't agree with them, as has been documented extensively in this book. Remember the "foot-dragging, knuckle-dragging Neanderthals?"

Now if you made it this far into this book, you may have picked up on the fact that I disagree with Obama and the Left a lot, an awful lot! I disagree with their policies on out-of-control spending, on the economy, on energy, on national security, on foreign affairs, on the environment, on illegal immigration, on appeasement of our enemies, etc. Not only do I disagree with those policies, I hate them. I hate their policies intensely, but I don't hate their guts. That, to me, is the big difference.

On Race

To me, all people are created equal; skin color, ethnic background, language, etc. don't make one bit of difference to me. What matters to me is how people treat each other, what they stand for. What matters is people's character. I wish everybody would share those views.

Obama's skin color and ethnic background should be totally irrelevant to everybody, but sadly enough that isn't the case for too many people, both for white people and people of color. Also sadly enough, Obama has not turned out to be the post-racial president he promised to be during his election campaign. Many people in his administration and supporters on the Left have made racially-loaded remarks and poisoned the atmosphere. As a result, race relations in this country have significantly deteriorated under Obama's presidency and have been set back by decades. Most of the time, it are the so-called enlightened, tolerant and supposedly post-racial Liberals who, instead of living by what they claim they are, play the race card. People who disagree with Obama's policies are either called an Uncle Tom or a sell-out if they are black or from another ethnic minority, or a racist if they are white. Let me give some examples:

Wow, That's Scary!
On the campaign trail, Obama claimed that Republicans tried to scare voters against a black President by suggesting that people say "he doesn't look like all those other presidents on the dollar bills." [77]

A Nation of Cowards
Eric Holder, Democrat, Obama's Attorney General and the first African-American to hold that post said: "in things racial, we have always been and we, I believe, continue to be in too many ways essentially a nation of cowards." [78]

Racism, Straight Up
Janeane Garofalo, radical-Left mouthpiece, commented on Tea Party attendants: "Let's be very honest about what this is about. This is not about bashing Democrats. It's not about taxes. They have no idea what the Boston Tea party was about. They don't know their history at all. It's about

hating a black man in the White House. This is racism straight up and is nothing but a bunch of teabagging rednecks. There is no way around that." [79]

The Beer Summit
When an out-of-control black professor and friend of Obama was arrested for disorderly conduct, Obama, while acknowledging that he didn't know all the facts, accused the policy of acting stupidly and racial profiling.

What Do Those White Males Know?
Sonia Sotomayor, Democrat, was confirmed as Supreme Court Judge for life, in spite of her racist remark: "I would hope that a wise Latina woman with the richness of her experiences would more often than not reach a better conclusion than a white male who hasn't lived that life." [80]

Oops, No Takers!
In March of 2010, near the end of the bitter health care debate, three black Democrat Congressmen, Representatives John Lewis, Andre Carson and Emanuel Cleaver, said that some demonstrators, many of them Tea Party activists, yelled the "N-word" and spat on them as the Congressmen walked from House office buildings to the Capitol. With so many media and citizen cameras at the demonstration, any epithets would have been caught on tape, but none were ever found, in spite of a $100,000 reward. [81]

We're Supposed to Enforce Laws?
When the state of Arizona enacted a law to fight illegal immigrations, the Obama Regime accused Arizona of racial profiling and violations of the Constitution. Nothing could be further from the truth and the Arizona law was even way

more restrictive than federal law, unanimously upheld by the Supreme Court in 2005.

I Didn't See That!

Several members of the New Black Panther Party were accused of violating the Voting Rights Act by using coercion, racial slurs, threats of force and intimidation against voters and campaign workers at a Philadelphia polling place. One brandished what prosecutors called a deadly weapon, a baton that he pointed at people. It was all recorded on video and there were several witnesses. And what was done about that? In May of 2010 the prosecutor was instructed by Eric Holder's Justice Department to ban the person brandishing the baton from Philadelphia polling places until 2014; it was apparently OK to have this thug show up in other cities and harass voters and in Philadelphia it was OK again after 2014! Charges against the others were dropped!

Eric Holder refused to explain. A Department of Justice lawyer, who had been involved in this case, testified before the Civil Rights Commission, that he and others handling this case were told by the higher-ups in the Justice Department, that no voter's rights violations lawsuits where the accusers were white and the accused were black would be pursued! [82]

She Is, She's Not, or Is She?

In July of 2010 a video surfaced that showed Shirley Sherrod, Democrat, USDA's black director of rural development for the State of Georgia, describing at an NAACP meeting how she withheld help to a white farmer facing bankruptcy. Under pressure from the White House, the USDA fired Sherrod on the spot, even before the video aired on TV. Oops. Examination of the whole video showed, that Sherrod continued to describe how she concluded, that her actions were wrong and subsequently helped the farmer to save his farm. Under pressure from the White House, the USDA apologized profusely and offered to rehire her the next day. Double oops. It soon surfaced that Sherrod was a racial bomb-thrower, who called people opposing Obama's agenda racist and who advocated closing down TV and radio stations and websites that opposed Obama's agenda! [83]

Republicans and Independents Are Racist

In January of 2011, James Moran, Democrat, Representative for Virginia, told the Arab television network Alhurra that Republicans won in the 2010 mid-term elections because many Americans didn't want a black president. He said that the Democratic losses in those elections "…happened because of the same reasons the Civil War happened in the United States. The Civil War happened because the Southern states, particularly the slaveholding states, didn't want to see a president who was opposed to slavery. In this case a lot of people in this country, I believe, don't want to be governed by an African American, particularly one who is inclusive, who is liberal, who wants to spend money on everyone and who wants to reach out to include everyone in our society. That's a basic philosophical clash." [84]

A Man with Foresight

In April of 2011, one and a half year before the 2012 presidential elections, PBS host Tavis Smiley used the race card preemptively on MSNBC: "I said over a year ago that this was going to be, this presidential race, Lawrence, was going to be the ugliest, the nastiest, the most divisive, and the most racist in the history of this Republic." [85]

Gurgling Baby Tells It Like It Is

It became obvious that Obama hadn't learned much from the Reverend Wright controversy. For Easter 2011 Obama and his family went to the Shiloh Baptist Church in D.C. Problem was that the church's African American Reverend Wallace Charles Smith's views were very similar to those of the Reverend Wright. According to Reverend Smith, this country was still blatantly racist. He even went so far in his sermon on this Easter day to say, that his grandson's gurgling was actually talking about how they tried to write him off as only 3/5 of a person, referring to the old U.S. Constitution. [86]

3. The Economy

Our economy is being hammered by high unemployment, out-of-control spending, government interference, disastrous energy policies, a lack of affordable energy, an obsession with the environment, devastating health care reform and illegal immigration. A weak recovery may turn into a double-dip recession or even a full-blown depression, but Obama continues his anti-free-market, anti-business policies on the road to economic collapse.

"The Worst Financial Crisis since the Great Depression" & Job Losses

Details about what Obama called "The Worst Economic Crisis since the Great Depression" and related job losses can be found in Chapter 5, Bailout and Stimulus – Choosing Winners and Losers.

Unemployment

Obama said that the Stimulus Bill would keep unemployment below 8%, but it went up sharply after the bill passed and has hovered between 9 and 10% for years. So much for the economic acumen of the Obama Regime! Most experts believe that any significant recovery of employment will take many years.

The unemployment information presented here in a graph is from the U.S. Bureau of Labor Statistics [1] and includes only those without work who have looked for a job in the preceding 4 weeks. People who haven't looked for a job in the preceding 4 weeks are not counted as being unemployed, as are people who have part-time jobs that let them work fewer hours than what they want.

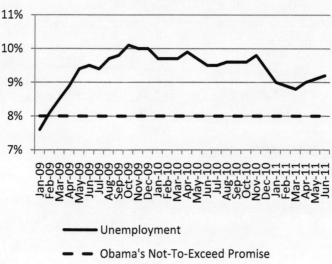

Unemployment

Unemployment

— — Obama's Not-To-Exceed Promise

Hostility towards Our Free-Market Economy System

Obama himself is an economic illiterate, who lacks any experience, skills or genuine interest in business. In his cabinet are less people with prior private sector experience, about 22%, than in any administration since 1900; for other administrations this percentage varied between about 28 and 58 percent. [2] Not only does the socialist Obama Regime run low on the needed economic experience and skills, they are downright hostile towards our free-market economy system. Their so-called economic policies are a disaster and as a result our economy, our freedom and our survival are in immediate danger. Let me give some examples:

Cap and Trade

Under the guise of protecting the environment, the Cap and Trade legislation would deal a deadly blow to our economy, jobs and the availability of affordable energy to sustain us.

The Stimulus That Wasn't

The so-called Stimulus Bill has done anything but. Our hard-earned tax money has been wasted on government chosen winners and losers and is no longer available to truly stimulate our economy.

Car Companies Nationalized

The administration's manipulation of the Chrysler and GM bankruptcies is a violation of bankruptcy law. These companies were in effect nationalized.

Gary Jason [3] wrote: "Consider first the facts. In these two cases, rather than let the free market and the legal system (specifically, the bankruptcy court) handle the reorganization of the failing auto makers in the normal way, the Obama administration spent tens of billions in taxpayers' dollars to take control of the companies and force the outcome it wanted. Obama, who received millions in contributions from the United Auto Workers union, has forced a settlement that will give UAW far more equity in the companies when they come out of bankruptcy than it was due compared to the secured debt holders. Obama's agents used threats and intimidation (calling holdout bondholders speculators and hedge funds at one point) to get the creditors to accept being shafted. (WSJ) The result is that the vast majority of the two companies will be almost clearly owned by the federal government and the UAW, and the UAW arguably controls the federal government."

Uncle Sam Takes Control
Large parts of the labor unions, communication media, banking-, mortgage-, insurance-, financial- and auto- and health care industries our now under government control.

Vilify Those Who Help You Live Healthier and Longer
Health care and pharmaceutical companies have been vilified.

Gag and Bind Them!
Health and Human Services Secretary Kathleen Sebelius issued *a gag order* to health insurance companies to prevent them from alerting patients, that ObamaCare could eliminate important Medicare and other benefits. [4] This gag order was a *flagrant violation of the First Amendment's freedom of speech.*

You Can't Do That!
In September 2010 Health and Human Services Secretary Kathleen Sebelius warned the health insurance industry, that the Obama administration wouldn't tolerate blaming premium hikes on ObamaCare. "There will be zero tolerance for this type of misinformation and unjustified rate increases" said Sebelius. [5] So the Big Brother Regime will

determine what rate increases are "justified"? Straight out of Marx' playbook!

Mr. Waxman Should Read the Law

After passage of ObamaCare and as required by law, companies announced their accounting charges as a result of increased costs of doing business, resulting from the health care reform bill. Apparently without studying the law, Henry Waxman, Democrat, chairman of the House Energy and Commerce Committee, promptly wrote threatening letters to AT&T, Deere and Caterpillar, the three companies with the biggest charge estimates, questioning the charges and ordering their top officials to testify at a hearing. They were ordered to bring with them any analyses related to the impact, any documents, including email, sent to or prepared or reviewed by senior company officials and an explanation of the accounting methods used. When real-life consequences of massive, radical, socialist redistribution entitlements start to be reported, you vilify the law-abiding messengers. Weeks later the hearing was cancelled. [6]

Big Brother is Watching Those Bad Insurance Companies

During the health care reform debates, House Democrats sent a letter to 52 of the nation's largest health insurance companies, demanding detailed information on compensation packages of the companies' highest-paid employees, information on the companies' boards, conferences and sponsored events, profitability of the individual health-care products they sold and revenues earned through government programs like Medicare and Medicaid. [7] Another 1984, Big Brother assault on the free-market economy system for political power gains. Way to go, Congressmen!

Unions Need All the Help They Can Get

In May of 2010 a 76-year-old rule for unionizing airlines and railroads was drastically altered in favor of the unions. The rule used to be that in order to unionize, more than 50% of the employees had to vote yes. The new rule is, that more than 50% of the employees that actually vote, need to vote yes. [8] This change will lead to more labor disputes and higher fares. Thank you, Obama Regime.

Bad Toyota; Bad, Bad Toyota!

The Obama Regime was quick to vilify Toyota publicly for allegedly cutting corners and trading off profits for safety and ignoring and covering up safety issues, once those issues showed up with their Toyota and Lexus vehicles. It was alleged that floor mats caused the gas pedal to get stuck, that gas pedals stuck for other, unknown reasons and that on-board computer anomalies caused sudden acceleration. Over 3,000 complaints were filed, including 75 fatal crashes involving 93 deaths. As more and more details emerged, it appeared most crashed were caused by the drivers themselves and not by any flaws in Toyota vehicles. Extensive investigations and testing by the National Highway Traffic Safety Administration (NHTSA) showed, that only one fatal crash in which 4 people died, was caused by a problem with the vehicle, a floor mat that had trapped the gas pedal in a depressed position. Toyota recalled millions of vehicles to remedy the mat interference problem. Moreover, testing by the NHTSA of dozens of on-board computers of other crashed vehicles showed that *drivers pressing on the gas pedal instead of the brakes had caused all those crashes*. [9]

These findings, favorable to Toyota, were suppressed by the Obama Regime. When asked about it, they claimed they couldn't comment because not all fact-finding and testing were 100% completed! They were very quick to demonize Toyota without solid proof, but when the facts mostly exonerated Toyota, they held back. A reasonable person would have to come to the conclusion, that the Obama Regime again showed their hostility towards business in general and Toyota specifically. They did not criticize General Motors or Chrysler, equally plagued by safety issues, but for the most part owned by the Obama Regime. Don't hold your breath for the Obama Regime to at least apologize to Toyota.

Hostile to Oil
The Obama Regime has shown an unprecedented hostility towards the oil industry, particularly towards BP, which I discuss elsewhere.

The Unholy Alliance between Labor Unions and Democrats

The union membership rate of all U.S. workers dropped from 20.1% in 1983 to 12.3% in 2009 and 11.9% in 2010. The union membership rate for public sector workers at 36.2% dwarfs the rate for private sector workers at 6.9%. About 12% of workers at U.S. subsidiaries of global companies have collective bargaining agreements. [10]

So, what do these numbers tell us? U.S. workers depend less and less on labor unions; public sector workers are way more unionized than public sector workers; the rate of unionization in U.S. subsidiaries of global companies is about the same as for all U.S. workers.

The steep decline in unionization since the eighties has caused a significant decline in union dues and the power the unions – and by extension the U.S. government - hold over the labor force. The unions and Democrats have been in an unholy alliance for decades. Unions take dues from their members and give large sums mainly to Democrats, who in turn empower the unions with lucrative concessions and preferential treatment for both the union bosses and union members. Union members have largely no say in who their bosses give money to. This is bad for the country, business and the economy. The Bureau of Labor Statistics data shows, that average union workers' pay is about 28% higher than pay for comparable jobs for non-union workers and benefits like health insurance and pension plans are even more out of balance. [11] These generous salaries and benefits make companies less competitive and hurt profits. In large part, the decline of the American car industry has been caused by excessive union demands.

Union big-shots, like AFL-CIO President Richard Trumka, are in bed with Democrats. By his own admission, Trumka visits the Obama White House 2-3 times a week [12] - more than any other non-government person - and talks to them every day. The AFL-CIO is the largest U.S. federation of unions, made up of 55 national and international unions, representing over 12 million workers. [13]

Twenty two states in the U.S. have right-to-work laws, giving workers the right to refuse to pay dues and fees to the unions that represent them. In the 28 states that don't have these laws, the unemployment is significantly higher by an average of 0.5 to 0.8 percentage points, [14] demonstrating the negative effect of unions on the economy.

In March of 2011 Obama's National Labor Relations Board or NLRB filed a complaint against Boeing. The NLRB accused Boeing of setting up a non-union production line in South Carolina as retaliation against unionized workers in Washington State for striking four times since 1989. If true, this would be illegal. The NLRB wanted to force Boeing to make all of its Dreamliner planes in the State of Washington, rather than make 30% of those planes in South Carolina.

So, let's cut through the Left's posturing and see what the facts were. Boeing said that it wanted to spread production to multiple sites to become less vulnerable to potential future strikes, which is legal. The Left took offense at what one Boeing executive told The Seattle Times about the main reason for starting a new production line in South Carolina: "we cannot afford to have a work stoppage, you know, every three years." Boeing also said that starting the production line in South Carolina would not lead to layoffs in the State of Washington. To the contrary, jobs would also be added there to produce the new airliner. [15]

The New York Times called yhe complaint "a welcome effort to defend workers' right to collective bargaining." [16] Never mind that what Boeing was planning to do was totally legal. The Obama Chicago-style thuggery kicked in when unions - together with lawyers the biggest Obama contributors - were not getting it their destructive way.

How Accurate are Government Numbers?

It all depends. It varies between reasonably accurate and totally misleading! To begin with, we should always be wary of and question information supplied by the government. A listing of highly inaccurate government-supplied information fills more pages than ObamaCare and the Tax Code combined. Inaccuracies range from the totally innocent and minor to the criminally-twisted and major. A sad example is Medicare. The House Ways and Means Committee estimated that Medicare would cost about $ 12 billion by 1990, but in 1990 the actual cost was 107 billion, nine times higher than the original estimates. [17]

Particular attention needs to be paid to data issued by the Congressional Budget Office (CBO). This government body is claimed to be "impartial" in that it supplies information requested by Democrats, Independents and Republicans alike and under that banner its numbers, figures and estimates are touted by many as being unquestionable. Particularly the Left has a habit of using CBO data selectively in an effort to confuse us, while accusing Conservatives of doing exactly the same thing. So, let's take a closer look.

We need to differentiate sharply between the different kinds of numbers the CBO gives out. When we talk about data concerning past events, like budget shortfalls in past years, we can assume great accuracy of the information. However, when we talk about estimates of future events, like projections of health care costs, budget deficits, etc. all bets are off and we need to be very, very wary! What are the underlying assumptions, what agenda is pushed, what political calculations are made? Estimates of future events the CBO comes up with depend to a major degree on the underlying assumptions *supplied by the very people who request the estimates!* For example, when asked to calculate future budget deficits, the CBO may use unrealistic *assumptions* about economic recovery supplied by the requestor, resulting in future deficit estimates that are way too optimistic.

Taxes

Taxes are at best a necessary evil. They should be as low as possible, but are not. Americans now pay more in taxes than they do in food, clothing and housing combined. [18]

Corporate income taxes, both the published or statutory rates and the effective rates, are among the highest in the world, according to the Organization for Economic Cooperation and Development and the World Bank. [19]

Our progressive taxation system increases the tax rate as the taxable amount increases and there are other provisions that also reward lower incomes and punish higher incomes. In 2008 the top 1% of income earners in the U.S. paid 38% of all federal income taxes, the top 10% paid 70%, the bottom 50% paid less than 3% and the bottom 49% paid nothing at all. [20] The bottom 40 percent gets *free money* from you, the taxpayer, because they get more money in tax credits than they would otherwise owe in taxes. [21] This is pure Socialism, theft and income redistribution. Estate Taxes, also called Death Taxes, add insult to injury since, upon a person's death, they tax *again* what's left of lifelong earnings *after paying taxes every year.*

Obama promised: "I can make a firm pledge. Under my plan, no family making less than $250,000 a year will see any form of tax increase. Not your income tax, not your payroll tax, not your capital gains taxes, not any of your taxes." [22] He broke the promise: read on.

Taxes may have to increase if spending by the Obama Regime is not cut dramatically. The Obama Regime has already suggested that a nation-wide federal sales tax or *value added tax* (VAT) would be necessary. [23] This would be over and above any current state and local sales taxes.

The Obama Regime has also suggested that *mortgage interest deductions* be killed or drastically reduced. Only a radical Socialist or a clueless, economic illiterate would even think of doing this, let alone talk about it and suggest it, as this *would devastate* homeowners, the construction industry, the banking and mortgage industry and the American economy in general.

Taxes on cigarettes, other tobacco products and indoor tanning services have gone up already. Starting in 2013 Medicare taxes will increase and those taxes will also - for the first time ever - be due on investment income, not just on earned income. Starting in 2014 people will be taxed when they don't buy health insurance. There are also new fees for health insurance companies and prescription drug manufacturers and a new tax on high-cost "Cadillac" health insurance plans.

All these tax increases will have a devastating effect on the economy, unemployment, inflation and prices for goods and services.

Expiration of the Bush Income Tax Rates
The Bush income tax rates were scheduled to expire at the end of 2010, unless they were extended or made permanent. If not extended at all, taxes would *increase by $3.8 trillion* over 10 years, [24] *the biggest ever tax increase in American history.* [25] Obama said that he would extend those tax cuts only for families making less than $250,000 per year, in which case taxes would **increase by $678 billion** for families making more than $250,000 per year, [26] but it remained to be seen if he would keep that promise. The issue had not been resolved less than a month before the Bush tax rates would expire. The House approved an extension for families making less than $250,000 per year, but the Senate voted it down. During a deep recession, businesses and individuals still didn't know what the tax situation would be in 2011, let alone beyond that timeframe.

Increasing taxes on "the rich" is a socialist and Democrat hallmark, but it would cause "the rich" to invest less and create less jobs. So how was this kind of extreme redistribution of wealth fair as Democrats claimed? Here is how taxes would change if the Bush tax cuts simply expired: [27]

2010 Income Tax Bracket	2011 Income Tax Bracket	Increase
10%	15%	50%
15%	15%	none
25%	28%	12%
28%	31%	11%
33%	36%	9%
35%	39.6%	13%
2010 Capital Gains Tax	2011 Capital Gains Tax	Increase
15%	20%	33%
2010 Dividend Tax	2011 Dividend Tax	Increase
15%	39.6%	164%

In addition, the "marriage penalty" would worsen, child tax credits would be cut, dependent care and adoption tax credits would be cut and the Death Tax would be reinstated.

The Tax Deal

After Obama and the Democrats suffered a defeat of historic proportions in the 2010 mid-term elections, Obama caved and gave in to Republican demands to not let the Bush tax rates expire on December 31, 2010, but extend them for two years for everyone, over strong objections from members of his own party. The deal was approved by Congress. Here are additional provisions of the deal: [28]

- Extends unemployment insurance benefits till the end of 2011
- Lowers Social Security payroll taxes from 6.2% to 4.2% during 2011 at a cost of $120 billion
- Continues tax cuts for families and students from the Stimulus Bill at a cost of $40 billion

- Allow 100% write-off of business capital purchases during 2011
- Sets the estate tax at 35% for 2011 and 2012 with a $5 million asset limit

The deal amounted to $858 billion in total over the next ten years, [29] but it was not offset by savings elsewhere thus adding to the deficit and the mounting national debt at a time when we urgently needed to reverse years of financial mismanagement by the government!

This deal was too much of a Republican compromise in many different ways. Republicans broke one of their promises of the September 2010 Pledge to America, to support only bills that addressed a single legislative issue; the deal was laden with pork and totally unrelated issues like unemployment benefits. It should have been deficit neutral and only include extending the Bush tax rates and spending cuts elsewhere to offset the costs; the cost of the deal far exceeded the original Stimulus Bill and would add dramatically to the deficit and national debt. Increasing unemployment benefits even more doesn't help the economy one bit; smaller government, less government spending and lower taxes do.

Spending Your Tax Dollars Illegally

More pages than the U.S. tax code have been written on how your tax dollars are wasted every day, so I won't go into that subject here. But I want to highlight just one example of how your hard-earned money is spent illegally, so read on.

The Planned Parenthood Tax Fraud

Planned Parenthood claims to be "a trusted health care provider, an informed educator, a passionate advocate, and a global partner helping similar organizations around the world. Planned Parenthood delivers vital reproductive health care, sex education, and information to millions of women, men, and young people worldwide." [30] They don't mention that they are the largest abortion provider in the U.S. [31]

Planned Parenthood tries to downplay their involvement in abortions. They don't disclose how much of their revenue comes from abortions. So, let's take a closer look, which requires some digging for data. In mid-June 2011 Planned Parenthood still hadn't published their 2009-2010 annual report - their fiscal year runs from July through June - so you have to look at their 2008-2009 annual report, which states that abortions are 3% or about 328,000 out of 10,943,609 "total services". Assuming conservative average revenues of $500 per abortion you arrive at total revenues for abortions of $164 million or 15% of their $1.1 billion total revenue. That's quite a different number from the 3% Planned Parenthood use for an argument of how little involvement they have in abortions.

During the same 2008-2009 fiscal year, Planned Parenthood received 33% of their $1.1 billion revenue or $363 million of your tax money, in the form of government grants. By law, tax money cannot be used for abortions. Planned Parenthood claims that 363 million of your taxpayer dollars are used to support non-abortion related "reproductive health" assistance to low-income people. Sounds good, right? Low-income people get non-abortion related "reproductive health" care with subsidies from the taxpayer and any abortions are not subsidized by the taxpayer. So how can Planned Parenthood possibly make sure that none of the $363 million of your money goes toward abortions? Well, they can't and for all we know, they don't even try to accurately separate all their non-abortion related activities and expenses from those related to abortions. They don't have a firewall between strictly separated organizations. And even if they could and would, it wouldn't make any difference because under such a scenario, each and every tax payer dollar that comes in to support non-abortion related activities would free up money to be spend on abortions. There is no way around it: your tax money helps support abortions performed by Planned Parenthood and that is a violation of law. Their claim that no taxpayer money goes for abortions is a fallacy.

We are supposed to believe their claim, that they work within the law, while they tell supposed pimps how 14- and 15-year old girls, who work for them as prostitutes, can get abortions at Planned Parenthood, no questions asked!

Thank goodness, some people are waking up and demand that laws are followed. After Republicans regained control of the House in the October 2010 mid-term elections, they started efforts to defund Planned Parenthood.

4. Spending, Deficits and National Debt

The Left is spending money we don't have to push through their radical, socialist agenda. Taxpayer money is wasted like there is no tomorrow. Deficits and debt are increasing rapidly to disastrous levels. Serious attempts to rein in our spending are dismissed with contempt. We are heading for economic collapse and burdening future generations with crushing debts.

Out-of-Control Spending

The Left continues the zealous pursuit of their socialist ideology of bigger government, more spending and bigger intrusion of government in people's private lives and freedoms. Out-of-control spending helps them to push through their radical agenda and buy votes in the process. Like in any other country where the socialist model of big government and big government spending and entitlements has been tried, we in the U.S. are in a death spiral of our own Welfare state.

Socialist Europe in particular has been on this path for decades and many countries in Europe are in financial crisis mode, threatening the economy of the European Union as a whole. Greece is on the verge of economic collapse and is forced to enact draconian austerity programs and cut Social Security payments and government workers pay, amongst others. Italy, Spain, Portugal, Ireland and England are also particularly vulnerable. In the summer of 2010 Italy announced that government workers' pay would be frozen and other expenses would be reduced. As a result, there would be a budget surplus and the Italian national debt would shrink; they would do this without increasing taxes. Germany decided to cut government spending drastically to stave off economic collapse. Denmark cut the duration of its unemployment compensation in half. As could be expected, the die-hard European Socialists protested loudly.

Our aging population has been promised huge, unfunded health and retirement benefits. Government spending outstrips revenues by huge amounts, resulting in massive budget deficits and steep increases in our national debt. Sooner or later this bubble will burst with extreme consequences: higher inflation, tax increases and ultimately, economic collapse.

Erskine Bowles, businessman, educator and political figure who co-chaired Obama's debt commission, testified in March of 2011 before the Senate Budget Committee, that we faced the most predictable economic crisis in history and that we had maybe two years left to act: [1]
"I'm really concerned. I think we face the most predictable economic crisis in history. A lot of us sitting in this room didn't see this last crisis as it came upon us. But this one is really easy to see. The fiscal path we are on today is simply not sustainable."
"This debt and these deficits that we are incurring on an annual basis are like a cancer and they are truly going to destroy this country from within unless we have the common sense to do something about it."

"I used to say that I got into this thing for my grandchildren. I have eight grandchildren under five years old. I'll have one more in a week. And my life is wonderful and it is wild. But this problem is going to happen long before my grandchildren grow up."

"This problem is going to happen, like the former chairman of the Fed said, or the Moody's said, this is a problem we're going to have to face up. It may be two years, you know, maybe a little less, maybe a little more. But if our bankers over there in Asia begin to believe that we're not going to be solid on our debt, that we're not going to be able to meet our obligations, just stop and think for a minute what happens if they just stop buying our debt."

"What happens to interest rates? And what happens to the U.S. economy? The markets will absolutely devastate us if we don't step up to this problem. The problem is real, the solutions are painful, and we have to act."

In December of 2010 [2] and again in January of 2011 [3] Moody's Investors Service warned that if the U.S. wouldn't get serious about reining in the budget deficit, its AAA credit rating might be downgraded in the following 12 to 18 months.

In April of 2011 the International Monetary Fund [4] stated that the U.S. lacked a promising strategy on how to curb its growing government debt, that the U.S. was the only advanced economy to increase its budget deficit, rather than decrease it, and that the U.S. should introduce more severe austerity measures.

Also in April of 2011 credit rating agency Standard & Poor's (S&P) changed its outlook on the U.S. debt from "stable" to "negative" and said there was at least a one-in-three likelihood that the U.S. could lose its AAA credit rating within two years for failure to reduce its debt burden. [5] Losing the AAA rating would mean that it would be much more difficult for the U.S. to borrow money and that we would have to pay significantly higher interest rates.

In yet another example of Chicago-style thuggery, the Obama regime had put pressure on S&P [6] not to lower its outlook, during a series of private meetings with the ratings agency. However, S&P did not give in to the pressure and stood by their opinion.

The Obama Machine went immediately into damage control mode. In April of 2011 Treasury Secretary Timothy Geithner said he disagreed that the U.S. outlook was negative and believed there was "broad consensus" to reduce the deficit. [7] See the subtle spin? While S&P looked at the key issue of the staggering U.S. debt, caused by out-of-control spending, borrowing and budget deficits, Geithner commented only - with a false claim of "broad consensus" - on reducing the deficit, not reducing the debt! Economics 101 note to Geithner: reducing the key driver of our credit rating, debt, requires not only reducing the deficit, but eliminating it altogether and turning it into a budget surplus.

The U.S. is a member of the Group of Twenty (G-20), a group of finance ministers and central bank governors of 19 countries plus the European single currency, the Euro. Collectively, the G-20 represents 85% of the global economy, 80% of world trade and two-thirds of the world population. At a meeting in Toronto in June of 2010, G-20 agreed that all their countries, except Japan, would cut their deficits in half by 2013. [8] Canada had already announced significant cuts before the G-20 meeting. [9] England announced massive spending cuts in October of 2010. [10] And what did Obama, the economic illiterate, do? Drastically increase spending and the deficit!

Even communist Cuba started to see the light! In September of 2010 the Cuban government admitted that their economic model had failed and announced that it would reduce public jobs by a million. [11] While socialist Europe and communist Cuba embarked on austerity measures to drastically reduce government spending to avoid the collapse of their economies, Obama argued for more government "stimulus" spending while at the same time saying that we needed to start living within our means! The Obama Regime's reckless spending to push through their radical agenda is not only economic suicide, but a grave moral misdeed by burdening future generations with crushing debts.

Government spending is a necessary evil at best and should be limited to the absolute minimum. But that's not what is happening. Federal, state and local governments spend our tax money like drunken sailors, with apologies to drunken sailors, who spend their own money, not someone else's. Every dollar spent by government is a dollar less available to individuals and the private sector to spend as they see fit, cater to their needs and create wealth. Government doesn't create wealth, but consumes it. This economics 101 principle also explains why government spending is not the cure for slowdowns, recessions, depressions, deficits and debts; it makes things worse, much worse, as history has shown repeatedly.

Spending, deficits and borrowing

Let's see how Obama's spending and deficits compare to Bush's. Also note that Congress controls the U.S. purse strings. The president can't spend a penny without approval from Congress. Democrats, who love to portray Bush as a big spender, controlled Congress during the last two years of the Bush administration and thus were instrumental in the deficit spending during those two years.

U.S. Federal Spending, Surpluses and Deficits					
President	Fiscal Year	Spending in Trillion $ [12]	Surplus or Deficit (-) in Trillion $ [13]	Borrowed of Every $ Spent	Cumulative Surplus/Deficit Under Each Pres
Bush	2001	1.863	0.128		0.128
Bush	2002	2.011	-0.158	8 cents	-0.030
Bush	2003	2.160	-0.378	18 cents	-0.408
Bush	2004	2.293	-0.413	18 cents	-0.821
Bush	2005	2.427	-0.318	13 cents	-1.139
Bush	2006	2.655	-0.248	9 cents	-1.387
Bush	2007	2.729	-0.161	6 cents	-1.548
Bush	2008	2.983	-0.459	15 cents	-2.007
Obama	2009	3.520	-1.416	40 cents	-1.416
Obama	2010	3.456	-1.294	37 cents	-2.710
Obama	2011	3.819	-1.645	43 cents	-4.335
Obama	2012	3.729	-1.101	30 cents	-5.456

Note: numbers in **bold** are actuals.

As the numbers clearly show, Bush was a big deficit spender most of his 8 years in office. However, Obama makes him look like Mr. Scrooge! Obama racked up more deficits in two years than Bush did in eight!

In 2009, spending under Obama increased by *18%* and represented *25% of GDP* - Gross Domestic Product, the size of the whole U.S. economy. Historically we were at 20%. So Obama took an extra 5% of GDP away from the private sector, the creator of most of the jobs. The deficit was *3x the previous year's* and representing *10% of GDP, the highest percentage since 1945*, at the height of the U.S. involvement in World War II.

For 2011 Obama proposed to freeze spending. Sure, let's keep spending at historically high and unsustainable levels! He did not propose this for 2009, his first year in office, not for 2010 when he voiced that idea in January, but for 2011. You know, *after mid-term elections*. Get the drift? However, there was nothing frozen about the budget for FY 2011: a spending *increase of 11%* and a staggering deficit increase of *27%!* Part of the revenues was claimed to come from Cap and Trade, a legislation that was nearly dead. So how come Obama counted on that income? Not to mention that the 2011 revenue estimates were based on overly optimistic expectations of economic recovery. This budget helped to create jobs? That's the kind of fiscal responsibility Obama talked about in his January 2010 State of the Union address to Congress, in a time of extreme economic hardship? Both Obama and his Democrat collaborators are either economic illiterates and truly believe that you can spend yourself out of debt, or they want to collapse our economy on purpose.

For 2012, proposed spending was barely less than 2011. Estimates were based on predictions of economic recovery that were, again, way too optimistic, assuming a 4-5% growth in our economy.

National Debt

Instead of living within our means and paying off our debt, our out-of-control government spends our tax dollars like there is no tomorrow, piles deficit on top of deficit and drives this country off the cliff! Our national debt is increasing at an alarming rate.

President	Fiscal Year	National Debt at end of Fiscal Year in Trillion $ Actual Are Bold [14]
Clinton	2000	**5.7**
Bush	2001	**5.8**
Bush	2002	**6.2**
Bush	2003	**6.8**
Bush	2004	**7.4**
Bush	2005	**7.9**
Bush	2006	**8.5**
Bush	2007	**9.0**
Bush	2008	**10.0**
Obama	2009	**11.9**
Obama	2010	**13.6**
Obama	2011	much more than 14.3?
March 2009 CBO estimate	2018	19
March 2010 CBO estimate	2019	23
February 2011 CBO estimate	2020	27

Note: number in **bold** are actuals.

Under eight years of Bush the national debt grew by *$4.3 trillion*, while under two years of Obama it grew by *$3.6 trillion!*

The CBO and many economists pointed out that the White House February 2009 10-year deficit estimate of *$7.1 trillion* was based on assumptions about economic recovery that were way too optimistic. In August 2009 the White House revised their prediction to *$9 trillion.* [15] This massive adjustment shows that Obama and his economic advisors are *incompetent, criminally dishonest or both.*

Obama's spending plans would almost double the 2008 national debt in 10 years, from $10 trillion to $19 trillion, an increase almost as big as the debt accumulated by all pre-Obama governments over the preceding 233 years since the Declaration of Independence in 1776!

In October of 2010 the national debt stood at *$13.6 trillion* or about *$45,000* **for** every man, woman and child in America. A child born in 2020 would inherit from us at birth a debt of about *$75,000!* This is nothing less than child abuse; it is stealing from future generations to further the Left's radical agenda now.

How Do We Pay For Our Government's Reckless Spending?

How are we going to pay for this government's reckless, out-of-control spending on their radical agenda? Because Obama will spend way, way more money than is coming in, we will have to borrow way more than we already have and/or drastically increase taxes. Borrowed money will have to be paid back sooner or later. If we don't start now to reduce our spending drastically and pay off our debts, then this will fall on the shoulders of future generations, so the term "generational theft", awful as it is, applies here.

If we don't get spending under control we are looking at:

- **higher taxes.** Not only for the rich, but for everybody. No doubt the rich will be hardest hit and with them the creation of jobs and wealth, the major driving forces of a free-market economy system, but there is only so much income of the rich to tax, so the middle class will not escape increases. Tobacco taxes have already been increased under Obama, his campaign promises notwithstanding. The Democrats have already proposed a nation-wide, federal sales tax or VAT, over and above any current state and local sales taxes. Then there are proposals for a soda-pop tax and taxing employer provided health insurance. The list will get longer and more painful over time, guaranteed.

- **printing more money** causing the devaluation of the dollar, higher inflation and steep price increases for goods and services for everybody.

- **ultimately, the collapse of the U.S. economy.** Unless steps are taken to drastically reduce government spending and the national debt, the reckless spending of this government will cause the collapse of the U.S. economy and with it, the world economy. When that happens, the Great Depression will look like a walk in the park in comparison.

Unfunded Liabilities

And then there's the nasty little issue of unfunded U.S. liabilities - future financial commitments that are not currently funded and for which no future funding has been identified. According to usdebtclock.org, total U.S. unfunded liabilities in June of 2011 were **$114 trillion**. The ingredients in this deadly mix were: Medicare liabilities of **$79 trillion**, prescription drug liabilities of **$20 trillion** and Social Security liabilities of **$15 trillion**. That's more than **$366,000** for every man, woman and child in America and more than **$1 million** for each taxpayer. Or to look at it from a different perspective: the **$114 trillion** of unfunded liabilities is more than twice the **$50 trillion** of the total wealth of the U.S.,¹⁶ adding up the value of all private, business and government possessions: houses, buildings, factories, furniture, cars, boats, trains, airplanes, arms, savings, investments, stocks, bonds, securities, etc. Now there's some food for thought! But the Obama Regime could care less: they **spend, spend, and spend**.

Social Security
FDR signed Social Security into law in 1935. The program was meant to be a safety net for the 1930's for those people fortunate enough to reach the age of 65; it was never meant to be what it is today: an entitlement program for everyone. Things have changed dramatically over the years, with people living healthier, longer lives. There is an ever-increasing imbalance between how much money comes in and how much goes out. In 1945 there were 42 workers putting money into the system for every Social Security beneficiary; in 2009 it was 3:1 and it is heading towards 2:1 in 2025. [17] The burden on workers to pay for beneficiaries is increasing and the unsustainable system is running out of money.

What hasn't changed is the Democrats' appetite for doling out other people's money. In April of 2011 almost 60 million people received Social Security and Social Security Income (SSI) benefits, averaging $1,077 per month. [18] In 2010 Social Security for the first time in its history **paid out more money than it took in** and the program would run out of money in 2036, [19] one year earlier than projected previously in 2010, compliments of the economic malaise.

Clearly, this unsustainable entitlement program is on a collision course with reality and needs drastic reforms. So what happens when more money is paid out than comes in? The shortfalls will have to come out of the budget, paid for by you, the taxpayer!

Bush tried to reform Social Security and proposed to allow younger people to put some or all of their contributions into selected low-risk, long-term investments if they chose to do so. His proposal made a lot of sense. But Bush was immediately and savagely attacked by the Left. He was accused of wanting to steal from grandpa and grandma and his initiative didn't go anywhere.

Obama promised to protect Social Security, but failed to indicate how he would do that. At the 75-year anniversary of Social Security in 2010 he played politics as usual by trumpeting Democrat support for the program and accusing Republicans of trying to destroy it. [20] If you have the guts to face a problem head-on and want to work on fixing it, Obama is there to accuse you of evil intent. He accused Republicans of wanting to privatize Social Security. He called privatization "an ill- conceived idea that would add trillions of dollars to our budget deficit while tying your benefits to the whims of Wall Street traders and the ups and downs of the stock market." [21] Obama could not resist the temptation to take yet another swipe at our free-market economy system in general and specifically those evil traders and the stock market.

Contrary to how Obama tries to paint it as a disaster, privatization would not affect Social Security for anyone over age 55 and would allow those younger to *opt* to put part of their Social Security payroll taxes into a limited and relatively safe group of investments similar to an IRA and overseen by the Social Security Administration. This would mean higher payouts for individuals and lower costs for the government, a win-win situation.

But economic illiterate Obama has no concept of investing for the long term in low-risk investments or worse he has, but attacks it to push his socialist agenda of tax-and-spend and ever-increasing power of the government over the individual.

Medicare

This program mostly provides health insurance for people age 65 and over and people under 65 with physical disabilities. Like Social Security, funding for Medicare comes from payroll deductions and employer contributions. Because of less and less workers paying into the system as compared to Medicare beneficiaries, Americans living longer and the cost of health insurance continuing to rise, this program is unsustainable over the long run. According to a May 2011 annual report by trustees who oversee the Medicare entitlement program, [22] it would run out of money in 2024, five years earlier than projected a year earlier, compliments of the economic malaise.

The 2010 Debt Commission

In April of 2010 Obama appointed a presidential deficit commission, the National Commission on Fiscal Responsibility and Reform. The commission was to suggest ways to address the mounting national debt. It should be clear to everyone, that staying the current course of social engineering and out-of-control spending will lead to the collapse of our country's economy. But instead of Obama facing up to the mess he created himself, heading a team effort with Pelosi and Reid and making the necessary changes, he appointed a commission in an effort to distance himself from suggestions the commission would necessarily have to make to get the debt under control.

One of the co-chairs of the commission, Erskine Bowles, seems to agree with my dire view on this country's financial and economic future if we stay the Obama course. He said that the government's current spending trends "will destroy the country from within."

In November of 2010 the two co-chairmen of the commission issued the draft of the recommendations, [23] including:

- eliminating/reducing the child tax credit
- eliminating/reducing mortgage interest deductions
- eliminating/reducing business deductions for employer-provided health care
- eliminating/reducing the tax-free status for employees of employer-provided health care
- increasing gas taxes
- increasing Social Security payroll taxes
- increasing the Social Security retirement age
- lowering of Social Security cost-of-living increases
- paying even higher Social Security benefits to people who have had lower-wage careers and even lower benefits to people with higher-wage careers than is currently the case; translation: even more aggressive redistribution of wealth
- curtailing Medicare spending even further
- making deep cuts in defense spending
- drastically reducing overseas bases
- freezing pay for most military and other federal employees for 3 years
- cutting the federal workforce by 10%

- reducing federal spending
- elimination of earmarks
- no changes to ObamaCare

In short: significantly higher taxes - *$1 trillion* over the next 10 years - , lower benefits for virtually everybody and further damage to our national security, but without balancing the budgets. Elimination of mortgage interest deductions would send the home mortgage industry in a further tailspin and raise taxes for most home-owners. It was claimed that the recommendations could reduce total deficits over the next 10 years by as much as *$3.9 trillion*. [24] Note however that this *would not eliminate* deficits, only reduce them! For instance, under this plan the deficit for 2015 would still amount to *$421 billion*.

The plan came under immediate attack from both the Right and the Left. Both chairmen of the commission acknowledged right away that their plan was so controversial, that it was dead on arrival; they just hoped that it might prompt a more realistic debate about what would be required to solve the nation's fiscal woes.

The full 18-member commission recommendations report was made public in early December 2010, but it did not obtain the 14 out of 18 votes to officially send the plan to Congress for consideration. [25] And so the orchestra continues to play and the deckchairs are being rearranged while the ship is sinking fast. Don't you love your government?

There was also talk on both sides of the aisle to apply *means testing* to Social Security, [26] meaning when you are finally old enough to qualify for Social Security, if and how much you get would depend on your financial situation. People with little financial means, either through no fault of their own, laziness, failure to save and invest, gambling habits, etc., would get the higher payments. People with substantial financial means, either through inheritance, luck or hard work, saving and investing, would get less or nothing. Pure redistribution of wealth!

The Lack of a 2011 Budget

Despite the fact that Democrats controlled the White House, the House of Representatives and the Senate, they did not establish a budget for 2011. Instead, expenses for 2011 were approved by Congress for limited durations like a couple of weeks or months at a time using a Continuing Resolution or CR.

Under this scenario, when Congress can't agree on approving the next amount of money, the U.S. Government will shut down except for essential services. The CR process and the possibility of government shutdowns create uncertainty and negatively impact the economy, businesses and jobs.

The Obama regime didn't want to go on record just before the 2010 mid-term elections as the big spenders they were and they apparently thought they could make political hay out of battles with Republicans over the Continuing Resolution.

The Obama 2012 Budget Proposal, Take One

Obama claimed that his goal was to reach a "primary balance" in the budget, meaning that expenses, not including interest payments on the national debt, would not exceed revenue. But, while pretending to care about our economic future and saying repeatedly that we need to live within our means, Obama continued to spend like a drunken sailor and showed a total lack of leadership and intellectual honesty, when he proposed his 2012 budget in February of 2011: [27] insane, unsustainable spending of **$3.7 trillion** and a deficit of **$1.1 trillion** in 2012 and projected deficits totaling **$7.2 trillion** over 10 years. It included massive tax increases by letting the Bush tax rates expire at the end of 2012.

In March 2011 the CBO released their assessment of Obama's budget proposal, [28] saying that he severely underestimated future budget deficits. The CBO, quoting Obama's overly optimistic projections of economic recovery and tax revenue and unsubstantiated claims of savings, estimated the deficits to total **$9.5 trillion** over 10 years.

Obama did not reduce any of the big entitlement programs by a single penny. He did not endorse any of the major elements of the debt commission's recommendations, so why did he appoint them in the first place? So he could claim that he at least tried? Obama totally ignored the message from voters in the 2010 mid-term elections and wanted to continue to spend us into oblivion. His budget director Jacob Lew opined that any drastic spending reduction plans offered by the president would simply become a target for partisan attack. [29] Boy, what a great excuse!

There was no way that this proposed budget would be approved by Congress and major cuts would have to be made. In my opinion there were several reasons why Obama didn't propose a drastically reduced 2012 budget, needed to avert an economic meltdown: he didn't really care about this country and its citizen; he wasn't interested to turn the country and our economy around; he wanted to push his radical, socialist agenda at any cost; he wanted the necessary, significant spending cuts to be spearheaded by Republicans, so he could blame them for the consequences, like the Democrats did when Bush proposed to address the Social Security crisis. Soon enough the Obama Regime would start blaming Republicans for being mean to the elderly, women, children, poor people, people of color, etc.

The Senate **unanimously** rejected Obama's $3.7 trillion 2012 budget on May 25, 2011. All 52 Democrats and all 45 Republicans voted against it.

The Disappearing 2011 Spending Cuts

Washington can be a mysterious place with lots of huffing and puffing, smoke, mirrors, and demagoguery. Results may vary and can be unpredictable, unreliable or sometimes plainly unbelievable. Take the case of the incredible shrinking spending cuts for 2011. Republicans campaigned for the 2010 mid-term elections with a promise to cut $100 billion from 2011 spending, but later prorated that to $61 billion, [30] arguing that almost half of the fiscal year had already passed. Sounds kind of reasonable, but you still wonder about the campaign promise. So the Republican-controlled House passed a resolution to cut 2011 spending by $61 billion or a mere 2%. That minute amount was apparently too much for the Left to swallow. Obama objected to such "deep cuts" and claimed to be willing to meet Republicans "halfway" and proposed cuts of first $4 billion and then $10.5 billion or 0.3%. Did he get any basic math education at all or is 10.5 really the middle between zero and 61? Now I'm beginning to doubt my own math skills!

Apparently Obama was right when he said in the past: "America has a debt problem and a failure of leadership." Meanwhile, the country was going to hell in the proverbial hand basket, compliments of the Left. But not to worry, the Democrats really got the message, upped the ante and offered a "courageous" $33 billion or 1% in cuts! [31]

In March 2011, New York Democrat Representative Anthony Weiner, after blaming Bush for Obama's record spending and deficits - "...and that's a tragedy that President Bush drove us into this cliff..." - proudly stated that he had proposed to cut – drum roll please – $400 million from 2011 spending, representing a whopping 0.01%! [32] Wow, the Congressman was really serious when he said that he too wanted to cut spending. Another way to look at that $400 million cut: in 2011 the Obama Regime spent that amount of money every 55 minutes!

In the fight on possible 2011 spending cuts, Obama was mostly AWOL, limited his involvement to a few pronouncements and showed not even a trace of leadership. The worst part of the whole spending cut debate was that Obama held military pay hostage. For decades, government shutdowns have been guided by a directive issued during the Reagan years. Under this directive, military paychecks would continue while politicians argued about budget issues. Bill Clinton kept military paychecks flowing during the last government shutdown. Not Obama! He decided to suspend military pay if it would come to a shutdown. Despicable!

It came very close to a government shutdown on Friday April 8 with just one more hour to go, when a compromise was reached and it looked like $38.5 billion or 1.0% in spending cuts through the end of September 2011, [33] not the $100 billion Republicans promised during the 2010 mid-term elections and not the $61 billion Republicans had sought. However, the CBO estimated that the deal would cut federal spending for non-war activities by just $352 million [34] or a measly 0.01%, because large amounts of money would not have been spent anyway. Worse yet, when war outlays were factored in, expenses would actually go up, not down, by $3.3 billion! [35]

So, the net result of all this bickering, posturing, threatening to shut down or at least slow down the government and compromising resulted in - drum roll please - spending cuts of **0.01%** for 2011 or an amount equal to what Obama spent each and every 48 minutes! It's amazing what honest, hardworking presidents and Congress-people can achieve if they really put their mind to it!

You could argue that the long-term reductions in spending would be way, way bigger and you would be right, sort of. What was promised by Republicans to be a $315 billion reduction in spending over a 10 year period [36] was estimated by the CBO to amount to only $122 billion over 10 years. [37] That's an average reduction per year of − drum loll please − 0.3%!

Defunding ObamaCare and Planned Parenthood were taken out of the resolution and would be voted on separately in the Senate - they were already approved in the House. It remained to be seen if the Planned Parenthood defunding would pass in the Democrat-controlled Senate. Using taxpayer money for abortions was - and still is - against the law, but the Obama regime hadn't exactly been playing by the rule of law, to say it mildly. Defunding ObamaCare in the Democrat-controlled Senate would require a miracle.

Republicans caved and didn't fulfill their promises made during the 2010 mid-term election campaign. You could say that $38.5 billion was better than nothing and it indeed was the biggest spending cut in U.S. history - at least on paper - as Obama was so eager to observe, without also mentioning the fact that he was the biggest spender in U.S. history. But if you couldn't win a battle to cut spending by $100 billion or $61 billion, how could you win the battle to cut $6.2 trillion, as the Ryan 2011 budget proposal sought?

We need to slash spending rigorously to save this country from economic collapse. It will be an enormous task. And expect it to get very, very ugly! Although everyone's wellbeing is at stake, the Left will do everything in their power, including name-calling, character assassination, demagoguery, manipulation, distortion, misinformation, lies and bribes to push through their radical agenda, even if it means the destruction of our society. Which begs the question: is the radical Left, with Obama in the lead role, destroying this country on purpose, to collapse the system and take total control? I don't think there is even any room for doubt!

Proposals to cut spending will be called draconian, severe or cruel. Spending cut proposers will be demonized, vilified and accused of stealing from women, children, minorities, people of color, the poor, and forcing the elderly to lose their houses and eat dog food. And sure enough, here we go:

Debbie Wasserman Schultz
Democrat, U.S. Representative for Florida, said that cutting federal spending would hurt people who have cancer. [38]

Nancy Pelosi
Democrat, House of Representatives Minority Leader, after the Republican controlled House passed a resolution to cut $61 billion from the 2011 budget: "When it comes to health and education, Republicans put women and children last." [39]

Debbie Wasserman Schultz

"If we don't fund early schooling for poor families their kids will become criminals." [40]

Harry Reid

Democrat, Senate Majority Leader, called the same $61 billion spending cut "mean-spirited" [41] and lamented that the GOP's proposed budget cuts would eliminate the annual "cowboy poetry festival" in his home state of Nevada: "The mean-spirited bill, H.R. 1 ... eliminates the National Endowment of the Humanities, National Endowment of the Arts," said Reid. "These programs create jobs. The National Endowment of the Humanities is the reason we have in northern Nevada every January a cowboy poetry festival. Had that program not been around, the tens of thousands of people who come there every year would not exist." [42] That's right, your tax dollars are wasted on Nevada cowboy poetry festivals and eliminating the funding is heartless!

Anthony Weiner

Democrat, Representative for New York, derided Republicans after the House passed a bill that would block federal funding for NPR, which aired the popular show "Car Talk": "What a relief. I'm glad we got the economy back going ... I'm so glad we secured our nuclear power plants. So glad Americans are going back to work ... The American people are not concerned about the economy around the world. They're staring at their radio station saying, 'Get rid of Click and Clack.' Finally my Republican friends are getting rid of them. Kudos to you." [43]

Nancy Pelosi

Referring to the original HR1 bill to cut $61 billion from 2011 spending, Nancy Pelosi, Democrat, House of Representatives Minority Leader, said: "In one of the bills before us, six million seniors are deprived of meals, homebound seniors are deprived of meals. People ask us to find our common ground, the middle ground. Is middle ground three million seniors not receiving meals? I don't think so. We've got to take this conversation from a debate about numbers and dollar figures and finding middle ground there to the higher ground of national values. I don't think the American people want any one of those six million people to lose their meals or the children who are being thrown off of Head Start and the rest of it." [44] Later she corrected herself and said that she should have said "six million meals" instead of "six million seniors". [45] Oh, yeah, now it makes a lot more sense, Nancy! Republicans are mean-spirited!

The Republican 2012 Budget Proposal aka the Ryan Budget

Our only hope to save this country form total collapse is for conservative Republicans, Tea Party favorites and the few remaining conservative Democrats to work together diligently to turn this country around.

In April 2011 House Budget Committee Chairman Paul Ryan, Republican Representative for Wisconsin, unveiled the Republican 2012 budget proposal. [46] It sought to downsize government, reduce spending by $6.2 trillion and the deficit by $4.4 trillion over 10 years compared to Obama's 2012 budget proposal, reach a "primary balance" by 2015, balance the budget by 2030 and pay off our debt over time. It emphasized social support, social mobility and personal choice.

Let's take a brief, overall look at what the Ryan proposal would do over 10 years as compared to Obama's first proposal:

- Cut spending by a total of $6.2 trillion
- Cut taxes by $2.7 trillion
- Lower interest payments on the debt by $ 900 billion
- Reduce the deficit by $4.4 trillion

Notes:
Repeal of ObamaCare will cut taxes by $800 billion
Lower interest payments are based on 5.1% interest

While the proposed cuts might not be deep enough, it was the most courageous and comprehensive budget reform proposal in our lifetime and showed leadership and accountability so lacking in Obama's irresponsible and out-of-control 2012 budget proposal. This Republican proposal might become the 2012 Republican elections platform.

Social Security, Medicare and Medicaid are the biggest drivers of our debt. None of those programs would see funding cuts, but would grow at a slower, more sustainable pace than under Democrat plans. *Social Security*, which covers about 60 million senior citizens and disabled Americans, would not be changed. *Medicare*, the huge health program for the elderly, would be replaced for those younger than 55 by a program similar to that for members of Congress. Rather than paying for seniors' medical costs outright, the government would help retired people financially to purchase private health insurance through an exchange. This would likely raise out-of-pocket costs and limit coverage, but the current system is simply unsustainable. On the bright side, Medicare would not see a *$732 billion* cut as planned under ObamaCare. *Medicaid* for poor Americans would be restructured to limit federal expenses by establishing block grant for states, giving states more flexibility on how to use the money for social Welfare programs. ObamaCare would be repealed and defunded.

The maximum tax rate for corporations and individuals would decrease from 35% to 25% to fuel economic recovery, while elimination of tax loopholes would result in net revenue gains.

The proposal also tackled agriculture subsidies and other corporate Welfare and consolidated job-training programs into a single adult scholarship. It reformed housing assistance and Food Stamps.

This Republican proposal would force Obama to sharply revise his first 2012 budget proposal, but in the meantime the attacks on the Ryan proposal began. Reaction from the Left was swift and predictable. For example:

Nancy Pelosi
Democrat, House Minority Leader, Representative for California: "A path to poverty for America's seniors and children." [47]

Xavier Becerra
Democrat, Representative for California: "Waging war on American workers." [48]

Debbie Stabenow
Democrat, Senator for Michigan: "Pulling the rug out from under seniors." [49]

Chris Van Hollen
Democrat, Representative for Maryland, House Budget Committee Ranking Member: "The tea party has hijacked the Republican caucus." [50]

The American Federation of Government Employees
The nation's largest public employees union: "His budget proposal contains so many inaccurate and outright preposterous claims that it wouldn't hold up to a middle school debate team." [51]

Paul Krugman, Democrat, mouthpiece for the Left and syndicated columnist for the New York Times: "voodoo economics", "mean-spiritedness and fantasy", "a sick joke", "savage cuts in aid to the needy and the uninsured" and "alleged cost saving were pure fantasy". [52] [53]

Krugman also claimed that "privatizing Medicare" would almost surely raise health care costs by adding a layer of middlemen. [54] The old and tired mantra of the Left: government can do things more efficiently and at a lower cost than private enterprises and even if they can't, it's all *for the common good*. A similar tactic was used in the attack on President Bush's attempts to reform Social Security.

The House approved the Ryan budget proposal in April 2011 [55] by a nearly-partisan vote: Republicans 235 yes, 4 no; Democrats all 189 no. This put the Republicans on a collision course with Obama and the Democrat-controlled Senate. As expected, the House rejected the Ryan budget proposal in May 2011 by a nearly-partisan vote: Democrats 52 no; Republicans 40 yes, 5 no.

The Obama 2012 Budget Proposal, Take Two

Let's remember that the Obama Regime planned to increase spending from $3.456 trillion in 2011 to $3.819 trillion in 2012, an increase of 11%. They didn't want to cut

2011 spending by a single penny and fought tooth and nail against the Republican proposed spending cuts for 2011, but were forced to agree to spending cuts anyway. Now, forced by the Republican budget proposal for 2012 to aggressively rein in out-of-control spending by the Left, Obama had to throw his own 2012 budget proposal, issued only two months earlier, out of the proverbial window. In April 2011 Obama unveiled a revision of his first 2011 budget proposal.

Instead of issuing a detailed document, he held a speech at George Washington University, outlining a rather vague plan, reading, of course, from his teleprompters. Only after being prodded by Republicans did this economic illiterate feel the need to cut trillions of dollars out of his first proposal. Where is the leadership of this man? Why should we take him seriously?

In a most despicable display of the worst possible partisanship he slammed the Republican 2012 budget proposal, while its main author, Paul Ryan, was right in front of him on the first row on invitation by Obama himself. His speech was loaded with fear mongering, class warfare, inaccuracies, gross misrepresentations and straightforward lies about what conservatives and Republicans stand for. Instead of bringing the parties together in a sincere effort to stave off the collapse of this country - for the most part brought on by his own doing - he poisoned the atmosphere with his reprehensible rhetoric. Instead of caring for the wellbeing of this country, the Political-Agitator-in-Chief was in full campaign mode for the 2012 presidential elections, demonizing his opponents.

Here are some of the worst remarks taken straight from Obama's speech: [56]

- "tell families with children who have disabilities that they have to fend for themselves"
- "putting at risk current retirees, the most vulnerable, or people with disabilities"
- "slashing benefits for future generations"
- "subjecting Americans' guaranteed retirement income to the whims of the stock market"
- "tax cuts for every millionaire and billionaire in our society"
- "the most fortunate among us can afford to pay a little more"
- "pay for tax cuts by making seniors pay more for Medicare or by cutting kids from Head Start or by taking away college scholarships"
- "fear that any talk of change to Medicare, Medicaid, or Social Security will usher in the sort of radical steps that House Republicans have proposed"
- "This is a vision that says up to 50 million Americans have to lose their health insurance in order for us to reduce the deficit. And who are those 50 million Americans? Many are someone's grandparents who wouldn't be able afford nursing home care without Medicaid. Many are poor children. Some are middle-class families who have children with autism or Down's syndrome. Some are kids with disabilities so severe that they require 24-hour care. These are the Americans we'd be telling to fend for themselves."

So let's look at what Obama proposed this time. [57] [58] Here's his revised proposal in brief:
- Reduce the deficit by $4 trillion over the next twelve years
- Cut spending by $2 trillion

- Lower interest payments on the debt by $1 trillion
- Cut about $1 trillion in spending from the tax code
- Reach a final agreement by June of this year

Let's take a closer look at each of the elements of the proposal.

Reduce the Deficit by $4 Trillion over the Next Twelve Years

Obama misleads us on purpose to make the numbers look better. The accepted standard method to evaluate budgets, spending, etc. is to look at a 10-year period, not 12 years. Called on it the next day, he said that over a 10-year time frame his plan would reduce the deficit by $3 trillion.

Cut Spending by $2 Trillion

A White House fact sheet has the following details:

- Cut non-security discretionary spending by $770 billion over 12 years
- Cut defense spending by $400 billion over 12 years
- Cut health care spending by $340 billion in 10 years, including cuts in Medicare of $200 billion and cuts in Medicaid of $100 billion, and $480 billion in 12 years
- Cut other mandatory spending by $360 billion over 12 years

Lower Interest Payments on the Debt by $1 Trillion

The Obama numbers assume a 5.1% interest rate on the debt. The rate was about 3% in early 2011, but is expected to increase significantly over the next ten years, so using 5.1% seems reasonable for this exercise.

Cut About $1 Trillion in Spending From the Tax Code
What a nice, progressive example of Orwellian doubles-peak! Translated into straight English it says: **increase taxes by about $1 trillion**. This is on top of massive tax increases in his first proposal, caused by letting the Bush tax rates expire at the end of 2012!

Reach a Final Agreement by June of This Year
This timeline is totally and utterly unrealistic. Obama excused himself from this task and volunteered Biden, who is supposed to make it happen and is doomed to fail.

Corrected for a time period of 10 years, Obama's revised 2012 budget proposal looks as follows:
- Cut spending by $1.6 trillion
- Increase taxes by $800 billion
- Lower interest payments on the debt by $600 billion
- The resulting reduction in the deficit is $3 trillion

Obama plays political games and/or doesn't get it and/or doesn't want to face reality. His revised pie-in-the-sky budget proposal, coming on the heels of his first budget proposal, is woefully unrealistic and inadequate to address this country's pending economic downfall:
- Spending cuts in this proposal are about ¼ of the Ryan proposal.
- Substantial cuts in defense spending may be unrealistic in the face of three wars, the global War on Terror and increasing unrest in the Arab world.
- Counting on significant cuts in Medicare and Medicaid spending without significant reforms is wishful thinking. These cuts are supposed to be in addition to the non-existing savings of *$732 billion* from ObamaCare!

- Obama may not be able to push through massive, **additional** tax increases since they will very likely slow down the economy, cost jobs, lower revenue, increase the deficit - not decrease it - and possibly send this country into another deep recession. The old, tired mantra of the Left, "the rich are not paying their fair share", may not cut it.
- This budget will not reach "primary balance" nor will it balance the budget.

Raising the Debt Ceiling, Again

Congress cannot increase the national debt beyond the statutory limit or debt ceiling. Such increases have occurred more than once a year on average during the past 50 years. While the most recent increase of the debt ceiling to $14.3 trillion occurred in February of 2010, we reached that new limit on May 16, 2011. Bookkeeping tricks like borrowing from retirement funds for federal workers, selling assets and other maneuvers could be used to delay by a few months the point at which the federal government would run out of money to pay its bills. Yet, a major battle loomed over increasing the debt ceiling again.

Under Obama our debt has been increasing at an alarming rate and it has reached a point where our economic viability and credit rating are in serious doubt. As discussed earlier, at the end of 2010 and in early 2011 Moody's Investors Service, credit rating agency Standard & Poor's, the International Monetary Fund and others warned that the U.S. lacked a promising strategy on how to curb its growing government debt and that we could lose our AAA credit rating within two years. Losing the AAA rating would make it much more difficult for the U.S. to borrow money, would significantly increase the interest rate on any borrowing and would severely damage our economy.

So what is the Left's position on increasing the debt ceiling? Their position isn't based on principles, but changes to whatever supports their political agenda at the time. In December of 2010, Obama's economic advisor, Austin Goolsbee, argued that a refusal to increase the national debt ceiling would be "catastrophic" and a sign of "insanity". [59] On the other hand, Obama voted against increasing the ceiling in 2006 and said: "The fact that we are here today to debate raising America's debt limit is a sign of leadership failure. It is a sign that the U.S. Government can't pay its own bills. It is a sign that we now depend on ongoing financial assistance from foreign countries to finance our Government's reckless fiscal policies... Increasing America's debt weakens us domestically and internationally. Leadership means that 'the buck stops here'. Instead, Washington is shifting the burden of bad choices onto the backs of our children and grandchildren. America has a debt problem and a failure of leadership. Americans deserve better." [60] These words deserve to be repeated over and over until even the Obama Regime understands them. In a May 2011 Gallup poll, Americans agreed by a wide 47% to 19% margin with Obama's 2006 pronouncements against raising the debt ceiling. [61]

These were the kind of words and pronouncements that got Obama elected in 2008, but as president he, once again, showed not to be driven by what's good for America, but by what advanced his radical-Left political agenda.

In the looming battle over increasing the debt ceiling, Obama and Congressional Democrats called for a "clean", unconditional, no-strings-attached increase in the debt ceiling. So you may ask yourself: what is so "clean" about increasing the debt ceiling without any conditions? It's more Orwellian double-speak. Radicals want to spend us into oblivion with no-strings-attached and by portraying that as "clean", they hope you automatically assume it to be good and anybody taking a stand against such irresponsible behavior somehow may be the opposite of "clean", or "dirty". I can see the headline already: "Dirty politics by Conservatives Sinks Obama's Attempts to Save Our Country from Default and Doom!"

The House rejected the proposal overwhelmingly by a 318-97 vote in May of 2011. Obama had claimed that not increasing the ceiling would cause the U.S. into a crippling default on its debt and could possibly trigger a worldwide recession. [62] That is a position fraught with intellectual dishonesty. Not increasing the debt ceiling does not mean that we automatically default on our debt payments. Debt interest payments, while large in absolute terms, are a small part of total spending. In 2010 those payments were $414 billion [63] or 11% of total spending of $3.729 trillion.

There are other possible outcomes. Instead of playing the crisis card again, Obama should get serious. We can live within our means, not increase the debt ceiling, pay our debt interest and not default, by cutting our other expenses drastically. It would hurt, but by not increasing our debt ceiling **and** continuing to pay our debt **and** curtailing our other spending, we would send a very strong, positive message and put us instantly on the road to economic sanity and recovery.

What will we ultimately do about our already humongous debt ceiling? I clearly see three alternatives:

- The **cold turkey approach** is financially the sanest, but it is also the most painful in the short term: don't increase the debt ceiling; don't spend more than we take in, aka live within our means, aka have a balanced budget; pay our debt obligations first and drastically cut all other expenses; lower taxes to stimulate the economy, which will lead to more, not less, tax revenue.

- The **compromise approach** is less painful, but might be more difficult to stick to: allow a limited increase in the debt ceiling; set specific spending limits; obtain a balanced budget within a specific time period. The spending limits, also called spending caps, should be very specific, like 20% of Gross Domestic Product (GDP). Historically spending has been around 20% of GDP, but under Obama it has increased to about 25% and will continue to rise rapidly if we don't take dramatic measures. This approach would ease some of the difficulties that the cold turkey approach would create, but it also increases the likelihood that we would abandon the needed drastic steps to balance the budget and start paying off our debt.

- And then there is the **liberal, business-as-usual, approach**: demonize proposals for the previous two approaches as mean-spirited and radical, pay lip service to "living within our means" and "needed reforms", compromise a little here and a little there, increase the debt ceiling, continue the out-of-control spending and push through the radical-Left agenda.

Which approach ultimately prevails will determine to a very large extent the future of this country and the viability of our free society.

Republicans favored the compromise approach: drastic spending cuts; an increase in the debt ceiling, not to exceed spending cuts; restrict spending; pass a balanced budget amendment to the Constitution; no tax increases. [64]

So, what was Obama's response? Proposals to increase taxes by hundreds of billions of dollars and more economic gobbledygook: "I have a larger vision for America, ...where we work together – Democrats and Republicans – to live within our means, to cut our deficit and debt, but also to invest in what our economy needs to grow." [65] Does this man even understand the definition of "living within your means", "deficit" or "debt"? By definition, when you live within your means, you don't have a deficit. Economy 101, anyone?

How to Save our Country from Economic Collapse and Return to Fiscal Responsibility

If we continue on our current path of running up huge deficits and debt, our economy will collapse. Even Obama admitted in his speech outlining his second 2012 budget proposal that, if we continued on the same path, by 2025 our revenue would only pay for health care programs, Social Security and interest payments on the national debt; there would be no money for national security, education, veterans' benefits or any other programs. [66] Our country would collapse way, way before 2025!

It is over-abundantly clear that we must take a u-turn on the radical tax, spend and deficit path to destruction. We must demand that our government immediately and drastically reduces spending and starts paying off our debts.

So where does all the money go? In fiscal year 2010, most of the federal budget, 61%, was spent on major health programs, Social Security and Defense. The breakdown of all expenses is as follows: [67]

Medicare, Medicaid, and CHIP: 21%

Social Security: 20%

Defense and Security: 20%

Safety Net Programs: 14%

Benefits for Federal Retirees and Veterans: 7%

Interest on Debt: 6%

Education: 3%

Transportation Infrastructure: 3%

Scientific and Medical Research: 2%

Non-Security International: 1%

All Other: 3%

So where do we cut expenses and how deep? The answer is clear: everywhere and very deep. Based on the spending and deficit levels of Obama's first two years in office, we must cut spending by about 40% in order to just balance the budget. While it would be a good start, just balancing the budget would not lower our debt by a single penny. So we really should cut spending in half and start living within our means **and** paying off our debt. Every program, large and small, must be included in drastic cuts and eliminations. These are some of the steps we must take to balance the budget, start paying off our debt and revitalize our economy:

- Drastically reduce the power, size and reach of the Federal Government.
- Stimulate the economy by getting the government out of the way, eliminating unnecessary regulations and reducing taxes.
- Close tax loopholes.
- Replace our current complicated, confusing and expensive-to-administer federal tax code with a simple flat tax

system like FairTax and save individuals and businesses hundreds of billions of dollars every year, money that will give the economy a significant, ongoing boost.

- Eliminate the IRS and good riddance!
- Drastically reform and reduce entitlement programs like Social Security, Medicare, Medicaid and Welfare to make them solvent; eliminate abuses.
- Curtail Defense spending.
- Repeal and replace ObamaCare with free-market solutions.
- Reform and rein in Freddie Mac and Fannie Mae.
- Eliminate the unholy alliance between the labor unions and Democrats.
- Reduce government employees' pay, health care, pensions and other benefits and perks to be in line with those in private business.
- Reduce union members pay, health care, pensions and other benefits and perks to competitive levels.
- Become energy independent; develop all our energy resources through private enterprise.
- Privatize all bailed-out companies.
- End corporate Welfare.
- Enforce immigration laws.
- End agricultural subsidies, bio-fuel subsidies, green technology subsidies and the like.
- Drastically cut Foreign Aid, particularly to countries hostile to the U.S.
- Cancel our membership in the U.N., an organization fraught with corruption and waste and where most member countries are hostile to the U.S.
- Drastically reduce or eliminate funding for every other program.

- Eliminate funding of programs that don't pass the common sense test, don't provide critical services, fall outside of the powers of the Federal Government as enumerated in our Constitution and/or violate law. To name just a few:
  - NPR (National Public Radio)
  - PBS (Public Broadcasting System)
  - Planned Parenthood
  - The National Flood Insurance Program (Why should the taxpayer foot the bill for rich people to rebuild their million-dollar-homes on the water's edge?)
  - The National Endowment for the Arts
  - The National Education Association
  - The National Endowment for the Humanities

5. Bailout and Stimulus – Choosing Winners and Losers

Obama made up "The Worst Financial Crisis since the Great Depression" to create an atmosphere of crisis and fear and push through the single biggest waste of taxpayer money in the history of the world: the nearly-trillion-dollar so-called "Stimulus Bill". Winners and losers do not emerge as a result of free-market forces, but are arbitrarily chosen by the Obama Regime.

The Bailout or TARP Bill

TARP stands for Troubled Asset Relief Program. This $700 billion bill, aimed at stabilizing the economy, was passed under Bush in October of 2008, [1] at the height of the financial crisis and was continued and misappropriated under Obama. For instance, car companies were not included in the program, but Obama, with the Democrat-controlled Congress' approval, used the funds to bail out the car industry anyway. It was claimed to be needed to prevent many financial institutions from going under and dragging down our whole economy. Opponents of the bill made strong arguments against this massive government intervention and propping up of Freddie Mac, Fannie Mae, banks and other financial institutions, which had caused the financial crisis in the first place.

One year later the U.S. Government Accountability Office reported: [2] " ...several factors will complicate efforts to measure any impact. For example, any changes attributed to TARP could well be changes that:

- would have occurred anyway;
- can be attributed to other policy interventions, such as the actions of FDIC, the Federal Reserve, or other financial regulators; or
- were enhanced or counteracted by other market forces, such as the correction in housing markets and revaluation of mortgage-related assets."

Translation: "We can't tell you if this massive program did anything to improve the economy." Although most of the taxpayer money spent on this bill would ultimately be recovered, this bill should have never been passed.

In March of 2011 the CBO reported on the bill's financial status. [3] Of the bill's authorized $700 billion, $410 billion was actually used and "only" $19 billion might not be recovered. To bail out banks $245 billion was used and it was expected that after the banks paid back the loans plus interest there would be a "profit" of $20 billion. Of the $80 billion used to bail out General Motors and Chrysler, $65 billion was expected to be recuperated. Of the 3 to 4 million people estimated by the Obama administration to be provided with mortgage relieve, only about 600,000 did so.

Simple math told us that we stood to lose $15 billion on the bailout of General Motors and Chrysler: $80 billion bailout - $65 billion paid back = $15 billion loss. But if you listened to Obama you would be misled to believe that the auto industry bailout actually made us money. In June of 2011 he said: "Chrysler has repaid every dime and more of what it owes American taxpayer for their support during my presidency." [4] Note that he didn't talk about the General Motors bailout, which will leave the taxpayers with about $14 billion in losses. He talked about Chrysler only, the lesser of the two evils.

So let's take a closer look at the Chrysler situation. Bush bailed them out with $4 billion and Obama with $8.5 billion. Obama's own Treasury Department acknowledged that we will not recoup $1.3 billion of the $12.5 billion of the two bailouts combined. So how can our Deceiver-in-Chief claim that Chrysler repaid more than owed? By telling us a *big, fat lie!* Notice he said "during my presidency". So his crooked math is as follows: $11.2 paid back - $8.5 billion bailout during my presidency = $2.7 billion profit, totally ignoring the first $4 billion bailout.

The Freddie Mac and Fannie Mae Bailout Sequel
To add insult to injury, in mid December 2009 both Freddie Mac and Fannie Mae got additional, taxpayer-funded financial support of $400 billion to stay afloat. [5] Oh yeah, the housing market is recovering just fine! Who says this country is going to hell in the proverbial hand basket?

"The Worst Financial Crisis Since the Great Depression" Fabrication

Obama made up a whopper of a lie about the state of the economy to mislead the American people and create an atmosphere of crisis and fear. He used that bald-faced lie during his campaign and later as president. During a presidential election campaign debate with McCain in October of 2008, then-candidate Obama said: "I think everybody knows now we are in the worst financial crisis since the Great Depression. And a lot of you, I think, are worried about your jobs, your pensions, your retirement accounts, your ability to send your child or your grandchild to college." [6] Question to Mr. Obama: How can you declare an ongoing recession – by definition a recession that hasn't ended yet – to be worse or better or equal to any other recession of the past? Answer for Mr. Obama: You can't and pretending otherwise equals intellectual dishonesty.

So let's take a closer look at this issue of the recession we found ourselves in during Obama's presidential campaign and during the first six months of his presidency. Let's look at how it really stacked up. The following table lists the numbers for four major measures of economic health - unemployment, inflation, growth of the GDP after inflation and prime interest rate – during the Great Depression and the recessions thereafter. I've also added the data for the Bush 43 recession as it had progressed up to January of 2009, the point where Obama used this data to push through his disastrous Stimulus Bill.

Recession Period	President(s)	Unemployment [7]	Inflation [8]	GDP Growth [9]	Prime Interest Rate [10]
Great Depression 1930 to 1939	Hoover/ Roosevelt	18.3%	-2.1%	0.6%	about 3%
January 1980 to July 1980	Carter	6.8%	14.4%	-3.3%	16.4%
July 1981 to November 1982	Reagan	8.9%	7.9%	-1.1%	16.7%
July 1990 to March 1991	Bush 41	6.1%	5.8%	-2.4%	9.8%
March 2001 to November 2001	Bush 43	4.7%	2.9%	0.6%	7.0%
December 2007 to January 2009	Bush 43	5.7%	4.6%	-2.3%	5.3%
December 2007 to June 2009	Bush 43/ Obama	6.5%	3.2%	-2.6%	4.7%

Note: percentages are averages over the periods indicated.

So, the dubious honor of being "***The worst financial crisis since the Great Depression***" goes to ***the recession under President Carter*** for all four major measures of economic health.

Many have started to use the term "The Great Recession" to describe the December 2007 to June 2009 recession. That is equally incorrect and reinforces the myth that Obama created for political purposes.

What Caused the Latest Recession?

So what caused the recession that officially started in December of 2007? To make a long story short: irresponsible social engineering by the Left caused an unsustainable housing bubble and when that bubble started to burst in 2006, it took the whole economy down.

The foundation for the disaster was laid with the Community Reinvestment Act, signed into law by Jimmy Carter in 1977. The law required banks and savings and loans to ease their requirements for approving loans and mortgages to the public in general and medium- and low-income people in particular. Both Freddie Mac and Fannie Mae, backers of about half the mortgages in the U.S., pressured financial institutions to approve mortgages to people who couldn't possibly afford them, often with little or no money down and so-called sub-prime interest rates, that started out below sustainable levels and would sharply increase afterwards. To minimize their exposure to these high-risk loans, the financial institutions in turn created so-called mortgage-backed securities and other derivatives, by bundling the risky mortgages and sell them to investors, like pension funds, life insurance companies and individual investors. This was a disaster just waiting to happen. Several attempts by concerned Republicans, including President Bush, to remedy the situation and avert a debacle, were blocked by Democrats, most notably Barney Frank.

The whole scheme started to unravel in 2006, when a mild economic downturn caused more and more people to default on mortgages they couldn't afford. That in turn caused massive losses for the financial institutions and the mortgage-based investments held by others and we entered into a deep recession. Socialism had failed yet again and dragged down the whole country.

Job losses

Only in the area of jobs lost - both in absolute numbers and as a percentage of the labor force - is the most recent recession, from December 2007 to June 2009, worse than the recession under Carter: [11]

Recession Period	President(s)	Jobs Lost	Job Losses as a Percentage of the Labor Force
January 1980 to July 1980	Carter	968,000	1.0%
July 1981 to November 1982	Reagan	2,824,000	3.1%
July 1990 to March 1991	Bush 41	1,249,000	1.1%
March 2001 to November 2001	Bush 43	1,599,000	1.2%
December 2007 to June 2009	Bush 43 Obama	7,490,000	5.4%

One thing is for sure: Obama made things worse, not better, with his nonsensical meddling in our economy and irresponsible spending like the so-called Stimulus Bill and job-killing initiatives like Cap and Trade and ObamaCare.

The Stimulus Bill

This bill is officially called American Recovery and Reinvestment Act or ARRA. This was Obama's first major blow to our economy during his first three weeks in office. You have to give the guy credit for expediency; not only is he, according to Mark Levin, "a human wrecking ball, destroying everything he touches", he does the dirty work really fast. Citing impending doom and disaster, "The worst financial crisis since the Great Depression", a crisis that was about to destroy the country, Obama pushed the bill through against the will of the American people; a majority of Americans, 43% to 37%, opposed it. [12]

Never mind the will of the American people; the Stimulus Bill was approved by Congress on February 13, 2009. The voting record was as follows: the House - Democrats 97% for, Republicans 100% against; the Senate - Democrats 100% for; Republicans 93% against. [13] So let the record show that Democrats voted overwhelmingly for this atrocity and that Republicans voted overwhelmingly against it.

The CBO initial cost estimate for this bill was $787 billion, but they increased it in January 2010 to $862 billion, [14] not including interest, or about *$3,000 for every man, woman and child in America*.

This "crisis" required the utmost speed in passing this bill, or so we were told. The final language of the 1,100-page bill was released only twelve hours before the Senate vote [15] so nobody had sufficient time to read the bill, let alone understand it completely and thoughtfully debate it, as required by law. On the campaign trail Obama had promised at least 5 days to study any new legislative proposals.

Obama claimed that his Stimulus Bill would immediately boost the economy significantly and unemployment would not exceed 8% and 3.5 million jobs would be ***created or saved*** by the end of 2010, but without it the economy would worsen and unemployment would rise to 8.5%. [16] The whole concept of "creating or saving jobs" is of course fake and phony, as no one can ever prove or disprove it.

After passage of the bill, the economy deteriorated even more and unemployment steadily increased. In October 2009 unemployment was 10.1%. Many experts believe that any significant recovery of employment will take many years.

In mid October 2009 it was reported by recovery.gov that the Stimulus Bill had created 30,380 jobs, but that number was suspected of being grossly overstated. Wow, even if the number of jobs created were correct, that was a ***full 0.9%*** of the goal of 3.5 million jobs created or saved by the end of 2010. So far, $173 billion or 22% had been paid out. That translated into $5.7 million per job created. Way to go, Obama. In 2009 over ***4 million*** jobs had been lost, [17] but Obama called the Stimulus Bill a great success!

At the end of October 2009 recovery.gov no longer reported the number of jobs created, but by applying more smoke and mirrors changed it to jobs created/saved as reported by Stimulus money recipients. Yeah, let's claim jobs saved because nobody can prove that one way or the other. They claimed that 640,329 jobs had been created or saved at a cost of $323,271 each. Jobs of people who had received raises or additional benefits were counted as jobs saved.

Give me a break! Obama's own Bureau of Labor Statistics reported that since the Stimulus Bill was passed *3.3 million jobs had been lost*. [18]

In an apparent attempt at deflecting the criticism on the term jobs created or saved, the White House in December of 2009 issued a memo announcing that those receiving Stimulus money no longer had to report whether jobs had been saved or created, but instead would report jobs funded by Stimulus money. [19] In other words, if the project was being funded with stimulus dollars – even if the person worked at that company or organization before and would work the same place afterwards – that was a stimulus job!

Just as the October 2008 $700 billion Bailout Bill, the Stimulus Bill should never have been passed. The bill funded projects that for many years had been rejected as not worthy of spending money on by Federal, State, County and City Governments, philanthropists and other organizations and individuals.

It has been proven over and over that the economy is depressed, not stimulated by increasing taxes and government spending, but is stimulated by reducing government spending and lowering taxes. This allows companies and individuals to keep more of their earnings and reinvests it, spend it on products and services they, not politicians and bureaucrats, deem important and thereby create more jobs and wealth and improve living conditions for the less fortunate.

According to recovery.gov, at the end of February 2010, more than a year after the bill was passes, only $279 billion or 32% had been paid out; in mid August 2010, 18 months after the bill was passes, only $502 billion or 58% had been paid out.

And what happened to all those "shovel-ready" jobs that Obama promised this bill would create? [20] In October of 2010 Obama had to admit that "there's no such thing as shovel-ready projects." [21]

Most Americans apparently agreed with my position that this so-called stimulus was a pork-barrel scam and didn't do anything at all to improve the economy. In July of 2010, nearly 75% were of the opinion that the Stimulus Bill had not improved the economy. [22]

In August of 2010 a member of Obama's Economic Recovery Advisory Board said that a second Stimulus Bill of $1 trillion might be needed because there was "far too much focus on the deficit and far too little on unemployment." A second stimulus could "boost job creation and economic growth." [23]

The Summer of Recovery That Wasn't
While the stimulus hadn't worked, the economy was still in the dumps, jobs were scarce, unemployment was persistently so high that longer unemployment benefits were deemed necessary and a double-dip recession looked like a real possibility, Obama and Biden went on what they called the "Summer of Recovery" tour, traveling the country in the summer of 2010 and making speeches to sing the praises of how the economy was recovering and Obama "saved or created" millions of jobs.

In August of 2010 we had lost a total 3.4 million jobs in the 18 months since the Stimulus Bill was enacted. [24]

Why the Stimulus Bill Isn't Working

Obama's economic and other policies have been flat-out disasters. Spending taxpayers' money on pork projects doesn't stimulate and doesn't entice companies to invest and hire more people.

Companies are barely investing and hiring people because of the business-hostile climate created by Obama. They face economic uncertainty, unknown tax increases, unknown cost increases due to health care reform, energy regulations like Cap and Trade and financial reform legislation. The free-market economy system and Socialism, as pushed by Obama, clash.

Private enterprise needs confidence in the future business climate, but Obama is doing the exact opposite by pushing his socialist, radical agenda. In order to turn this economy around we need to repeal ObamaCare, kill Cap and Trade, make the Bush tax cuts permanent and lower taxes, lift the drilling bans, reduce spending, start paying off the national debt and drastically reduce the size and impact of government.

Stimulus II, the Sequel

In December 2009 the House passed a *$155 billion* so-called jobs creation bill to promote employment in the construction industry and prevent layoffs of teachers, police and other public employees. [25] Pelosi didn't say how this bill would be paid for, but you get the drift, don't you? To hell with concerns about deficit spending! Nancy Pelosi, single-handedly if needed, will spend us out of debt! Of course, the Senate could not sit idling by. In March of 2010 they created their own *$149 billion* so-called job creation bill to extend unemployment benefits and tax breaks for business-es. [26]

In the face of growing concern about the federal government's out-of-control spending, the Democrats were not able to push through such a huge bill, particularly since spending for the first Stimulus Bill was far from complete and had shown not to work as claimed.

Despite Obama's promise of no more bailouts made in July of 2010, a final bill, HR1586 - Education Jobs and Medicaid Assistance Act of 2010, of *$26 billion* to bail out cash-strapped states, was voted on mainly along party lines and signed into law by Obama in August of 2010. [27] So much for a promise made only weeks before! *$10 billion* of it went to school districts and was claimed to save or reinstate 161,000 education related jobs. Doesn't that sound familiar? Oh yes, "create or save" was now called "save or reinstate". Payback time for the unions, with trial lawyers the two biggest contributors to Democrats! *$16 billion* of it would be used to extend for six months FMA, a program to help financially strapped states pay for additional Medicaid coverage under the first Stimulus Bill. This would allow states to meet other budget priorities, including keeping more than 150,000 police officers and other public workers on the payroll.

So how long are we going to bail out states? Another half year, a year, a decade? But don't despair! The Democrats claimed the bill was paid for by increasing taxes on some U.S.-based multi-national companies and reductions of *$12 billion* in the food stamp program, *serving more than 40 million poor people*. Who said Democrats don't care about the poor?

I have to object to the notion that this bill was paid for and therefore would not have any negative impact on the country. If we responsibly can come up with $26 billion in extra revenue and savings, then that money should be used to pay off the humongous national debt before it will send us all to the poorhouse. They claim to have found responsible ways to increase revenue, but then they squanders it away on yet another radical-Left, socialist spending binge. And of course this *$26 billion* could not be taken from the still enormous unused balance of the original Stimulus Bill - *$362 billion* in August of 2010 according to recovery.gov. No, no, we have to spend more and more and more! Way to go Obama Regime!

Financial Reform Legislation

The Stimulus Bill didn't stimulate and unemployment was still very high, so it was time for the Obama Regime to play the "crisis" card again. It had served them so well to force the Stimulus Bill and ObamaCare upon the American people, so it was time for a repeat performance!

Claiming to address the "financial crisis", a new, 2300-page so-called financial reform legislation, called the "Dodd-Frank Wall Street Reform And Consumer Protection Act", was pushed really hard in the spring of 2010 under the guise of "protecting the little guy" (socialist double-speak for seizing control of private companies, also known as nationalization).

Let's take a look at the main components of the bill: [28]

- create the Bureau of Consumer Financial Protection, within the Federal Reserve, to regulate consumer financial products like mortgages and credit cards

- regulate processing fees and use of credit and debit cards
- regulate lender verification of borrowers' ability to re-pay mortgages; eliminate prepayment penalties
- regulate credit score disclosure to borrowers
- empower the FDIC to liquidate failing firms
- create the Financial Stability Oversight Council to mon-itor systemic risk in the financial system
- no efforts to address the problems and sustainability of mortgage giants Fannie Mae and Freddie Mac
- no Resolution Fund
- limits on banks' ability to invest in private equity groups or hedge funds
- regulate how banks can trade in so-called derivatives
- study and address the conflict of interest issues with credit rating agencies
- allow the General Accounting Office (GAO) to audit the Federal Reserve

Looks good, right? Well, maybe not! The liberal answer to any real or perceived problem is always the same: bigger government, more spending. This legislation would require hiring hundreds or even thousands more bureaucrats.

Surprise, surprise, this legislation would not apply to Freddie Mac and Fannie Mae, the two government-controlled lending institutions that underwrite over 50% of all mortgages in the U.S. These institutions, under liberal, Democratic direction, engaged in a disastrous effort of so-cial engineering by pressuring lenders into issuing mortgag-es to people who couldn't afford them and in doing so trig-gered the mortgage crisis and severe recession.

Why did we need yet another new agency, the Bureau of Consumer Financial Protection? It was claimed to help protect consumers from abuses, but it would not apply to Freddie Mac or Fannie Mae. Never mind that we had already 21 federal agencies to protect consumers and investors.

And that was not the only new agency. I counted four in a Senate summary of the bill: [29] the Bureau of Consumer Financial Protection, the Financial Stability Oversight Council, the Office of National Insurance and the Office of Credit Ratings.

The bill would give the FDIC the authority to seize control of any financial company deemed to be in trouble, whether they received government aide or not, remove management, dissolve the board of directors, take over management or liquidate or sell the company.

This legislation originally would have included a *$ 50 billion* or *$150 billion* Resolution Fund, a slush fund for future bailouts of financial companies. Talk about rewarding bad behavior for perpetuity and institutionalizing bailouts! This provision was dropped.

Democrats had also tried the idea of "taking" $10 billion from the TARP fund to help pay for the expenses of this legislation. [30] Never mind that this was illegal as TARP funds could not be used for this purpose. Never underestimate the ability of Democrats to come up with illegal activities "for the greater good."

The bill was signed into law in July 2010. At the signing ceremony Obama said: [31] "The American people will never again be asked to foot the bill for Wall Street's mistakes…, …There will be no more taxpayer-funded bailouts. Period…, …And there will be new rules to make clear that no firm is somehow protected because it is 'too big to fail." Many Republicans, however, disputed the notion that financial reform ends government bailouts of big banks. House Minority John Boehner, Republican of Ohio, contended the bill "provides permanent bailouts for his Wall Street allies at the expense of community banks and small businesses around the country." [32]

The U.S. Chamber of Commerce commented on their website, uschamber.com/capmarkets, that the bill "does not address the core causes of the financial crisis. Instead, it adds new regulatory agencies to the already antiquated system and grows a bloated, ineffective bureaucracy while leaving critical areas unaddressed, including the future of Freddie Mac and Fannie Mae." An analysis by the same chamber concluded that the bill required creation of at least 533 new regulatory rules. [33]

To everybody's surprise, the federal Securities & Exchange Commission (SEC) told Fox Business Network that under new rules brought on by the 2300 pages financial reform legislation the SEC *no longer has to respond to public requests for information*, previously required under the Freedom of Information Act (FOI). [34] See, everybody is having a field day reading and interpreting 2300 pages of legislation *after* it has been signed into law. So this is the transparency and openness Obama has talked about? This is the kind of protection of our freedoms that the Obama Regime is giving us?

Labor Union Pension Funds Bailout?

In May of 2010 Bob Casey, Democrat, senator from Pennsylvania, introduced legislation to bail out union pension funds in financial trouble. [35] If passed, taxpayers could be on the hook for $165 billion or it could be much higher since pensions need to be paid until the workers' deaths. The bill was claimed to – drum roll please - save jobs and help people. Only one week before Obama had promised that there would be no more bailouts.

And More "Stimulus"

In September of 2010 Obama, claiming to revive the economy, pushed for a *$50 billion* bill to upgrade the nation's roads, railways and runways and create a ***government-run bank*** to finance innovative transportation projects. [36] It was claimed that the spending program would create middle-class jobs in manufacturing, construction and retail and thereby stimulate the economy. Of course there was no mention of the negative effects of this program: higher taxes and/or deficit and less money available for economic activity selected by our free-market system, which would be way more effective in stimulating the economy and creating jobs.

Funding had not been determined, but could be offset in part by higher taxes and lower subsidies for the oil and gas industry. And why not harm the evil oil and gas industry, you know, the creators of jobs, profits and wealth?

The utterly-failed, original $862 billion Stimulus Bill still had, according to recovery.gov, an unused balance of $362 billion, it hadn't created any jobs, 3.4 million jobs had been lost since the original Stimulus Bill had been signed into law and unemployment was still a staggering 9.6%, but Obama wanted to spend more, more and more of our money. Again, the socialist knee-jerk reaction is to spend more of the taxpayer's money on a problem, any problem.

6. Energy

The Left's devastating energy policies choke off the supply of oil, drive up the price of energy and strangle our economy. The thought of having sufficient energy to support our economy and making us independent from foreign energy sources as much and as fast as possible, appears alien to Obama and many others on the Left.

Obama's Disastrous Energy Policy

One of the major factors driving Obama's so-called energy policy is a deep-seated aversion to energy derived from fossil fuels like oil and natural gas. As his many actions in this area have clearly and over-abundantly shown, Obama is doing anything and everything in his power to destroy the fossil energy industry. Instead of encouraging the development of *all* our available energy sources, Obama has issued one drilling ban after another and falsely accused those who should be his allies in providing the energy sources our country needs.

The Drilling Bans

Obama, driven by political considerations, not concern for our environment or well-being, ordered a six month moratorium on all deepwater oil drilling in May of 2010, halting 33 exploratory drilling projects and suspending new permits, putting thousands of Americans and other nationals out of work and causing big losses for oil drilling operations. [1] This ill-advised measure would put tens of thousands of people out of work in the state of Louisiana alone. [2] It also causes oil drillers to move to other regions of the world, further increasing our dependence on foreign oil and driving up energy costs; drilling rigs left the Gulf to relocate to drill for Egypt, the Republic of Congo, Nigeria, Brazil, etc. [3] The cost of this ban was estimated to be up to *$330 million per month* in direct wages alone. [4]

Obama's Interior Secretary, Ken Salazar, Democrat, was the major force behind this moratorium. He *falsified* a federal panel's scientific report by inserting a blanket drilling ban recommendation and presenting it as the scientists' opinion. All scientists on the panel came out and stated that they did not favor or recommend a blanket drilling ban. [5] Let me emphasize here: *Salazar lied and committed fraud to advance Obama's anti-oil, anti-free-enterprise agenda.* Salazar should have been fired immediately!

Cooler heads prevailed, but only for a while: a federal judge lifted the ban, saying that the Obama Regime had failed to demonstrate the need for such a drastic measure. [6] Obama appealed and lost, but not to worry: he issued a new deepwater drilling moratorium in July 2010, claiming new evidence of lack of sufficient safety for deepwater drilling. [7] A judge declared that second moratorium unlawful in October of 2010, but Obama continued to block any deepwater drilling. Only after a judge intervened again was the first drilling rig allowed to resume operations on February 28, 2011, but Obama immediately appealed that decision.

Moreover, the Obama regime had been stalling for months to make a decision on whether to approve permits for seven proposed deepwater drilling projects. In February 2011 a federal judge found Obama in contempt and *ordered* him to make a decision within 30 days. [8] The Obama regime responded by stating that the applications were "flawed or incomplete" and would possibly be rejected.

To further damage our oil industry and sabotage the development of our energy resources, in December 2010 Interior Secretary Ken Salazar announced that expansion of offshore oil exploration into the Eastern Gulf of Mexico and along the Atlantic Coast approved in March 2010 had been rescinded and that the ban would be in place for seven years. [9]

While sabotaging the development of our own oil resources, Obama has loaned billions of dollars to Petrobras, the Brazilian national oil company, to drill for oil and natural gas off the coast of Brazil. [10] Instead of "Drill, Baby, Drill", a slogan used by proponents of developing our own oil resources, it is "Drill, Brazil, Drill" for Obama. During a March 2011 visit to Brazil, he praised Brazilian energy policies and commitment to offshore drilling for oil and natural gas. Funny, isn't it? Obama praises Brazil for doing what he sabotages here in his own country! [11]

As oil and gasoline prices increased sharply and posed a serious threat to the economies of our country and the world, Obama continued to push unproven renewable energy sources, sabotaged development of our own, ample energy sources and did nothing to lessen our dependence on foreign oil. The price of crude oil rapidly climbed to more than $100 a barrel and the national average for one gallon of gasoline to more than $3.50, mostly as a result of unrest in the Middle East, particularly Tunisia, Egypt, Libya and Saudi Arabia and a falling dollar.

During all this Obama was mostly mum. At a March 11, 2011 news conference he pretended to address the oil and gas situation, but he mostly produced misinformation and political rhetoric. He claimed to favor boosting domestic drilling in a responsible way and stated that improvements in energy efficiency and boosting renewable energy were the only ways to break U.S. dependence on foreign oil in the long term. He dismissed claims that his environmental policies had choked off drilling as political posturing.

He said: "We need to continue to boost domestic production of oil and gas. Last year, American oil production reached its highest level since 2003. Let me repeat that. Our oil production reached its highest level in seven years. Oil production from federal waters in the Gulf of Mexico reached an all-time high... Any notion that my administration has shut down oil production might make for a good political sound bite, but it doesn't match up with reality."
It's amazing how this guy can distort reality with a straight face! Oil production didn't go up thanks to him, but in spite of him and thanks to measure taken by presidents Bill Clinton and Bush.[12] And oil production in the Gulf of Mexico will fall for the foreseeable future, thanks to Obama. Oil production in the Gulf was indeed the highest in 2010 at 1.64 million barrels per day. However, it peaked in May and then declined for the rest of the year as a result of Obama's drilling bans. It is expected to further decline to 1.4 million barrels per day in 2011 and 1.2 million barrels per day in 2012. [13]

In order to stabilize oil production at a constant level, not even increase it, Obama would need to issue deepwater drilling permits for the Gulf at a rate of between 30 and 40 each month. As of April 2011, Obama had issued only 22 such permits in total since October 2010! [14]

Did Obama announce he would try as much as possible to undo the damage he had caused by his drilling bans and accelerate the approval of drilling permits? NO. Did he overturn Interior Secretary Ken Salazar's December 2010 offshore drilling ban for any new areas through 2017? NO. Did he announce to stop pouring our tax money into as-yet-unproven renewable energy technologies and let the free-market system develop and apply those technologies? NO. But he said that he was possibly willing, maybe, to open up the strategic oil reserves! As if the strategic oil reserve, meant to be used only for strategic purposes in case of disruptions in oil supplies like during hurricanes or war, is anything more than a drop in the bucket.

Obama also said that he directed the Interior Department to assess how many onshore and offshore oil leases already held by industry, are going undeveloped so that companies can be encouraged to produce from those leases. Note to Obama: those leases are not being developed because there is no oil there that can be extracted economically, in spite of subsidies to the oil companies; there are enough oil, natural gas and coal reserves elsewhere in the country to economically provide all of America's energy needs for the next 200 to 300 years, but those reserves have been banned from being developed! He also said the administration was looking at the potential for new production in Alaska and elsewhere. Yes, Mr. President, we have known about those potentials for decades and there is no need to yet again *look* at them. It's time to *act*, get out of the way, lift the bans and let the free-market develop our resources and make us energy-independent!

As if we needed any more proof of the Obama Regime's objective to choke off oil supplies and drive up fuel prices, the Democrat-controlled Senate rejected a Republican plan to allow more coastal oil and natural gas exploration and speed up the granting of oil drilling permits. Fifty Democrats, five Republicans and two Independents opposed the plan, while forty two Republicans supported it. While the plan included the requirement that companies develop spill response and containment plans, Democrats claimed that it lacked necessary safeguards for increased drilling in the Gulf of Mexico and along the East Coast. [15]

Instead of doing everything in his power to ensure an ample supply of affordable energy, Obama announced with much fanfare a token effort of releasing 30 million barrels of oil from the Strategic Petroleum Reserve in June of 2011. [16] It was claimed that this was done "to offset the disruption in the oil supply caused by unrest in the Middle East". How about lifting drilling bans and issuing permits, Mr. Obama?

How much difference would this make anyway? The 30 million barrels from the U.S. plus the 30 million barrels pledged by other countries equaled – drum roll please – about 16 hours worth of world consumption of crude oil and other liquid fuels. [17] Obama in full re-election mode will say and do the darndest things to keep his fans happy, without - of course - saying or doing anything useful!

The Gulf of Mexico Oil Spill

How Obama reacted to the Gulf of Mexico oil spill is a telling and sad example of Obama's total lack of leadership. For weeks he mainly ignored the Deepwater Horizon disaster in the Gulf of Mexico, set off by an explosion on April 20, 2010. Then he said he was fully in charge, had been on it *from day one*, [18] and would do everything needed and folks just had to call him if they didn't get what they needed.

Louisiana, for one, didn't get what it needed; Obama turned a deaf ear. Louisiana wanted to build 24 offshore berms to protect their wetlands from the oil sludge. BP would do the actual work at a cost of around $360 million. It took the Obama Regime more than 3 weeks to respond and approve *only six* berms! The feds would pay for only one berm and Louisiana had to pay for five while waiting for BP reimbursements. [19]

Just when you thought it couldn't get any more ludicrous, in June 2010 the Obama Regime ordered Louisiana to halt the sand dredging that was being done to create the protective berms, because sand was being removed temporarily from a "sensitive area". This sand was going to be replaced in a couple of days, but common sense has been in very short supply for the Obama Regime. [20]

Obama *rejected* help from other countries and U.S. and foreign companies to help with the clean up. For instance, the Dutch government, only 3 days after the Deepwater Horizon explosion, offered to send several ships equipped with oil skimmers capable of removing 20,000 tons of oil and sludge per day. The Dutch also proposed a plan for building sand barriers to protect sensitive marshlands, but both BP and the Obama Regime rejected this. [21]

The outdated Merchant Marine Act of 1920 - also referred to as the Jones Act - would require that the crews of ships helping with the disaster be American, i.e. union members. Obama was asked to suspend that law for fighting the oil spill (Bush immediately suspended the law for the Katrina clean-up) but he did not do so for *10 weeks* while there was not enough equipment and personnel to fight the oil slick, thus destroying sensitive wetlands and coastlines and killing wildlife. Labor unions - one of the two biggest groups of money contributors to Obama, lawyers being the other group - were protected at the cost of our environment and economy of the Gulf States and the whole nation

Nobody yet knew what the root cause or causes for this disaster were. Right after the explosion an effort was made to close the blowout preventer valve, but it did not function. But that didn't stop the Obama Regime from quickly assigning blame to BP and accusing them of reckless behavior. And, wonder oh wonder, Bush was blamed as well. BP was found guilty without due process, was ordered to pay for any and all damages and faced stiff penalties of tens of billions of dollars. Never let an opportunity to demonize or better yet, destroy a free-market enterprise or better yet, a whole industry, go to waste!

Obama appointed a so-called independent commission to investigate the cause or causes of this disaster. [22] [23] None of the seven members had any experience in or knowledge of drilling, be it on land or in shallow or deep water. The two co-chairs were a former senator/governor and former head of the EPA. Two more members had natural resource and geography backgrounds, while the remaining three members were academics, with only one with an engineering/science background. At least three members had opposed offshore drilling in the past and most had shown a heavy anti-oil/BP bias even before any commission activities had started. It was clear that the outcome of this investigation had been pre-determined to be anti-oil and anti-drilling.

By contrast, when Reagan appointed a 13-member commission to investigate the Challenger shuttle disaster in 1986, seven members had hands-on experience in aviation and space exploration and there were three more scientists, one being world-renown physicist Richard Feynman.

Of course the Obama Regime wasn't talking about their failure to properly oversee BP's drilling operations. The oil industry is one of the most heavily regulated industries and anything they do is meant to be checked and rechecked, but oversight had been failing miserably.

Until June 2010, eight weeks into this ecological and economic disaster, Obama had not once talked to BP CEO Tony Hayward. Lame excuse #1: Obama said he "assumed CEO's just told presidents things they wanted to hear." Lame excuse #2: the White House Propaganda Minister, eh Press Secretary Robert Gibbs said that "the CEO alone isn't the final word on company decisions, which were made by the board of directors." [24] Either Gibbs/the White House doesn't know how the free-market works - not entirely unthinkable - or even worse, they play dummy to deflect blame. Anyway, did Obama instead talk with anyone on the BP board of directors then? Of course not! What about working closely, personally with the man heading the company that has the resources and knowledge to remedy the catastrophe? What about working with BP and other oil companies and experts instead of demonizing them? What about showing some leadership? Don't hold your breath!

Obama engaged in a Chicago-style shake-down of BP and other oil companies:

- The Obama Regime coerced BP into not paying dividends to their shareholders for the remainder of 2010. [25] Since when could an administration coerce a private enterprise into harming their shareholders? Since Obama was hell-bent on destroying the free-market system!

- The Obama Regime coerced BP into coughing up *$20 billion* for a four-year escrow compensation fund to pay for damages. [26] According to Obama that $20 billion was not a cap but a "good start"; the total cost of cleanup was estimated at **$37 billion** or more, way more. The plan was to have an independent third party oversee this fund and the disbursements from it, but as it turned out Obama coerced BP into accepting Obama's compensation czar Kenneth Feinberg to head the fund. An Obama crony was supposed to be an independent third party? It looked more like Obama now also had a Gulf Payout Czar!

- Obama coerced BP into setting aside **$100 million** [27] to pay for any income and other losses stemming from Obama's moratorium. So BP was paying for Obama's rash, politically motivated actions! Saul Alinsky would have been proud. And then again, maybe not: the $100 million set-aside was a drop in the bucket compared to the real cost of the ban.

- In an effort to further demonize and harm the oil industry, Obama announced plans to increase taxes on all oil companies by a factor of four. [28]

Using this crisis to advance his radical-Left agenda to the maximum extent possible, Obama pushed his devastating Cap and Trade bill in a belated address almost two months after the explosion. [29] He claimed that the U.S. had only 2% of the world's oil reserves and that the U.S. was running out of places to drill for oil on land and in shallow water. [30]

Fact is that the U.S. has way more oil reserves and an even larger share of natural gas reserves. For coal, natural gas and oil combined, the U.S. has probably the largest reserves in the world, and certainly ranks among the top three. [31] America has enough oil to provide for all of America's energy needs for **300 years**! [32] So we could be fully independent from foreign energy sources. And no, we are not running out of places to drill for oil; there are enough places to drill, but those have been declared off-limits, compliments of the environmental whackos.

In a despicable display of free-market-enterprise-bashing, the House Energy and Commerce Committee, lead by Free-Market-Destroyer-in-Chief Henry Waxman, Democrat, grilled BP executives in a clear attempt to draw attention away from the government's lack of oversight and abysmal failure to act effectively in the management of this crisis. The BP CEO was asked if he thought he would keep his job much longer and if BP had cut corners and acted recklessly, yes or no. Every time the CEO started to reply he was rudely interrupted, because he didn't say what these hypocritical bureaucrats wanted to hear. [33]

Then finally, finally on **day 71** of this disaster, Obama accepted assistance from 12 countries of the over 30 that offered to help. Would this take effect immediately? Probably not, as the press release stated: We are currently working out the particular modalities of delivering the offered assistance. Further details will be forthcoming once these arrangements are complete." [34]

In mid July of 2010 BP placed an improved cap on the Deepwater Horizon well that hopefully would cut off any more oil spilling into the gulf.[35] After placement, the cap needed to be tested to ensure it could withstand the high pressure when relieve valves would be closed. BP was ready to start testing, but out of the blue the Obama Regime expressed fears that this could make matters worse, and delayed the process. The government, it was stated, wanted to *carefully review the risks*. So here is BP working for months to design, build, transport, lower and install the new cap and here is the Obama Regime, asleep at the wheel, suddenly wondering about the risks and throwing a monkey wrench into the process. At best a horrible display of incompetence and possibly a deliberate act to prolong the crisis for political gains. Remember: never let a good crisis go to waste!

Four preliminary reports issued in October of 2010 by Obama's own presidential commission to investigate the oil spill, stated that the Obama Regime failed to act upon or fully inform the public of its own worst-case estimates of the amount of oil gushing from the blown-out well, resulting in slowing response efforts, loss of faith in the government's ability to handle the spill and a continued breach between the federal authorities and state and local officials. [36]

In November of 2010, *two months* after it had been raised from the seafloor, the 300 ton Deepwater Horizon blowout preventer, owned and maintained by Transocean, was still waiting for federal investigators to begin their root-cause investigation, allowing it to corrode and thus compromising forensic analysis. [37] Federal investigators also failed to perform flushing of the control pods with fluids to prevent their corrosion, agreed upon to have been performed in September of 2010. What the heck was going on here and what were federal investigators trying to hide?

Ultimately, the failure analysis of the blowout preventer was commissioned to a Norwegian company, Det Norske Veritas. They concluded in March 20111 that neither BP, nor Cameron International, which manufactured the preventer, nor Transocean, which owned and maintained it, were responsible for the preventer malfunction. The report confirmed that the blowout preventer, an industry-standard device designed to prevent drilling disasters, was designed and tested to industry standards and was in proper operating condition, as tests, conducted just days before the blowout, confirmed. A sudden pressure surge, exceeding worst case expectations and the approved design limits of the device, caused it to fail. This newly-gained knowledge might help to improve the design of these devices in the future. [38]

The report completely rebuked all the criticism lobbed by Obama at BP, Cameron International and Transocean and the whole oil industry. So, was Obama going to profusely apologize for his bashing of BP and the other companies? I didn't think so. After all, Obama was not looking out for us or our energy needs; he was pushing, as always, his radical-Left agenda and used any crisis to advance it.

The Renewable Energy Pipedream

The Left wants you to believe that we have an environmental, climate and energy crisis and that our own energy sources are close to being exhausted. They tell us that the U.S. only has about 2% of the world's oil reserves and that we use 20 to 25% of the world's oil. Fact is that the U.S. reserves of oil alone, not including coal and natural gas, is sufficient to supply all of our energy needs and make us totally independent from any foreign oil and other energy sources for the next *300 years*. [39] Fact is that the U.S. has the highest amount of proven fossil fuel reserves – coal, oil and natural gas combined - in the world, followed by Russia, China, Iran and Saudi Arabia. [40] However, the Left is sabotaging the development of these abundantly available energy sources.

In 2008 the lion's share, 84%, of our energy was supplied by oil, coal and natural gas. The total picture looks roughly as follows: [41]

Fossil fuels: 84%

- oil: 37%
- natural gas: 24%
- coal: 23%

Nuclear: 8%

Renewable: 7%

- hydropower: 3%
- wood: 2%
- bio-fuel: 1%
- geothermal: 0.4%
- wind: 0.6%
- solar: 0.1%

So, in spite of many decades of development of the so-called renewable, alternative or green energy sources with the aid of huge subsidies by taxpayers, little has been achieved in this area and only a measly 2% of our energy is currently supplied by bio-fuel, geothermal, wind and solar. By-and-large renewable energy is not cost-effective, yet the Left continues to push it. Government keeps interfering with the energy market with legislation that forces the use of expensive and often unproven energy sources. This infringes on our freedom, raises the cost of doing business, raises the cost of living for every American and hampers economic growth.

Obama's Energy Secretary, Steven Chu, fits right in with the "green" craze. He backs higher gasoline taxes to force people to buy cars that are more fuel efficient and buy homes closer to work. He said: "Somehow we have to figure out how to boost the price of gasoline to the levels in Europe," [42] at a time when gasoline cost less than $3 a gallon in the U.S. and $7 to $9 a gallon in Europe.

Renewable Energy in Oregon [43] [44]

Supporters of Oregon's Business Energy Tax Credit (BETC) claim that the subsidies under this program have created thousands of jobs, but can't say how many with any certainty, not even the Department of Energy, which approves and administers the subsidies. Incentives under this program have sharply increased from $30 million in 2007 to $150 million in 2010.

These are examples of Oregon and federal taxpayer funded programs in Oregon:

- Eastern Oregon's Horizon Wind Energy wind farm received $11 million in state tax credits and employs 36 full-time workers

- Portland's solar manufacturer Solaicx received $9 million in state tax credits and employs 127 full-time workers

- Cascade Grains, a bio-fuel startup, received $12 million in state subsidies before going out of business

- Reklaim Technologies received $3.4 million in state subsidies to recycle tires into oil; after two years it employs 8 people but hasn't deliver any products yet

- SolarWorld received $22 million in state tax credits for construction of a $400 million solar panel production facility in Oregon and is slated to get $74 million more.

- The Shepherds Flat wind farm under construction in Oregon is scheduled for completion in 2012. It will be the largest and most modern in the world with 338 wind turbines on 30 square miles. The total cost is $1.9 billion and 65% or $1.2 billion will be paid for with state and federal tax dollars and higher electricity rates. That's right, even with the developers only paying 35% of the real cost of the wind farm, this cutting-edge renewable energy project is not cost-effective and electricity rates will go up, not down. But this massive project will surely create many new jobs, right? Even that may not be the case. After the initial construction, there will be only 35 permanent jobs for operating and maintaining the facility and it is not know how many other jobs like farming will have been lost because of loss of farm land. So, less than 35 jobs created at a cost of more than $34 million each of taxpayers' money. We could pay 35 people $100,000 per year tax-free for one hundred years for doing nothing and spend only $0.35 billion instead of $1.2 billion of taxpayers' money and not see an increase in electricity rates!

The city of Portland, Oregon found out how unavailable and expensive renewable energy still is today. They defined it as solar, geothermal, wind, ocean wave and small hydroelectric, excluding large hydroelectric, currently a major energy source in Oregon and Washington. In an effort claimed to reduce global warming by decreasing carbon emissions, the city approved a plan in 2001 to have 100% of power used by city government come from renewable energy sources by 2010. They utterly failed to achieve their goal, mainly due to high cost and limited availability; in 2010 only 9% of the city government's power came from renewable sources.

In 2005 the State of Oregon set a goal to get 25% of state agencies' energy use from renewable sources by 2010 - again excluding existing, large hydropower - and upped the goal in 2007 to 100% by 2010, in spite of no noticeable success to meet the earlier goal. This too failed miserably. In 2010 only 1 to 2% of state government's power use came from renewable sources and the goal was yet again modified to 100% by 2025.

Bio-Fuels

And then there are bio-fuels like bio-ethanol and bio-diesel! What a great idea! Let's burn our food to make those fuels and pay more for both food *and* fuels! Food prices world-wide are increasing as a direct result of more and more food products being diverted from actually feeding people and livestock to producing fuel.

In the U.S. 40% of corn crops grown in 2010 were diverted from the food chain and used to make corn-ethanol, a fuel far more expensive than fossil fuels in spite of heavy tax-payer subsidies. The financially struggling ethanol industry is kept alive artificially by anti-free-market tax credits total-ing $6 billion in 2010: a 45-cents-a-gallon tax credits and a 10-cents-a-gallon small-producer tax credit. To further pro-tect this food-destroying scam, imported ethanol is hit with a 54-cents-a-gallon import duty. [45] A bio-diesel subsidy of a dollar-a-gallon was reinstated by Congress for 2011. [46]

Algae Fuel

And then there is algae fuel! Yes, we bend ourselves into pretzel shapes while paying through the nose (what an awkward picture I'm conjuring up here) to make – drum roll please – fuel out of algae. Mind you, it doesn't look like it can ever be produced on any meaningful scale or at com-petitive prices, but we – meaning our elected officials - sink our tax money into it anyway. And some fine results the algae contingent of the radical renewable energy crowd can point at: in 2011 you can buy, thanks to generous taxpayer subsidies, the equivalent of one barrel of crude oil in the form of algae fuel for the mere amount of – drum roll please - $400, while crude oil costs about $100 a barrel. [47]

Renewable Electrical Energy in California
California carries the torch of the radical renewable energy crowd. Already the law required the state's utilities to get 20% of their electricity from renewable sources like geothermal, wind and solar. While the actual percentage was only 14 in September of 2010, they upped the ante and increased the requirement to 33% by 2020. [48] To put more pressure on the energy industry, Governor Jerry "Moonbeam" Brown went even farther and in April of 2011 he signed that requirement of 33% by 2020 into law, his first major legislation since taking office. [49] This law would no doubt drive up the cost of electricity and put manufacturing in California into a further disadvantage, but who cared? Not the radicals who claimed the new law would create green jobs and reduce air pollution and - drum roll please - global warming!

Electric Cars
Contrary to claims from the "environmental movement", driving an electric car pollutes more and uses more energy than driving a gasoline-powered car. Similarly, the claim of the so-called "zero emissions" of electric cars is a sham. The electric car itself may have no or very low emissions of polluting waste products and may use low levels of energy, but energy-providing system for electric cars emits more pollutants and uses more energy than that for gasoline-powered cars. To make a valid comparison, we have to look at the total systems that provide either the electricity to charge the batteries or the gasoline to power the engine. For electric cars the total system includes:

- Mining, drilling for, excavating fuels like coal, oil, natural gas, radioactive materials and so on
- Transporting the fuel to the processing plants

- Processing the fuels
- Transporting the processed fuels to the power plants
- Operating the power plants
- Transporting the electricity from the power plants to the electric car charging system

For gasoline-powered cars the total system includes:

- Drilling for oil
- Transporting the oil to the refinery
- Refining the oil
- Transporting the refined fuel to the gas pumps

An in-depth study of pollution and energy use of the total support structure for electric cars and comparable gasoline-powered cars shows that pollution and energy use are way worse for electric cars. [50] On average, the total system for electric cars caused 55% more pollution and used 8% more energy. When taking into consideration the total life cycle of the electric car, which - in addition to driving - includes production, frequent replacement and disposal of the hi-tech batteries, it is even more of a burden on the environment. And then there is the issue of having to build an extensive and expensive network of charging stations.

So, who is worried about the claims of the radical environmental movement flying in the face of science and the facts? Certainly not Obama, who thrives on radicalism! In his January 2011 State of the Union address, he called for having one million electric vehicles on the road by 2015. Reuters called it "a renewed push for clean energy". [51] You call a significant increase in pollution "clean energy"? Well, I guess it's not the facts that count, but radical support for a radical president.

Electric cars are expensive and heavy, mainly because of the batteries, which require frequent charging and replacement. In 2011 there was only one model of an all-electric car that was more or less mass-produced, the Nissan LEAF. Its advertised range was 100 miles but many users reported a much lower actual range. Not very practical for anything more than short-distance commutes and shopping! Required recharging stations were almost non-existent.

Oregon was selected in 2009 to participate in the six-state EV Project; a $230 million Stimulus-Bill-funded study, geared to put thousands of all-electrical vehicles on the road in 18 cities, with a network of more than 8,000 public charging stations. Ecototality of San Francisco had been awarded a $130 million contract by the Department of Energy to install the public charging stations, but at the end of June of 2011 Ecotality had not installed any of the 1,100 stations they should have installed in Oregon. At the time only a handful of charging stations funded by private companies and municipalities had been installed in western Oregon and only 375 Nissan LEAFs had been ordered by Oregonians. [52]

Solar Energy
Energy from solar cells is more expensive than energy from coal-, natural gas- and oil-fired power plants, but that doesn't discourage the true believers. Spain heavily promoted and subsidized solar energy for many years, believing that it would create additional jobs. However, the reality was that the efforts resulted in net job losses and as a result Spain drastically curtailed those programs. [53] [54] Australia also has de-emphasized its solar programs. [55]

For the most part, solar cell production and use need hefty taxpayer subsidies to even happen!

Evergreen Solar opened an 800-worker solar cell manufacturing plant in Massachusetts in 2009 with the aid of a

$58 million award in the form of infrastructure subsidies, grants and tax credits. It closed in 2011. [56]

In 2011 SoloPower, a California startup, was going to build a $340 million thin-film solar panel manufacturing facility in Portland, Oregon. [57] [58] The facility would initially employ 170 people, with a possible increase to 500 within five years. They would receive hundreds of millions in tax breaks and government loans:

- $2 million property tax abatement from Portland
- $18 million enterprise-zone tax abatement from Portland
- $20 million Business Energy Tax Credit from Oregon
- $20 million energy loan from Oregon
- $197 million U.S. Department of Energy loan guarantee for expansion

In April of 2011 the U.S. Department of Energy approved a $2.1 billion loan guarantee for a Solar Trust of America (STA) solar power plant in the Mojave Dessert in California, the so-called Blythe Solar Power Project. [59] STA is owned by two German companies, Solar Millennium and Ferrostaal. A German bank, Deutsche Bank, would likely end up being the lender. If that would be the case, the guarantee would mean that if one or both of the German owner companies fails to repay the German bank, U.S. taxpayers would foot the bill. And how many positions would this massive loan guarantee create? Drum roll please – 1,000 temporary construction jobs and 220 permanent jobs, meaning the U.S. taxpayer is bearing the risk to the tune of $9.5 million for each job beyond initial construction. Isn't "green" energy wonderful?

Portland General Electric (PGE) supplies electricity to customers in Portland, Oregon and surrounding areas. They have a program that pays customers who install solar power-generating equipment to supply power to the electric grid. Under this program, a farmer installed solar power-generating equipment, consisting of 2,100 solar panels, on two acres of former farmland outside of Portland. The total cost of the project was $2,900,000. He received a $900,000 rebate from the federal government, paid for by you the taxpayer. PGE will pay 39 cents per kilowatt-hour delivered to the electrical grid under a 15 year agreement. [60] So what's up with this excessive price of 39 cents per kilowatt-hour? PGE charges residential customers less than 8 cents per kilowatt-hour, [61] so we know that it costs PGE less than that to either generate the electricity themselves or buy it elsewhere. So PGE overpays for electricity generated by their customers by more than a factor of five! For what? For the radical-Left to feel good? First, the federal taxpayer has to fork over close to a million dollars to have someone generate electricity at a non-competitive rate. Second, other PGE customers will have to pay more to offset the cost increase. What a scam!

For the most part, renewable energy sources are currently too expensive and are a greater burden on the environment than coal, natural gas and oil. We must fully develop *all* our energy sources, including oil, natural gas, coal, nuclear and renewables, *using free-market principles*. The government must get out of the way, stop interfering with and sabotaging the energy industry and stop spending our tax money.

7. Obsession with the Environment

Despite ample proof to the contrary, the Left continues the hysterical claim that human activity causes "catastrophic, global warming" or "climate change" and wastes our tax money on unproven and non-competitive so-called "renewable energy." Never mind that science shows that solar activity, planetary interactions and natural processes cause global temperature variations.

Global Warming Hysteria

The claim that human activity and particularly emission of CO_2 and other so-called greenhouse gases are the main cause of global, catastrophic warming is false. The scientific method - based on honesty, logic and evidence - teaches us that solar activity, the wobble in the Earth's rotation and natural processes on earth like volcanic and oceanic activity and rotting of dead vegetation, not human activity, are the main cause of global temperature variations. Temperature variations on other planets in our solar system correlate with temperature changes on earth, pointing to solar activity as a major cause of changes in Earth temperatures, not human activity. [1] Wobbles in Earth's rotation cause huge climate changes called ice ages and warming periods. [2] As all these processes vary, so will global temperatures. Warmer and colder periods will continue to come and go as they have for millions of years.

Since the "common good" cause of Marxism has been discredited everywhere it has been tried, by the stark realities of oppression, tyranny, hunger, economic collapse and more than 100 million dead people - more than 70 million in Communist China alone -, the radical-Left minority has latched onto "global warming" as a means to oppress and control the rest of us.

When "global warming" ran into major scientific problems, they quickly changed the terminology to "climate change". After all, it's easier to extol the virtues of more government control whenever temperatures go up or down, as they always do and always will! The radical Left is doing all they can, in the name of saving the planet, to force their anti-free-market, anti-capitalism ideology onto us. Cap and Trade legislation and the EPA are some of the main vehicles they use in America.

When the data did not support global warming alarmists' claims, they falsified the data to show continued warming during the first decade of the 21st century, when honest assessments showed flat or slightly declining temperatures. The warming period of the past decades was not as warm as the Medieval Warm Period, something climate alarmists deny ever existed or conveniently omit from what they claim to be historical data.

The much heralded "hockey stick curve" theory claimed to prove that global temperatures slowly declined for hundreds of years and then sharply increased starting with the industrial revolution as a result of human activity, but mysteriously did not show the Medieval Warming Period or subsequent Little Ice Age. The theory was later debunked as fraudulent. [3]

Climate alarmists claim they can predict climate changes over long periods of time, in spite of all the evidence to the contrary. For example, the British Meteorological Office, the United Kingdom's national weather service, predicted a warmer than usual 2010-2011 winter in Britain, with temperatures even warmer than the previous winter. [4] Instead, as Gordon Fulks wrote, it was way colder than normal. [5] How come people that can't explain yesterday's weather believe they can forecast the climate years and decades ahead?

To quote Gordon Fulks: [6] "But what if the New York Times, President Obama, the National Academy of Sciences, the U.N. Intergovernmental Panel on Climate Change, Yale University, and The Oregonian all say to be very worried? Perhaps you should question their expertise.

President Obama relies on scientists whom he funds to give him the answers he wants. The National Academy of Sciences is run to support government programs by an electrical engineer. He discovered that global warming is far more lucrative than electrical engineering.

The UN IPCC is run by a railroad engineer who writes romance novels. Yale University promoters are really psychologists who want you to believe that they are climate experts when their real expertise is propaganda. The Oregonian relies on all the above."

A large and growing number of scientists from around the globe, currently over 31,000, more than 9,000 of who hold Ph.D.s, challenge man-made global warming claims made by the U.N. Intergovernmental Panel on Climate Change (UN IPCC) and former Vice President Al Gore. [7] These prominent, international scientists, include many current and former UN IPCC scientists. They have turned against the UN IPCC and voiced skepticism about the so-called global warming "consensus". They compare to just 52 U.N. scientists who authored the media-hyped "IPCC 2007 Summary for Policymakers."

Electric Cars

The radical environmental movement, headed by Obama, is not driven by logic, facts or science, but an ideological agenda. They keep promoting their flawed ideas against all reason, including the use of electric cars as a more environmentally friendly means of transportation. I discussed the environmental issues with electric cars in Chapter 6, Energy.

Cap and Trade

This legislation, officially called the National Energy Tax, squeaked by in the U.S. House of Representatives in June of 2009 by a mostly partisan vote of 219-212. Democrats voted 83% for, Republicans 95% against. This bill is stalled in the U.S. Senate and appears dead.

This massive, new National Energy Tax would be the largest tax increase in American history and would hit poor and middle-income families the hardest. [8] With high unemployment we can't afford to weaken our economy even further with such a disastrous tax. The change in global temperature as a result of this legislation may not be noticeable and more likely will not even occur. We can't afford Cap and Trade. Not now. Not ever.

Our nation struggles to get the economy moving again and put Americans back to work. Instead of weakening our country, shouldn't we work to increase environmentally-safe energy, reduce energy cost, lower prices, create jobs, and clean up our air and water?

Just as for the Stimulus Bill, Obama said we urgently needed to pass this bill. There was no time to lose. A disaster was pending unless Obama came to the rescue and to hell with the campaign promise of at least 5 days to review and debate the bill; more than 300 additional pages of this legislation were released after 3am the day of the vote. [9]

This Bill Would Have the Following Results:

- The biggest tax increase in U.S. history
- Increase government's size and control over the U.S. economy, particularly the energy and manufacturing industries
- By the year 2050 this bill would reduce global temperatures by a paltry ***0.05 degrees*** Fahrenheit. [10] Overwhelming evidence shows that global warming is caused by sun activity and wobble of the Earth's rotation, not by greenhouse gases.
- Reduce Gross Domestic Product by $9.4 trillion between 2012 and 2035 [11]
- Destroy millions of American jobs [12]
- Raise an average family's utility costs by $800 per year [13]
- Raise electricity rates 90% [14]
- Raise gasoline prices by 58% [15]
- Drive up the cost for all goods and services
- Greatly reduce America's competitiveness
- Cause a steady decline in American manufacturing
- Drive more American jobs overseas to countries like China, India, Brazil and Mexico

The ClimateGate Scandal

In November 2009, leaked emails and documents showed a climate related scandal of major proportions. One of the world's leading climate research institutes and promoters of the man-made, catastrophic global warming hoax and key contributor to the U.N. Intergovernmental Panel on Climate Change, the University of East Anglia's Climatic Research Unit and other so-called leading climate researchers, engaged in criminal activities of conspiring to exaggerate warming data, manipulate and suppress evidence, destruct contrary information, admit in private but not in public to flaws in their climate theories, etc. [16] This may well be the undoing of the environmental whackos and their man-made, catastrophic global warming hoax, as well as the Cap and Trade disaster. Some of the scientists and meteorologists involved have been advisors to Al Gore. Way to go, Al!

More than likely as a result of ClimateGate, Australia unexpectedly voted down their version of Cap and Trade in early December 2009. [17]

In July of 2010 a review commissioned by the University of East Anglia was published. It claimed that the researchers in question, despite some injudicious comments about skeptics, had been honest in their science. And the Climate Research Unit hadn't done anything wrong other than reacting unprofessionally to criticism by dragging its feet in sharing data and responding to Freedom-of-Information Act requests and that there had been a consistent pattern of failing to display the proper degree of openness. [18] But besides those itty bitty issues, basically nothing to worry about and let's all sing Kumbaya! The fox guarding the henhouse has totally convinced me that all is just fine!

The UN IPCC Himalayan Glaciers Scandal

In January 2010 so-called U.N. climate experts had to admit, that a 2007 U.N. IPCC report, that Himalayan glaciers were melting faster than glaciers anywhere else in the world and might be totally gone by 2035, was not based on any scientific data. [19] Way to go again, IPCC!

The EPA Replaces Congress

In December 2009 the Obama administration's EPA (Environmental Protection Agency) declared that so-called greenhouse gases produced by burning coal and oil are a danger to public health. Said EPA administrator Lisa Jackson: "Look at the droughts, the flooding, the changes in diseases, the changes in migratory habits, the changes in our water cycle and climate that we now find affect human health and welfare." [20] This "finding" is a key step in a process that would allow the EPA to act on its own authority – without further action or approval by Congress – to enforce new rules on emissions and would allow Obama to regulate emissions anyway if Cap and Trade fails.

In May of 2010 the EPA did indeed issue new restrictive rules for any big facility that emits CO_2, methane, nitrous oxide or several other classes of chemicals. [21] To hell with science; let's hijack "the environment" to force radical-Left, socialist ideology and evermore government control onto the American people.

Republicans tried to block the new EPA regulation, but the effort was blocked by the Democrat controlled Senate. So now the Democrats are on record to support undermining the power and role of Congress to write U.S. law. The fact that six Democrat senators supported the effort to block the regulation didn't bode well for Obama's chances to pass the much more restrictive Cap and Trade legislation that year, but he tried again and again.

The American Power Act

This was the Senate's sequel to the House Cap and Trade bill. In May of 2010 Senators John Kerry and Joe Lieberman introduced this so-called climate and energy bill. [22] This rewrite of the House Cap and Trade legislation claimed to reduce pollution, curb foreign oil dependence and create domestic clean-energy jobs. Senator Lindsey Graham, the only Republican supporting this legislation initially, withdrew from crafting it in April because of White House politics. [23]

The legislation's main provisions were: [24]

- cut emissions of carbon dioxide and other so-called greenhouse gases by 17% below 2005 levels by 2020 and more than 80% by 2050

- a new gasoline tax on American motorists

- a controversial Cap and Trade system for electric utilities

- a new carbon fee that oil companies, referred to as "refined product providers," must pay to the federal government for the right to emit carbon dioxide

According to one analysis this bill would reduce global temperatures by only 0.2 degrees Fahrenheit by 2100. [25]

The effects from enacting this legislation would be disastrous and similar to those of the House Cap and Trade bill. See the comments above.

The Great Garbage Patch Deception

To support their radical agenda in general and their desire to dictate that you can't use plastic bags, bottles, etc. in particular, environmental wacko scientists have persistently claimed that a plastic mass twice the size of Texas floats in the Pacific Ocean. [26] It was also claimed that this garbage patch was growing tenfold each decade and that the oceans were filled with more plastic than plankton. Bad, bad people! Shame on you!

Not so fast! A scientific study by the Oregon State University and others concluded in January of 2011 that none of these claims were true. The amount of plastics in all our oceans combined was estimated to be less than $1/100^{th}$ the size of Texas. [27] Still too high by any standards, but his kind of junk-science exaggeration clearly shows that irresponsible environmental wackos will do anything, including lying through their teeth, to push their radical agenda.

Pelosi's "Green the Capitol" Fiasco

Pelosi launched the "Green the Capitol" initiative, aimed at reducing energy and water consumption. Part of the initiative was a composting program for the Capitol's cafeteria, replacing the polystyrene of cups and plastic of trays and utensils with biodegradable material made of cornstarch. Like so many "green" projects, this one may have felt good to the greenies, but fell short on delivering the promised benefits. Cornstarch take-away boxes leaked and utensils melted and broke. After four years and $475,000 of expenses a year, it was cancelled, since it was neither cost-effective nor energy-efficient. [28]

8. Health Care

Our world-class health care system is under siege. The Left forces ObamaCare down our throats using scare tactics, gross exaggerations of issues with our current system and the number of truly uninsurable people, bribes and a myriad of false claims about the advantages of ObamaCare. Never mind that universal or socialized health care hasn't worked anywhere else it has been tried.

"Health Care Reform" aka ObamaCare

Obama's so-called health care reform, or ObamaCare, will destroy our health care system and bankrupt this country. It needs to be recalled and replaced with free-market solutions.

As a U.S. senator, Obama never created or co-authored any health care legislation and voted against all such legislation in the Senate, so why the rush for ObamaCare now? Obama's aim is to grab more and more power, take over as much of the U.S. economy as possible and decide "what's best for us". After all, Big Brother is so much smarter than the American citizens. Just as with the Stimulus Bill, Cap and Trade and taking over parts of the banking, mortgage and car industries, he wants to take over and control the U.S. health care system.

Socialized medicine, aka universal health care or government-run health care, has been a dream of every self-respecting Liberal for decades and Obama and his collaborators in Congress have made this a top priority; higher than addressing the War on Terror, the economy, unemployment, deficit spending and the national debt. A government takeover of health care, representing one sixth of our economy [1] and providing 1 out of every 10 jobs, [2] is the top priority of the Obama Regime. Power, control and dependency are the driving forces behind all this, not concern for our health.

There have been numerous health care bills from both the House and the Senate. An overwhelming majority of Americans oppose these, but a punch-drunk Obama and Congress have gone full-steam ahead and forced health care reform down our throats.

Obama has not been able to explain ObamaCare or support his claims that it will make health care more available, more affordable and more effective without increasing the deficit. It will destroy our health care system, increase the cost of health care and bankrupt the country.

It is clear that our current system has issues, with the cost rising faster than inflation. There is room for improvement. Even one American without health insurance who really needs and wants it, is one too many.

The House Bill

After several iterations, the House presented the final version of their health reform bill, House Bill: H.R. 3962 or Affordable Health Care for America Act (AHCAA). Don't you love those impressive titles and acronyms? This bill, with amendments, narrowly passed in the House in October of 2009 with 220 for (219 Democrats, 1 Republican) and 215 against (176 Republicans, 39 Democrats). It could never pass in the Senate and ultimately it stalled in the House.

The bill was developed behind closed doors without any Republican input. It replaced three earlier House bills. It had 1990 pages; apparently the 1017 pages of a previous bill were not enough to weave a sufficiently tangled web. Illegal aliens were claimed to be excluded, but they would be covered, as I will explain later. The bill initially covered abortion, but that provision had to be taken out to get it passed. However, the pro-abortion Democrats hoped to reverse that and get abortion covered in a final bill.

The bill was claimed to have a major emphasis on preventive care and would lower patient costs. Riiiiight! It had a government-run insurance option and was claimed to extend coverage to 36 million uninsured Americans but still would leave 4% or about 12 million Americans uninsured. [3]

Obama in his infinite wisdom pronounced that health care reform should not cost more than $900 billion [4] and – surprise, surprise – the cost for this bill was claimed to be just under that amount, $894 billion, and it was claimed to reduce the deficit by $104 billion. [5] As we would see, both were **big, fat lies**. Also, keep in mind that these numbers were wishful thinking in the sense, that if this bill would be enacted in real life, it would more than likely cost **many times the estimates**; the entire Medicare program cost us 9 times the amount of the original estimates. [6]

The Misleading Ten-Year Estimate of This Version of ObamaCare [7] [8]

Congressional Budget Office (CBO) gross total cost: $1,055 billion

Plus, associated costs: $6 billion

Minus, penalties for not being insured, paid by individuals and employers: $167 billion

Net cost: $894 billion

Minus, cuts in Medicare and other federal health programs: $426 billion
Minus, tax increases: $572 billion
Deficit reduction: $104 billion

First, claiming a cost of $894 billion was intellectually dishonest; the cost of the program was $1,055 billion.

Second, cutting – arbitrarily, as far as I can tell - $426 billion out of Medicare and other health programs was a totally separate issue and it should not be included in the calculations to make it look like ObamaCare would reduce the deficit. Whether or not those cuts could be gotten by efficiency improvements, fraud reduction and other problem solving techniques or by simply paying doctors, hospitals and other health care givers less for the same medication and procedures, those reductions could be gotten independent from ObamaCare. The CBO later came to the same conclusion: the Medicare and Medicaid trust funds are separate from the government's overall expenditures; any reduction in Medicare and Medicaid expenses would automatically generate a government IOU, thereby leaving the overall expenditure liabilities the same; therefore no reduction in deficit or debt.

Third, there was still the issue of the "doc fix". The Senate "Medicare Physicians Fairness Act of 2009" would cut Medicare reimbursement rates to physicians by 21% in 2010 and 40% in 2016. The so-called "doc fix" bill would undo those cuts and was necessary to salvage Medicare at a cost of $245 billion. [9] The House did not have the guts to include the "doc fix" issue in this bill, but copped out and decided to deal with it separately.

So, this led me to make some major corrections to the flawed and misleading numbers of the Obama Regime:

<u>My Ten-Year Estimate</u>
Cost: $1,055 billion
Plus, associated costs: $6 billion
Minus, penalties for not being insured, paid by individuals and employers: $167 billion
Minus, tax increases: $572 billion
Deficit increase: $322 billion

Observations:

- Obama's claim that health care reform would not add one dime to the deficit was a *big, fat lie*
- Part, but not all, of the cost was paid for with $167 billion in penalties – aka taxes in my book – for the uninsured and other hefty tax increases of $572 billion
- The elderly would still be hit with $426 billion in cuts in Medicare, Medicaid, etc.
- The "doc fix" would still require $245 billion

The Senate Bill

After several iterations, the Senate presented the final version of their health care reform bill, Senate Bill: H.R. 3590 or Patient Protection and Affordable Care Act, aka The Affordable Care Act.

Not to be outdone by the House, this merger of the two previous Senate bills was 2074 pages long! Harry Reid, Senate Majority Leader commented "it's an important way to level the playing field for patients with the insurance industry".

Since the bill ran into major opposition among Democrats - Republicans were united against it -, Harry Reid announced in early December 2009 that the government-run public option would be removed in order to secure the 60 votes needed to finish debate and advance the bill to final voting where 50 votes were needed to pass it. Give up the golden standard of liberalism so easily? What was going on? Was there another shoe to drop? But of course! Just a couple of days later Reid announced that to "compensate" for giving up the government-run public option, people aged 55 through 64 – about 55 million - would be able to "buy into" the Medicare program. [10] At the time the normal, mandatory Medicare program for people 65 years of age and older covered about 40 million. People called it *"the Mother of All Public Options."* [11] Drop the government-run public option and replace it with another massive, government-run Medicare program. That made perfect sense to the average liberal bureaucrat Democrat, hellbent on running this country into the ground.

Soon after pushing for the Medicare "buy-in" provision and even before the CBO came out with an estimate, good old Harry Reid dropped it, after getting an earful from many of his Democrat colleagues.

What would be next? Were Democrats so desperate that, instead of coming up with real solutions for health care the majority of Americans would approve, they would throw just about anything up against the wall in the hope that something would stick and they could claim victory?

So the "buy-in" for Medicare was out and the public option was back in, but states would be allowed to *opt out* of the federal program. Would they also be allowed to opt out of paying for the program through increased taxes and higher inflation? I didn't think so! Abortion and long-term care insurance were also included. The bill was supposed to extend coverage to 94% of the population or 31 million additional Americans, but 23 million Americans would still not be insured.

Extortion and Bribes Used to Push the Senate Bill Through

When Nebraska senator Ben Nelson, Democrat, objected to the abortion provisions and other issues with the Senate health care bill and indicated he would not vote for it, the White House, in retaliation, threatened to close the Nebraska Offutt Air Force Base, home of the U.S. Strategic Center. [12] So now the White House was willing to compromise our national security and play politics with our military to crush objections from their own rank and file! Chicago-style politics!

In order to secure Nelson's holdout vote for this bill (all 60 Democrat and Independent votes were needed to finish debate and go to a final vote where only 50 votes are needed) he was bribed with taxpayer money. [13] To overcome objections on the issue of abortion, taxpayer funded abortions were limited, not eliminated and Nebraska would not ever have to pay Medicaid increased costs under this bill, a **bribe of $45 million** for the first 10 years alone. This bribe became known as the "Cornhusker Kickback".

All Americans are supposed to have equal protection and rights under the laws of the United States, so the special treatment for Nebraska was a violation of law and Nelson knew it. He made a token effort to correct this by proposing that the special treatment for Nebraska be expanded to all 50 states. [14] He knew full well that the Democrat-controlled Senate would vote his proposal down, which they indeed did. But this way he could claim to do the right thing AND get special treatment for his state. How corrupt is that? Very!

Nelson was cheap by comparison. While he was bought with "only" $45 million, Louisiana Senator Mary Landrieu, Democrat, was bought to vote for this bill with a *$300 million* fix of taxpayer money in the form of special Medicaid subsidies given to the state of Louisiana and not to any other state. [15] Oh yeah, hope, change, transparency, etc.! This bribe became known as the "Louisiana Purchase".

And then there was Florida senator Bill Nelson, Democrat, who got an even bigger bribe of *$5 billion* for the Medicare Advantage program, mostly for the State of Florida. [16] A handful of states didn't have to pay their share of the expenses of the liberal Obama agenda at the expense of people in other states, clearly violating the Constitution's Equal Protection Clause. This is not legislation. ***This is taxpayer-funded corruption by our government.*** The bribe became known as the "Florida Flim-Flam".

At the end of December 2009, Republican attorney generals from at least 13 states threatened to sue over the Nebraska deal if it was not removed. It was good to see that at least some people in our government had a spine!

However, these bribes were child's play compared to what the labor unions got! In January of 2010 it was learned that negotiations behind closed doors were held to ensure support for health care reform by labor unions. It was decided that labor union "Cadillac" plans would not be subject to the 40% excise tax for eight years. A ***bribe of $60 billion!*** [17] Labor unions are one of the two biggest contributors to Democrats, the other being lawyers. Apart from being unconstitutional - but who cares about the Constitution anyway? -, how would the Obama Regime fill this $60 billion hole? Well, by taxing other people $60 billion more, of course. Can't you do this simple arithmetic yourselves? What's wrong with you people? Said Pelosi: "We received the good news that there had been some accommodation arrived at by the White House." [18] Isn't "Crazy Eyes Pelosi" great, or what?

And then there was a 767 page Single Payer Amendment by Vermont Senator Bernie Sanders, Democrat. This amendment would make the U.S. government the single payer, meaning that any and all health care related payments to doctors, HMO's, hospitals, physical therapists and any other person or entity providing any form of health care, would be paid through the government. Right on! Let's create more government bureaucracy. After all, the government bankrupted Social Security, Medicare, Medicaid, Fannie Mae, Freddie Mac, the flood insurance program and the FDIC (Federal Deposit Insurance Corporation); an ideal track record to ensure we destroy our health care system.

After a Republican senator demanded Senate rules be followed and the amendment be read aloud, unless all senators would state that they read and understood it, it was pulled. [19]

It should be noted that the "new and improved" bill that Reid and a handful of others worked on **behind closed doors** had, with very few exceptions, not been made available to the same senators that would have to vote on it. What happened to transparency yet again? The last 383 pages of changes to the bill were released to the full senate only five days before the final vote, [20] not giving them a chance to carefully read it, let alone understand it and properly and carefully debate it.

The bill passed the senate on December 24, 2009. All 58 Democrats and 2 Independents voted for, all 39 present Republicans (1 was absent) voted against.

The Misleading Ten-Year Estimate of This Version of ObamaCare [21]

Congressional Budget Office (CBO) gross total cost: $875 billion

Minus, excise tax on high-premium insurance plans: $149 billion

Minus other effects on tax revenues and outlays: $60 billion

Minus, penalties paid by uninsured individuals and employers: $42 billion

Net cost: $624 billion

Minus, cuts in Medicare, Medicaid and other federal health programs: $478 billion

Minus, tax increases: $264 billion

Deficit reduction: $118 billion

Making corrections similar to those for the House bill, I arrived at the following:

My Ten-Year Estimate

Cost: $875 billion

Minus, excise tax on high-premium insurance plans: $149 billion

Minus other effects on tax revenues and outlays: $60 billion

Minus, penalties paid by uninsured individuals and employers: $42 billion

Minus, tax increases: $264 billion

Deficit increase: $360 billion

Observations:

- Obama's claim that health care reform would not add one dime to the deficit was a *big, fat lie*
- Part, but not all, of the cost was paid for with $149 billion of taxes on so-called "Cadillac Plans", $42 billion in penalties – aka taxes in my book – for the uninsured and other hefty tax increases of $264 billion
- The elderly would still be hit with $478 billion in cuts in Medicare, Medicaid, etc.
- The "doc fix" would still require $245 billion

If you think that these amounts are scary, hold on to your seat! Republican staff on the Senate Budget Committee estimated that spending would cost more than $2.5 trillion over the first ten years of full implementation of the bill, 2014-2023! [22]

This was the most corrupt major legislation ever to be passed in America. The Obama-Pelosi-Reid trio of socialist, dictatorial power needs to be stopped before this country is damaged beyond repair.

Both Bills Stalled

The final Senate and House bills should have been reconciled in committee and approved by both the House and the Senate. However, a bill that very likely would differ substantially from any of the previous ones, was being cobbled together by Obama, Pelosi and Reid and a few other members of Congress. Every Republican and all American citizens were excluded from these secret meetings. Obama's promises of transparency and conducting all health care reform debates on C-Span be damned! The new bill could then go through endless amendments and bribes; the whole circus could possibly start all over again. Business as usual! Oh no, wait: Hope and Change We All Can Believe In and Transparency to boot!

After Democrats lost their 60-seat supermajority in the Senate, all hope for Democrats to force health care reform down our throats seemed lost. [23] The Obama Regime wanted the House to approve the Senate bill without any changes. When that seemed very unlikely, the Obama Regime wanted to force health care reform through by using the so-called reconciliation process, a process that would further enrage the American public. So Obama faked a last-ditch effort to salvage his failing health care reform agenda. He called for a health care summit at the end of February 2010, a so-called bipartisan dog and pony show for both Democrats and Republicans to meet with the goal of forcing major health care reform onto the American public, you know, the dummies that are just too stupid to know what's good for them. He indicated that they should build on the existing House and Senate bills, rather than reset totally and start from scratch. Starting from scratch would be *the only way* to develop truly bipartisan, meaningful, effective and low-cost reforms.

The Obama Proposal

On February 22, 2010, just three days before the so-called bipartisan health care summit, Obama issued what he called his "own" proposal for health care reform. [24] Instead of going to the meeting with an open mind, he told everyone in advance what outcome he wanted. Obama offered really nothing new. The proposal followed the general framework of the bill that passed in the Senate, including the scandalous *bribes*, but was even larger and more expensive, with a first 10 year cost estimate of *$950 billion*. There he was again, pushing his radical-Left, socialist agenda.

One "improvement" was the creation of a federal authority to oversee the health insurance industry's rates and other practices. States already performed that task, so this was another case of growing government for the sake of growing government.

The summit accomplished nothing, except to reconfirm the Obama Regime's rigid, radical-Left agenda. [25] They refused to start over. The Democrats did not even want to consider allowing competition across state and district lines. They paid some lip service to Republican ideas of improving health savings accounts provisions and token efforts to battle Medicaid and Medicare fraud.

The Final Bill Pushed Through

Less than one week after the summit, Obama urged Congress to ram through health care reform anyway by abusing the budget reconciliation process. Under this scenario, the Senate bill without any changes would be passed by the House and signed into law by Obama right away. Right after that, a bill - with amendments to iron out issues for both the right and left wings of the Democrat party - would be passed by the House, an unprecedented abuse of the budget reconciliation process.

The budget reconciliation process had never before been abused to such extent to push through massive, partisan social engineering and destroy such a large part of our economy. The budget reconciliation process – applied frequently in the past - is meant to be applied when House and Senate bills have significant bipartisan support, but differ slightly in matters of *cost* only.

However, there was doubt that Pelosi would have the votes in the House to pass the unmodified Senate bill. Moreover, House Democrat didn't have the guts to go on record to vote for or against it. So what did Pelosi do? She proposed to use the so-called "***Slaughter Rule***" [26] or "***deem and pass procedure***" – the House would not vote on the Senate bill at all; they would go straight to abusing the budget reconciliation process, amending a House bill - in fact the Senate bill - that hadn't even passed in the House! This mumbo jumbo, sleaze maneuver would very clearly be a violation of the U.S. Constitution and a flagrant abuse of U.S. government power. Obama, the supposed law expert, went on record on Fox News that he didn't worry about how or if the House voted on the Senate bill. [27] Never before had we seen such a disregards and contempt for the U.S. Constitution - and American citizens - on such major legislation, legislation that lacked *any* bipartisan support. After withering criticism from both the Right and Left, Pelosi gave up on this idea of using "deem and pass", but she would have used it if she could have gotten away with it. There seemed to be no limit to how corrupt Washington could get.

The Misleading Ten-Year Estimate of This Final Version of ObamaCare: [28]

Congressional Budget Office (CBO) estimate of gross cost: $1,390 billion

Minus, penalties paid by uninsured individuals and employers, excise tax on high-premium insurance plans and other effects on revenues and spending: $348 billion

Net cost: $1,042 billion

Minus, cuts in Medicare and other federal health programs: $732 billion

Minus, tax increases: $520 billion

Deficit reduction: $210 billion

Making corrections similar to those for the House and Senate bills, I arrived at the following:

My 2012-2023 Estimate

Cost: $1,390 billion

Minus, penalties paid by uninsured individuals and employers, excise tax on high-premium insurance plans and other effects on revenues and spending: $348 billion

Minus, tax increases: $520 billion

Deficit increase: $522 billion

Observations:
- Obama's claim that health care reform would not add one dime to the deficit was a *big, fat lie*
- Part, but not all, of the cost was paid for with $348 billion of taxes on so-called "Cadillac Plans", penalties – aka taxes in my book – for the uninsured, "other effects", whatever they might be and other hefty tax increases of $520 billion
- The elderly would be hit with $732 billion in cuts in Medicare, etc.

- The "doc fix" would still require $245 billion

After much arm-twisting and special deals and without giving the CBO time to update their cost estimates, the Senate bill passed on March 21, 2010 in a 219-212 vote; all 178 Republicans opposed it, along with 38 Democrats. Obama signed the bill, ***including the multi-billion dollar bribes***, into law on March 23, 2010, clearly violating the Constitution on multiple issues. This was a dark day in the history of the U.S. This monstrosity, called the Affordable Care Act, will destroy our current health care system and virtually guarantee our economic destruction.

The budget reconciliation bill passed a week later in the Senate. Democrats paid heavily for these transgressions through harsh disapproval by the American public and losses of historic proportions in the November 2010 mid-term elections. ObamaCare will also be a major issue in the 2012 presidential elections.

It should be noted that this bill does not apply to any and all past, current and future presidents, senators, representatives and their staff! Talk about hypocrisy and arrogance!

To the surprise of most Americans, the Democrats included in the reconciliation bill a total takeover of all student loans in the country, redirecting income from banks and student loan companies to the federal government for advancement of their ultra-Left, radical socialist agenda. [29]

Fact and Fiction about Health Care Reform

In this section I look at claims being made about health care in America and comment on their validity.

Claim: Our Health Care System Is Broken and in Severe Crisis

This is yet another example of the Obama Regime scare tactics, used to frighten Americans into going along with the radical-Left agenda. The system is not broken and people are in general happy with their health insurance. Poll after poll shows that about 80% or more of Americans are satisfied with their health insurance. [30]

The claim is *false*.

Claim: 46 Million Americans Are Without Health Insurance [31]

This number was thrown around repeatedly by the Left. It was more than likely taken from a Census Bureau estimate of 46 million uninsured in 2007. That same Census Bureau study stated that the number included 10 million noncitizens. That brings down the number of Americans without health insurance to 36 million.

The claim is *false*.

Claim: More Than 30 Million Americans Cannot Get Health Insurance [32] [33]

This is a more honest approach to the problem since it looks at how many Americans want health insurance but cannot get it. However the number is way, way off. For starters, people temporarily without insurance, like people in-between jobs, will regain insurance once they return to work. About 14 million or more uninsured people qualify for existing government programs like Medicaid and SCHIP, but simply haven't bothered to sign up. Then there are millions who can afford health insurance but don't' get it for one reason or another; 18 million of the uninsured in 2007 had incomes of more than $50,000 and 9 million earned more than $75,000. About 18 million of the uninsured in 2007 were under 34, many of whom may simply have felt that they were young and healthy enough to go without insurance.

The net result - according to a 2003 BlueCross Blue Shield study - was that there were about *8 million* or about 3% of Americans who were truly uninsured: they were too poor to buy health insurance, but were not poor enough to qualify for government assistances. Ninety seven percent of Americans had health insurance or could readily get it.

The claim is *false*.

Claim: the Obama Regime Seeks to Insure "Everybody"

Are they talking about 46 million, 30 million or 8 million? The Obama Regime first used 46 million exclusively, but later switched to 30 million without explaining why. Yet all the proposals for reform leave millions uninsured.

The claim is *false*.

Claim: Health Care Reform Will Not Add One Dime to the Deficit

As I showed earlier, the deficit will increase by over $500 billion in the first 10 years alone.

The claim is *false*.

Claim: "Cadillac Health Insurance Policies Will Be Taxed to Help Pay for Health Care Reform

There was going to be an excise tax on so-called "Cadillac" health plans. One can ask how the government is authorized to selectively tax health insurance agreements between individuals, companies, institutions and insurance companies. Be that as it may, there is more to this issue than one would think. Labor union members enjoy many "Cadillac

plans. Labor unions support the Obama Regime. As we saw earlier, labor union "Cadillac plans are exempted from this 40% taxation. Can you spell "corruption"?
The claim is *false*.

Claim: Health Care Reform Will Exclude Illegal Aliens
34

Health care reform is claimed to exclude illegal aliens, but nowhere is it specified if and how illegal aliens will be identified. Obama knows full well that if this is challenged in court, the Constitution's Equal Protection Clause will be upheld, meaning illegal aliens *will* be included. Amendments to specifically exclude illegal aliens were voted down. The claim is *false*.

Claim: Health Care Benefits Will Be Preserved; You Can Keep Your Own Doctor

Over $500 billion will be cut out of the Medicare program, yet ObamaCare is supposed to have no negative effects. And we are supposed to believe this. In June of 2010 Sebelius, Democrat, Secretary of Health & Human Services, sent out a glossy political propaganda letter to Medicare beneficiaries – including me - that claimed: greater savings, increased quality health care, ensured accountability, greater control over your care, new benefits and cost savings, increased focus on quality, accurate information, your choice of doctors will be preserved, etc. etc.

Obama claimed that, while not reducing any coverage, these Medicare cuts will be realized by reducing inefficiencies, fraud and payments to health care providers. First, if inefficiencies and fraud can be drastically reduced, then this should be done anyway, independent of other health care reform and such savings will not make the other health care reform any less expensive.

Second, what effects will cutting payments to health care providers have? Before any Medicare cuts had even taken place, the American Medical Association reported that Medicare rejected more health care claims than private health care companies. [35] The program significantly under-pays providers, [36] leading many providers to refuse additional Medicare patients.

A telling example is the Mayo Clinic. Obama praised them as an example of healthcare with better outcomes at a lower cost. However, one of the famous medical center's facilities in Arizona will no longer accept Medicare patients as part of a two-year trial period to see if they should no longer accept Medicare patients at facilities in Arizona, Florida and Minnesota, where over 500,000 seniors are served. [37]

Reducing payments further as part of health care reform, will cause providers to reject more and more treatments and many will simply stop treating Medicare patients. Also, many doctors and other health care professionals indicate that they will leave the profession because of ObamaCare, further contributing to major shortages, long wait times and rationing of care. [38]

The claim is *false*.

Claim: Health Care Reform Will Increase Competition and Offer Choices among a Number of Different Plans

Fact is, there are already over 1300 health insurance companies in America, [39] There is no need for yet another big government program to increase competition. What we need is a recall of state government regulations that prohibit health insurance companies from freely competing in all districts in all 50 states.

Instead of increasing competition like Obama claims, he wants to eliminate all employer provided and private health care and establish a single payer system like the one in Canada, England and many other countries. His own words: "I happen to be a proponent of a single-payer health care program.", "But I don't think we're going to be able to eliminate employer coverage immediately.", "There's going to be potentially some transition process — I can envision a decade out, or 15 years out, or 20 years out, where we've got a much more portable system." [40] And in the words of Health and Human Services Secretary Kathleen Sebelius: "I'm all for a single-payer system". [41]

Obama's claim that if you are happy with your current insurance, you can keep it, is a bold-faced lie. A government-run plan, funded and subsidized by taxpayer money, will not need to make a profit and will unfairly compete with the low-profit-margin private health insurance industry and ultimately cause private insurance companies to go under, exactly what Obama wants.

The Obama Regime has increasingly targeted health insurance companies as the villains of health care. After all, these "mean" and "greedy" companies are making profits - a dirty word for any Left-winger - and need to be destroyed. Fact is that health insurance companies make less profit than most other industries. Their profit margin in 2009 was only 2.2%. [42] So it will not take much for a non-profit, taxpayer funded and subsidized government program to force the private health insurance companies out of business, exactly what the Obama Regime wants.

They embark on an all-out attack on the industry and facts be damned. Obama: "health insurance companies and their executives have reaped windfall profits from a broken system". [43] Democrat Speaker of the House Nancy Pelosi: "immoral profits being made by the insurance industry" and "obscene profits". Maryland Democratic Representative Chris Van Hollen: "their profits have skyrocketed". MoveOn.org: "Health insurance companies are willing to let the bodies pile up as long as their profits are safe". [44]

House Democrats sent a letter to 52 of the nation's largest health insurance companies, demanding detailed information on compensation packages of the companies' highest-paid employees, information on the companies' boards, conferences and sponsored events, profitability of the individual health-care products they sold and revenues earned through government programs like Medicare and Medicaid. [45] Another 1984, Big Brother assault on the free-market economy system for political power gains. Way to go, Congressmen!

Employers will face the choice between offering company sponsored insurance and paying a penalty if they don't offer insurance. They will more than likely choose the lower cost option of dropping their insurance, forcing employees to join a government-run program.
According to the CBO, *9 million* mostly low-pay and part-time workers will lose their employer-provided health coverage. [46] Another study found that 30% of employers will definitely or probably stop offering employer-sponsored insurance by 2015. [47]

Because of the above-mentioned factors, an estimated **80 to 100 million** people will lose their private health insurance.
48

All throughout 2010, as a result of the immediate and future cost increases of ObamaCare, many health insurance companies increased premiums or cancelled insurance programs and many companies announced limiting or dropping health insurance for their employees. These trends will intensify as we get closer to the 2014 full-implementation year for ObamaCare.

The claim is *false*.

Claim: ObamaCare Will Improve the Quality of Health Care

In countries with universal, government-run health care like Canada, England, Germany, etc. wait times for health care are significantly longer and death rates for cancer and other deadly ailments are significantly higher than in the U.S. Here are some facts: [49]

- Breast cancer mortality is 88% higher in the U.K., 52% higher in Germany and 9% higher in Canada as compared to the U.S.
- Prostate cancer mortality is 604% higher in the U.K., 457% higher in Norway and 184% higher in Canada as compared to the U.S.
- Colorectal cancer mortality is 40% higher in the U.K. as compared to the U.S.
- Colon cancer mortality is 10% higher among British men as compared to the U.S.
- 89% of middle-aged American women have had a mammogram versus 72% in Canada

- 54% of American men have had a prostate cancer screening test versus 16% in Canada
- 30% of American have had a colonoscopy versus 5% in Canada
- Canadian and British patients wait about twice as long to see a specialist, have elective surgery or get cancer radiation treatment as compared to the U.S.
- 51% of Americans are very satisfied with their health care services versus 42% of Canadians
- There are 34 CT scanners per million in the U.S. versus 12 in Canada and 8 in the U.K.
- There are 27 MRI machines per million in the U.S. versus 6 in Canada and the U.K.
- Of the 13 most important recent medical innovations, 10 originated in whole or in part in the U.S. versus 4 in the U.K., 2 in Japan and 1 each in Sweden and Switzerland

In 2010 the largest government-run health insurance provider in Greece would no longer pay for special footwear for diabetes patients because amputation was deemed to be cheaper. Greece's government-run health insurance was created in early 1980, when Andreas Papandreou was Prime Minister. This academic won the election with the slogan "Change". [50] Sounds familiar?

The quality of health care in this country will take a serious hit under ObamaCare. The Government will have to ration health care and limit access. Bureaucrats will decide which medical treatments are available to you and which are not. To help pay for this program, massive cuts are planned for Medicare so health care for the elderly will be rationed even more.

Obama's health policy advisor, Ezekiel Emanuel - brother of Obama's Chief of Staff Rahm Emanuel - has very radical views on rationing of health care. [51] He believes doctors try too hard to apply the Hippocratic oath to everyone as equally as possible, driving up costs. Instead he thinks we need to ration basic, guaranteed care to only those who can "fully participate in society" at the expense of those that cannot "fully participate in society" like people with dementia, the elderly and people with disabilities. [52]

The claim is *false*.

Claim: ObamaCare Will Reduce Health Care Cost

Social Security, Medicare and Medicaid are government-run, massive social programs fraught with problems, fraud and inefficiencies. They will have a devastating effect on our economy in the near future when they go broke. We have no reason to believe that a massive, government-run health care system, in whatever form, will fare any better.

It should be noted that the Government has grossly underestimated the costs of other large social entitlement programs like Social Security, Medicare and Medicaid. The 1965 Medicare Part A so-called conservative cost estimate was *$9 billion*, but the actual cost was *$67 billion*. Medicaid's original, so-called conservative estimate for the year 1992 was *$1 billion*, but the actual cost was *$17 billion*. The Medicaid special hospitals subsidy so-called conservative cost estimate was *$100 million*, but the actual cost was *$11 billion*. So ObamaCare more than likely will cost many times more than what is claimed.

The government's own actuary for Medicare estimated in early 2010 that, contrary to White House claims, Obama-Care would increase national health care spending by **$311 billion** over ten years. [53]

Obama claims that under his plan health care will cost less because substantial savings will result from applying more preventive care. He is either ignorant or misleads us on purpose. Studies have shown repeatedly that more preventative care will **not lower** cost, but **increase** it. The health of the patients will improve, but it costs more. Strictly speaking from a cost perspective as Obama does here, it costs less to only start treatment when an illness actually occurs. And preventive care will definitely increase under ObamaCare since co-pays for it will be eliminated. [54] [55]

More than 15 million additional people will be covered by the Medicaid program. [56] Since Medicaid routinely under-pays doctors and hospital, [57] health care providers will have to increase costs for other people to make up the difference.

To cover current and future cost increases due to Obama-Care, many health insurance companies have started to raise their premiums after passage of the law, making a joke of Obama's claim that health care costs will go down. Of course Big Brother couldn't have any of that. In September of 2010, Health and Human Services Secretary Kathleen Sebelius warned the health insurance industry that the Obama administration wouldn't tolerate blaming premium hikes on ObamaCare. "There will be zero tolerance for this type of misinformation and unjustified rate increases" said Sebelius. [58] So the Big Brother Regime will determine what rate increases are "justified"? Straight out of Marx' play-book!

The claim is *false*.

Claim: Computerizing Medical Records Will Lower Cost

A Harvard Medical School study of 4,000 hospitals shows that centrally computerized medical records will increase, not lower, cost. [59]
The claim is *false*.

Claim: Health Care Reform Will Create Additional Jobs

In March 2010, after passage of the health care reform bill, many companies - including AT&T, Caterpillar, Deere, Valero and 3M - announced their estimates of accounting charges to be made against the current quarter because of reduced deductions for health care plans for retired employees. They also announced likely future reductions in health care coverage for current employees and retirees. AT&T announced a *$1 billion* charge or 1/3 of their quarterly profits. [60] The total cost to American companies is estimated at *$14 billion*. [61] Higher costs and lower profits mean fewer jobs.
The claim is *false*.

Claim: "Death Panels" Are Not Part of Health Care Reform

So-called "end-of-life" planning was initially included in ObamaCare, but it touched off a debate about "death panels' and the provision was removed. So this claim may appear to be true. But not so fast! Obama, unable to achieve his goals through democratic means, used a dictatorial approach and achieved his objective through regulation. Starting January 1, 2011 new Medicare regulations would pay for so-called "end-of-life care", including withholding life-sustaining treatments. [62] This must have been a field-day for avowed *Socialist* Donald Berwick, Obama's recess appointee as administrator of the Centers for Medicare and Medicaid Services, who issued the rule!

The Obama White House had the nerve to comment that this new regulation was just a continuation of Bush's policies. ***Big, fat lie!*** Bush ***vetoed*** a similar provision! [63]

The ultimate goal of avowed radicals, including Obama, is of course to allow the government to cut off care for the critically ill and others deemed not worthy, all at the sole discretion of the government. Big Brother is working on it every day!

The claim is ***false.***

Confuse and Conquer

First the term "public option" was used to refer to the government-run plan. When it became clear that there was a lot of opposition to ObamaCare, the Obama Regime played word games and replaced the term "public option" with "co-ops", "trigger", "health insurance exchange", "public option with a state opt-out" or "consumer option". Wordsmithing of the worst kind!

More Misinformation from Our "Leader"

During a news conference in February of 2010, Obama claimed that "...for the first time this year you saw more people getting health care from government than you did from the private sector..." [64] What was he smoking? According to the latest available data from the U.S. Census Bureau, 87 million people had government health insurance in 2008 against 201 million with private health insurance. [65]

A Preview of Rationings to Come

In November 2009 the U.S. Department of Health and Human Services' Preventive Services Task Force issued new guidelines for breast cancer prevention that radically departed from current guidelines by the Government, the American Cancer Society and others. [66] Instead of getting a mammogram every year after age 40, the guidelines called for getting a mammogram every other year after age 50. The guidelines also claimed that self-examinations were not effective. After strong condemnation by medical and health professionals, the Government made an about-face and hastily retracted - kind-of - the guidelines, by saying that the Government was not changing its recommendations and advised to ignore the newly issued guidelines. This disaster was surely a harbinger of government-run-health-care rationing to come!

Universal Health Care in the State of Maine Is a Disaster

Maine, a State with about 1.3 million residents, started universal health care in 2005 with the goals of covering the estimated 130,000 residents without health insurance, improve the quality of health care, lower the cost and improve access; [67] pretty much what Obama claims he wants to do for the country as a whole.

So how has the Maine program, called Dirigo, fared? Here are the disastrous results as of October 2009: less than 10% of the original uninsured are covered; costs have skyrocketed; health insurance premiums have gone up by more than 70%; access is worse; taxes will have to be increased to cover the costs of the program.

Universal Health Care in the State of Massachusetts Is a Disaster

The program, started in 2006, requires all residents to buy health insurance. [68] It was supposed to reduce cost, but that's not what happened. The results have been premium increases, tax increases, rationing, coverage restrictions and increased wait periods. Premiums, already the highest in the nation before health care reform, have been increased by as much as 56% and are now twice the national average. The overall cost of the program in 2008 was more than $400 million, 85% higher than originally estimated.

The ObamaCare Waiver Scandal

By May of 2011 1,372 waivers to ObamaCare had been granted [69] to labor unions, companies and other organizations offering health insurance to more than 3 million Americans, so they don't need to comply with the Obama-Care law! U.S. Health and Human Services explained that the criteria for granting these waivers were if ObamaCare would result in premium increases or dropping health insurance altogether. Now wait a minute! Why those waivers? Wasn't this going to be good for everybody? And how is it that premiums could increase or health insurance be dropped as a result of ObamaCare? Didn't the master-deceiver himself ensure us over and over that premiums would go down, not up, and that you would be able to keep your existing insurance if you wanted to?

ObamaCare Challenged in Court

According to the Justice Department, as of mid-May 2011 a total of 31 lawsuits had been filed challenging ObamaCare in court,[70] including a lawsuit by 26 states against the federal government. The main objections are that the feds cannot force you to buy anything, including health care insurance, and that the feds are overstepping their authority, since health care is clearly the domain of state government. This will very likely go all the way to the Supreme Court.

Repeal and Replace ObamaCare

Conservative Republicans, many supported by the Tea Party movement, promised to do their utmost to repeal ObamaCare and replace it with sensible, affordable free-market solutions. It was one of their main promises during the 2010 mid-term elections and after their victory in those elections, the most sweeping in 70 years, they kept their promise: in January of 2011 the Republican-controlled House approved a bill to repeal ObamaCare, [71] but it was voted down by the Democrat-controlled Senate. [72] Even if it would have passed, it would more than likely have been vetoed by Obama and there wouldn't be enough votes to override such a veto. So why go through this exercise? To live by your principles, keep your promises and put the Left on notice that you are serious.

In addition, Republicans will fight ObamaCare in the courts to defund ObamaCare, avoid any tax dollars being used to pay for its myriad of expenses and nullify as many of its hideous provisions as possible. If not during the remainder of Obama's first term, repeal will happen if and when a Republican is elected as president in 2012.

What is Really Needed to Reform Health Care

We need common-sense solutions to reform health care and make it more accessible and affordable.

Free-Market Solutions
We need free-market solutions. Fair and open competition will lead to the best health care at the lowest possible cost.

Tort Reform
Tort reform will reduce unnecessary tests and procedures, frivolous lawsuits, outrageous awards and doctors' and hospitals' malpractice insurance expenses. Of the $2.2 trillion spent in 2009 on health care, about $210 billion was spent on over-testing or so-called defensive medicine, when doctors order unnecessary tests and procedures to avoid lawsuits. [73] ObamaCare doesn't include tort reform.

Allow Health Insurance Companies to Compete in All Districts in All 50 States
There are over 1,300 health insurance companies in America, but they are severely restricted by state government regulations, so only a handful of companies compete in many districts. ObamaCare doesn't have this provision and Democrats have expressly stated that they will not seek it.

Make Health Insurance Portable from State to State
This would allow people to keep their current insurance if they move to another state. ObamaCare doesn't have this provision.

Expand Health Savings Account Provisions

Health savings accounts allow people to set aside money tax-free for future medical expenses. ObamaCare doesn't include this.

Tax Credits for Low-Income People

This would make health insurance more affordable for low-income people. ObamaCare doesn't include this provision.

9. Illegal Immigration and Open Borders

Illegal border crossings, drug running and crime are rampant at the U.S.-Mexico border, but Washington claims things are under control and largely ignores the issue for political gains. A partial fence doesn't stop illegal activities. State laws to protect American citizens are attacked by the federal government. "Comprehensive immigration reform" aka "amnesty for illegals" is the slogan of the Left.

Illegal Immigration

Illegal immigration is a huge problem in this country. The Department of Homeland Security estimates that there are **11 to 12 million** illegal immigrants in the U.S., with more than 60% of those being born in Mexico. [1] Many of these people don't pay taxes. They send billions of dollars of what they earn in the U.S. back to their home country every year, instead of spending it in the U.S. economy. Illegal immigration puts a heavy burden on our society. It is estimated that it costs the U.S. taxpayer over **$100 billion a year** in expenses for education, medical aid, administration of justice, Welfare, public assistance, etc. [2] California, Arizona, New Mexico and Texas are particularly hard hit.

Open Borders

Instead of taking effective action, the federal government has largely ignored the open borders problem. Homeland Security Secretary Janet Napolitano claims that it is "inaccurate to state, as too many have, that the border is overrun with violence and out of control." [3] I beg to differ. Illegals, drugs and violence still pour into this country from the South.

While the rate of people entering the U.S. from Mexico illegally has declined over the years, people still cross the U.S. Mexico border in massive numbers. U.S. Customs and Border Protection (CBP) apprehended over 445,000 people in 2010 trying to cross the U.S.-Mexico border illegally. With only one person out of three being caught, that adds up to more than *1 million* people coming into the U.S. illegally in 2010. [4] That cannot be called "border security" by any stretch of the imagination.

Drugs are brought into the U.S. across the US-Mexico borders every day in large quantities and drug related crimes are rampant, particularly in Arizona. The out-of-control drug war in Mexico is spilling over into our country and U.S. citizens are getting killed. Entire drug-growing operations are brought into this country from Mexico. In July of 2010 a sweep in the California Sierra Nevada netted more than *$1.7 billion* worth of marihuana and 97 arrests of mostly Mexican nationals. Several Mexican drug cartels were involved in the grow operations. More than 400,000 marijuana plants were destroyed. [5]

What Border Fence?

The much-discussed border fence doesn't appear to help much in keeping illegal immigrants, drugs and violence out. Construction of a physical border fence along parts of the border with Mexico was approved when Bush signed the "Secure Fence Act of 2006". A later amendment greatly watered down the effectiveness of that fence. So how does this fence fit into the total picture? Here's the situation in May of 2010: [6] its total length of 649 miles is only 1/3 of the 1,954-mile border with Mexico; only 36 miles of it, 2% of the total border with Mexico, is double or triple fencing, which has proven to be very effective in stopping pedestrians; there's another 299 miles, 15% of the border with Mexico, with vehicle barriers.

The Left has tried to play the severe shortcomings of the physical fence down by claiming that the "virtual fence" would fill the gaps very effectively. So, where is this "virtual fence"? Read on! The SBInet "virtual fence" of integrated technology to keep watch on most of the 1,954-mile border with Mexico, was ordered by Congress in 2006. So, that was supposed to make our border secure and everybody could start feeling really safe, right? Wrong! After spending $1 billion to complete only 53 miles of it, Homeland Security Secretary Janet Napolitano cancelled the project in January of 2010, citing problems and cost overruns. [7] She never came up with a plan to replace this virtual fence to secure the border.

So, given the lack of an effective fence, either physical or virtual, how well do we control the U.S.-Mexico border? Not too well! In February of 2011 the U.S. Government Accountability Office (GAO) issued a report on border security, [8] stating that Border Control had achieved "varying levels of operational control" of 873 miles or 44% of the U.S. Mexico border at the end of fiscal year 2010. The number of reported miles under operational control increased an average of 126 miles per year from fiscal years 2005 through 2010. Even if this rate would continue – something that is very doubtful given the Obama Regime's attitude towards border security – it would take another nine years or until 2019 to achieve "varying levels of operational control." Note that "varying levels of operational control" doesn't mean that we have a situation that you and I would define as "border security".

Not Securing Our Borders for Political Gains

Arizona senator John Kyl has stated that during a private conversation, Obama said that he was not securing the border because otherwise he would not get support for "comprehensive immigration reform". [9] The White House denied Kyl's claim. Arizona senator John McCain came out in defense of Kyl and said that Obama had said as much during a lunch with the Republican senators. [10] Who are you going to believe: senators who are well respected for their integrity by many on both sides of the aisle or Obama? I think the choice is obvious.

"Comprehensive immigration reform" is a euphemism for amnesty. Amnesty would ensure that a great percentage of those people getting amnesty would vote for the party that got it for them, the Democrats. I am fully convinced that Obama is not enforcing our immigration laws and not securing our borders for the purpose of pushing through amnesty for millions of illegal aliens and enlarging the liberal voter base.

"Fair Pay" for Illegal Immigrants

You would think that the U.S. Department of Labor respects and follows our laws, but you would be wrong. Obama's Labor Secretary Hilda Solis, Democrat, overtly thumbs her nose at our immigration laws. She doesn't make a distinction between people who work here legally and illegal aliens. Never mind that the department's mission statement reads in part: "To foster, promote, and develop the welfare of the wage earners, job seekers, and retirees of the United States". [11]

Solis ran a TV ad, paid for by – you guessed it – taxpayers, to push for "fair pay" for illegal aliens and offer free and confidential help. The ad touted: "You work hard and you have the right to be paid fairly..., ... it is a serious problem when workers in this country are not being paid every cent that they earn..., ...every worker in America has a right to be paid fairly, whether documented or not. So, call us – it is free and confidential..." [12] More of your tax dollars at work to advance Obama's radical agenda!

"Comprehensive Immigration Reform"

So what does "comprehensive immigration reform" mean? Whether it goes by this name or by "path to citizenship", it really means amnesty for illegal aliens, rewarding those who violate our sovereignty and putting them ahead of those who seek entry into the U.S. legally. To get any bipartisan buy-in for immigration reform that would include some kind of path to citizenship, effective border control would need to come first. Calls for "comprehensive immigration reform" under Bush went nowhere because there were no serious plans to control our borders, particularly the border with Mexico. Obama also talks about "comprehensive immigration reform", but he too is not serious about securing our borders, enforcing our immigration laws and dealing with illegals.

Any promises from the Left about controlling our borders should be seen as highly suspicious. President Reagan found out how you can trust promises from the Left to control our borders. He tried sweeping immigration reforms. The deal was supposed to include tight control of the Mexican border, stiff penalties for anyone hiring undocumented workers and amnesty for millions. The provision of penalties for hiring illegals was taken out of the bill before Reagan signed it into law in 1986. Almost 3 million illegals got amnesty, but tight control of the Mexican border never happened. [13]

Green Cards for Illegal Aliens!

With his approval ratings tanking, Obama renewed his push for "comprehensive immigration reform". He clearly hoped that reigniting the issue in the 2010 mid-term election year would take some attention away from the oil spill, a weak economy, and high unemployment.

The issue failed to gain traction in Congress, again. But not to worry, you can always try to go around those pesky, opinionated lawmakers. The Obama Regime explored ways to let illegal immigrants stay in the U.S. and grant them the status of *"lawful permanent residents"!* An April 2010 internal memo by the USCIS (U.S. Citizenship and Immigration Services), [14] written in radical double-speak, mentions "administrative relief options to promote family unity, foster economic growth, achieve significant process improvements and reduce the threat of removal for certain individuals present in the United States without authorization" and "In the absence of comprehensive immigration reform, USCIS can extend benefits and/or protections to many individuals or groups." To hell with American law, to hell with American citizens' and legal aliens' safety and well being; let's extend benefits and protection to those who violate our laws and sovereignty!

The Arizona Immigration Law

The State of Arizona got tired of the federal government not enforcing immigration laws, sealing off the border and fighting illegal immigration. They got tired of the resulting budget, drug and crime problems. The Republican governor of Arizona Jan Brewer, signed a new Arizona State law in April of 2010. [15] The bill made it a crime to be in the country illegally. It required police to ask people their immigration status, if there was suspicion that they were in the country illegally. It also made it illegal to hire or transport illegal immigrant for day labor. The law requires that a) someone has been stopped for legal reasons other than immigration status and b) that law enforcement officers after stopping that person can ask for immigration status only if they, during their interaction with that person, have reasonable doubt about the person being in the country legally and c) the race of the person is not a valid reason to base that doubt on. While more than 60% of Americans across the country supported this law, [16] more than 90% of the mainstream media reports were against it. [17]

Obama appeared to either not have read the law or distort if for political expediency. He pronounced: "...but you can imagine if you are a Hispanic American in Arizona, your great, great grandparents may have been there before Arizona was even a state. But now suddenly if you don't have your papers and you took your kid out to get ice cream, you're going to be harassed, that's something that could potentially happen." [18] That's not at all what the law says, but Obama doesn't care about facts or laws; he cares about demonizing those who don't agree with his radical-Left, socialist ideology. Instead of doing his job and upholding and enforcing our laws, as he swore to do during his inauguration, he joked about this issue: "We all know what happens in Arizona when you don't have ID: Adios, amigos!" [19] Real classy and so presidential!

Many others in the Obama administration attacked the Arizona law as well. Problem was, they didn't read it either or didn't have sufficient knowledge about it to justify strong opinions. But lack of knowledge never prevented radicals from forming strong opinions!

Attorney General Eric Holder criticized this law from day one as racist and possibly unconstitutional. However, when he appeared before the House Judiciary Committee *three weeks later,* he had to admit that *he never even read* the 10-page law. [20]

Homeland Security Secretary Janet Napolitano and State Department spokesman J.P. Crowley similarly had to admit to criticizing the Arizona law without reading it carefully. [21]

Mexican President Felipe Calderon denounced the Arizona immigration law in front of Congress, and Democrats and White House officials, including Biden, Pelosi, Holder and Napolitano cheered on Calderon. [22]

To add insult to injury, John Morton, assistant secretary of Homeland Security for the U.S. Immigration and Customs Enforcement (ICE) said that ICE would not necessarily process illegal immigrants who would be referred to them by Arizona authorities, [23] no doubt on direct orders from Obama. So, ICE isn't going to take custody of those illegals or release them without taking any action? When is Obama going to uphold and enforce our laws or step down because he isn't doing either?

In July of 2010 the Justice Department filed suit against the Arizona immigration law, [24] citing interference of Arizona in federal immigration issues. Surprisingly enough, racial profiling wasn't mentioned. The federal government sued state government over a state law that mimicked federal law, but had more restrictions! What a travesty of justice! Could it get any more crazy or Orwellian? Very likely! After all, Obama still had a couple of years left - unless he would be forced to step down sooner - and there were Georgia, Utah, Indiana and Alabama, which had also enacted illegal immigration laws of a nature similar to or more restrictive than the Arizona law.

If Arizona's law, supporting federal immigration law, is bad and warrants a law suit, why isn't the federal government suing the many so-called "sanctuary cities" that thumb their noses at federal immigration laws, welcome illegal aliens and refuse to refer them to the federal authorities, even if those illegals commit severe crimes?

Apparently as a reaction to criticism, that the first federal lawsuit didn't mention the key concern of many critics of the Arizona law, - racial profiling - the Justice Department announced days after filing the first lawsuit, that they might file a second lawsuit in about six months, regarding racial profiling. [25] Advice to Mr. Holder: get your act together and READ THE LAW!

On July 28, 2010, just hours before the Arizona law would go into effect, a federal judge issued an injunction against some of the toughest provisions of the law. [26] As a result, Arizona, for the time being, cannot *require* its law enforcement officers to determine the immigration status of anyone they stop or arrest for other reasons. The officers still *can do it*, but they *don't have to*. Also struck down, for now, were the provisions that made it a crime not to carry immigration status papers or for illegal aliens to seek or perform work.

This will have to go all the way to the U.S. Supreme Court to get resolved and force the federal government to fulfill its duties of upholding the law and protecting its citizens.

In May of 2011 the U.S. Supreme Court upheld an earlier Arizona law that punished businesses for hiring illegal immigrants. [27] This ruling invalidated the Justice Department's claim that states had no role to play in enforcing federal immigration laws. It paved the way for progress in Arizona's fight against the federal government over its more recent and farther-reaching immigration law.

10. National Security

Our security has been diminished greatly. The military is attacked from within. Our intelligence capabilities are diminished. An apologetic and waffling president has damaged our standing in the world. Our enemies no longer fear us. The biggest threats to our security and peace in the world, an Iran with nuclear weapons and radical Islam, are largely ignored. Obama's so-called outreach to the Muslim world has failed miserably.

Weakening our Military

The military is attacked from within by both the Obama Regime and the military brass. One example of many: Navy SEALs captured a terrorist responsible for killing four Americans in Fallujah, Iraq, dragging them through the streets and hanging two of their corpses from a bridge. The terrorist mastermind behind the atrocity was captured and somewhere in the process he ended up with a bloody lip. The military decided to prosecute the Navy SEALs when the terrorist complained of mistreatment to investigators. [1]

Obama targeted Defense for 80% of the cuts in the 2010 budget for discretionary spending. [2] He said: "We can no longer afford to spend as if deficits do not matter and waste is not our problem". Excuse me, Mr. Big Spender, are you for real or what?

Obama the presidential candidate apparently wanted his own *"civilian army"*! During a July 2008 speech in Colorado Springs, Colorado Obama said: "We cannot continue to rely only on our military in order to achieve the national security objectives that we've set. We've got to have a civilian national security force that's just as powerful, just as strong, just as well-funded." [3] When you hear that kind of rhetoric, that kind of twisted logic, you have to ask yourself: is this the Alinsky-type community organizer speaking or do we have amongst us an admirer of communist dictator Mao tactics?

In April of 2010, in spite of increasing nuclear threats from North Korea, Iran and terrorism, Obama publicly ruled out the use of nukes against non-nuclear nations in response to chemical or biological attacks. [4] This significantly reduces the deterrent against such attacks and can only embolden our enemies. Our nuclear capability, whether you like or hate it, has kept us safe for over 60 years and helped us win the Cold War and end the Soviet superpower tyranny without firing a single shot. What happened to peace through strength? Oh wait, that was another president, who was told by the Liberals that we simply couldn't win against the Soviet Union and that we and the rest of the world just had to accept this evil empire and its satellites and learn to live with it.

Weakening Our Intelligence Capabilities

Three former CIA directors – George Tenet, Porter Goss and Michael Hayden – had stated that terrorist suspects, subjected to enhanced interrogation techniques, including waterboarding, had provided major parts of our knowledge about al-Qaida. [5] Barely two days after his inauguration as president in January 2009 and claiming the moral high ground, Obama declared harsh interrogations like waterboarding to be torture and banned them. [6] This would make gathering terrorist intel much more difficult.

At the same time, Obama ordered Guantanamo to be closed within a year, without having a plan for what to do with the captured terrorists, other than to transfer terrorists to whatever countries would be willing to accept them. As it turned out, very few countries were willing to accept detained terrorists and most held at Guantanamo were just too dangerous to be released and Guantanamo stayed open.

Also in January 2009, Obama suspended military trials of the captured terrorists held at Guantanamo as enemy combatants, forcing any prosecution of those terrorists to take place as criminal cases in civilian courts. But then in March of 2011 Obama did one of his many flip-flops and reinstated the military trials.

So, did the Obama Regime finally wise up and give up on the foolish idea of closing Guantanamo? That would have made too much sense. In May 2011 Obama's Attorney General Eric Holder said at a news briefing during an official visit to Paris, France: "Although we have not closed Guantanamo within the time period that we initially indicated ... it is still the intention of the president, and it is still my intention, to close the facility that exists in Guantanamo. We think that by closing that facility the national security of the United States will be enhanced." [7]

In April of 2009 Obama released memos detailing U.S. enhanced interrogation techniques [8] for all-the-world to see, but refused to release memos detailing the terrorist attacks we have been able to prevent using the information gained from those techniques.

To add insult to injury, Obama's Attorney General Eric Holder started a shameful, criminal investigation in August of 2009 of CIA officers for alleged crimes in carrying out the enhanced interrogation methods found to be lawful before being implemented under Bush. [9] Even after Osama bin Laden had been tracked down and killed, thanks in part to those methods, as detailed below, Holder refused to end the investigation and the CIA people, who helped to keep us safe, were still living in fear of being indicted and prosecuted. Shame on the Obama Regime!

After fierce criticism, Holder finally caved in June of 2011 and dropped most of the secretive investigations against the CIA, except for two cases where a detainee died while in U.S. custody. [10]

Osama Bin Laden Killed

On May 1, 2011 al-Qaida leader Osama bin Laden's hideaway compound in Pakistan was attacked by U.S. Navy SEALs and bin Laden was killed. Identifying the whereabouts of bin Laden was made possible by subjecting al-Qaida terrorists to "harsh" interrogations. Obama stated that the compound was identified in August 2010 as a likely home for a senior al-Qaida member and that in late April of 2011 U.S. intelligence concluded that the compound was bin Laden's and an attack was ordered.

Days later, on May 3, 2011 CIA director Leon Panetta confirmed during an interview with Brian Williams on MSNBC that enhanced interrogation techniques, including waterboarding, were among the tactics used to extract the intelligence that lead to bin Laden. [11]

Without President Bush's enhanced interrogation techniques – banned by Obama – bin Laden would very likely still be at large. In his televised announcement, that bin Laden had been killed, Obama did not mention any of Bush's efforts to hunt down bin Laden or that harsh interrogations ordered by President Bush had played a key role. During the announcement Obama only bragged about what happened during *his* administration: "And so shortly after taking office, I directed Leon Panetta, the director of the CIA, to make the killing or capture of bin Laden the top priority of our war against al Qaeda." and "Then, last August, after years of painstaking work by our intelligence community, I was briefed on a possible lead to bin Laden…" [12] So in effect Obama, clearly campaigning for his reelection in 2012, bluntly accused Bush of *not* making a top priority of finding and capturing or killing bin Laden! What a despicable lie!

If Bush's determined efforts over seven years didn't deserve to be acknowledged in Obama's speech to the Nation and the world, then Obama should not get *any* credit for what happened during two years of *his* administration. If Obama had been president all along, we would have never hunted bin Laden down, given his ban on enhanced interrogations like waterboarding.

It should be noted that bin Laden was killed on the spot without due legal process and I have no problem with that whatsoever. It should also be noted that Obama has continued - and stepped up - Bush's program of killing terrorist suspects with CIA Predator missile attacks in Iraq, Afghanistan and Pakistan. And again I have no problem with that. It should also be noted that the Left ties themselves into pretzel-like knots, when asked how they can justify killing bin Laden with a bullet to the head and killing terrorist suspects remotely with deadly Predator attacks, but object to waterboarding terrorists, a procedure that provides information to save lives and has not resulted in any injury or death to those subjected to it.

In another display of misplaced political correctness, Obama refused to release photos of bin Laden's corpse or his burial ceremony on board the aircraft carrier USS Carl Vinson, claiming that it might inflame radical sentiment against the U.S. We are *at war* with radical Islam, Mr. President! Release the photos and show what will happen if you try to terrorize America's freedom-loving people!

Another serious issue here is Pakistan's increasingly hostile attitude towards the U.S. We have know for a long time that they harbored and protected Taliban and al-Qaida terrorists and now we found out that they harbored al-Qaida's founder and top leader, Osama bin Laden! Despite all this, Obama had the gall to praise Pakistan in his speech announcing bin Laden's demise, saying: "But it's important to note that our counterterrorism cooperation with Pakistan helped lead us to bin Laden and the compound where he was hiding." [13] We need straight talk, Mr. Obama, not some unbelievable, meaningless drivel!

This situation becomes even more absurd when you consider how much military and civilian aid Pakistan receives from us: since 9/11, a total of $20 billion for the period 2002-2010 and $3 billion each for 2011 and 2012. [14]

Oh, and then there was the "Chinese Connection": Pakistan might allow Communist China to inspect the wreckage of the stealth attack helicopter that crashed during the raid on the bin Laden compound! [15]

Why do we even pretend that Pakistan is somehow friendly to the U.S.? Why do we give them even one penny of our tax money? Why?

Appeasement of Our Enemies and Denial of Muslim Terrorism

Appeasement of our enemies - Iran, North Korea, terrorists, radical Islam, etc. - is clearly more important to the Obama Regime than protecting American citizens and supporting our allies. Obama's sympathy for Islam runs deep, but his so-called outreach to the Muslim world has failed miserably. More disturbingly, instead of forcefully condemning radical Islam, he has repeatedly been an *appeaser* and *sympathizer* to the point of legitimizing and encouraging it. He didn't support demonstrators against the brutal, anti-American, anti-free-world, terrorism-supporting regime of Iran, but immediately jumped in to support demonstrators in Egypt, an ally in the War on Terror and vulnerable to a take-over by the radical Muslim Brotherhood.

Appeasement of Russia

Cancellation of Missile Defense Shield in Europe
Under pressure from Moscow, Obama waffled on prior agreements to install anti-missile defense systems in Poland and the Czech Republic to protect Europe from attacks by Iranian missiles that could potential carry nuclear weapons. Of course such systems could also be used against Russian missile attacks. In an apparent attempt to curry favor with Moscow and seek their support for tougher sanctions against Iran, Obama cancelled those agreements on Sep-

tember 17, 2009, [16] exactly on the 70th anniversary to the day of the Soviets' invasion of Poland in 1939. Was that particular date just one more fumble by the Obama Regime, a brazen disregard for the suffering of the Polish people, a deliberate insult to Poland or a shameful appeasement of Russia? Even under the best possible scenario, this was gross foreign affairs incompetence. The Wall Street Journal stated it aptly: "It's better these days to be a U.S. adversary than its friend." [17]

Whatever the case may have been, Russia must have been delighted with the cancellation of the systems. Instead of rewarding our Appeaser-in-Chief, Russia refused to support any additional sanctions against Iran in the U.N. Security Council.

the New START Treaty

The 1991 START (Strategic Arms Reduction Treaty) agreement with Russia expired in December 2009. In October 2009, as part of negotiations for a new strategic arms treaty, the U.S. apparently agreed to the most intrusive nuclear weapons inspection program ever, allowing the Russians to visit our nuclear sites in America to count our missiles and warheads! Secretary of State Hillary Clinton said that the U.S. would be as transparent as possible and "We want to ensure that every question that the Russian military or Russian government asks is answered". [18] Why not give away all our strategic military secrets right away and get it over with?

Under the new treaty, called "New START" the numbers of deployed nuclear weapon delivery vehicles - which include missiles and bombers - is to be reduced to 700 for both the U.S. and Russia. This means that the U.S. has to reduce theirs from 832 while the Russians can increase their existing 566 to 700! [19] With lopsided agreements like this one, it's easy to see why the Kremlin may come to love Obama.

While the U.S. already deactivated over 50 percent of its nuclear warheads during the Bush administration alone - without compulsion from any binding treaty - the number of warheads on each side – 1,968 for the U.S. and ~2,600 for Russia - is to be reduced further to 1550. [20]

While these reductions in nuclear warheads and delivery vehicles are seen by some as a step toward a safer world, others see it as a further weakening of our ability to maintain world peace and keep countries like Iran and North Korea from increasing their nuclear threats.

The major flaw in the treaty is the fact that it "imposes sweeping restrictions on U.S. missile defense options" [21] This treaty as written should have never been ratified.

Against better judgment, the Senate ratified the treaty by a vote of 71-26 on December 22, 2010; all 56 Democrats, 2 Independents and 13 Republicans voted for, and 26 Republicans voted against. [22] Without the 13 Republican yea votes, the required 2/3 majority would not have been achieved. Thanks to Obama, the Democrats, Independents and those 13 we-need-to-get-along Republicans, we squandered U.S. and world security and abandoned, again, the peace-through-strength principle.

Failure to Act on Iran

Iran is one of the biggest threats to world peace and the global economy. Its fanatic regime is hell-bent on spreading radical Islam and destroying Israel and the West. They supply money and weapons to the Hezbollah and Hamas terror organizations.

Iran is developing nuclear weapons capabilities under the disguise of peaceful power generation. A nuclear armed Iran will be a major threat to the balance of power in the Middle East and world peace. Iranian nukes could be used against Israel directly or they could be supplied to terrorist groups to do the dirty work for the Iranians. After all, Iran has repeatedly threatened to wipe Israel of the map. Nuclear weapons in the hands of the mad Iranian Mullahs have the potential to set off a conflict of major proportions in the Middle East and beyond and would throw the world economy in disarray, to say the least.

So, what has the supposed leader of the free world, Obama, done to contain the Iranian threat? Little, if anything! His so-called outreach and offer of unconditional discussions have been abject failures, as even the most clueless could have predicted. Obama said that he wanted to engage in dialogue with Iran without preconditions - like Iran recognizing Israel's right to exist. Of course, Iran didn't take him up on the offer.

Iran continues on a major collision course with the Middle East and the free world and continues on the road to nuclear weapons. And Obama is basically AWOL.

In September of 2009 Obama, as the first American president ever, presided over the U.N. Security Council meeting and as such set the agenda. The U.S.-drafted resolution on nuclear disarmament presented at that meeting did not even mention Iran or North Korea, in spite of the growing nuclear threat from those countries. [23] A nearly completed Iranian site near the city of Qom was specifically aimed at producing nuclear bomb-grade material. [24] This intelligence was known to Obama for a long time, [25] but was only recently made public.

Iran has been fooling the Europeans for decades with empty promises of cooperation about nuclear issues without any tangible result. Three previous U.N. sanctions did not cause Iran to live up to their obligations as signers of the Nuclear Non-Proliferation Treaty.

Instead of speaking out forcefully about the right of people to seek their freedom from tyranny, Obama said he didn't want to meddle in Iran's internal affairs [26] when Iranian citizens demonstrated in the summer of 2009 against Iranian rigged elections. Then Obama "played tough" and gave Iran till the end of 2010 to come around and start cooperating on the issue of the nuclear weapons threat. [27] Of course, nothing happened.

In January of 2010, Defense Secretary Robert Gates warned in a memo to top White House officials, that the U.S. lacked an effective long-range policy to deal with Iran's steady progress to a nuclear weapons capability, in case diplomacy and sanctions failed. [28] Diplomacy and sanctions never made any difference. It became clearer every day that the Obama Regime had either no clue how to deal with Iran or, worse yet, had no intention to deal with the threat.

In May of 2010 the United Nations atomic watchdog organization IAEA reported that Iran had amassed enough enriched uranium to make two nuclear bombs. [29] In June of 2010 the U.N. Security Council approved a fourth round of watered-down sanctions against Iran's nuclear program, [30] but there was widespread doubt that they would halt Iran's production of nuclear fuel. The new sanctions weren't "*crippling*" nor did they have the "*bite*" that Secretary of State Hillary Clinton had advocated. Iranian President Ahmadinejad promptly announced that talks about Iran's nuclear program would be postponed and that Iran would retaliate, if in-bound ships were searched to enforce U.N. sanctions. [31]

None of the previous sanctions had any effect. For instance, the U.S. was to freeze Iranian assets as part of the previous sanctions, yet in April of 2010 the U.S. had frozen "less than $43 million, or roughly a quarter of what Iran earns in oil revenue in a single day." [32] The U.S. - and the rest of the world - continued to pretend that we were acting against the Iranian nuclear threat, while Iran continued to pretend they were not working on it. What a maddening situation; a game with Israel's survival and world peace at risk.

Denial of Muslim Terrorism

KSM

In November of 2009 Attorney General Eric Holder announced that Khalid Sheikh Mohammed (KSM), mastermind of the 9/11 terror attacks, and four co-conspirators would be transferred from Guantanamo to New York to stand trial in civilian court, instead of stand trial before a military commission in Guantanamo. [33] This meant that they were not treated as enemy combatants in the War on Terror, but they would get the same rights as American citizens, something never before granted to enemy combatants. It also meant that much of the information these terrorists provided could not be used in court, because they were not read their Miranda Rights and information obtained through harsh interrogation techniques would be inadmissible in court! If they would be acquitted, they would have to be released in this country or somewhere else! The CIA and other intelligence operations would be forced to divulge sensitive information. The terrorists would be presented with the greatest propaganda platform imaginable, from which to proclaim the glory of jihad and the criminality of infidel America. The expense for this, what was believed to be a multi-year, trial was estimated to be over $200 million per year. [34]

Obama is more concerned about the presumed rights of terrorists than the safety of Americans. He treats terrorism as an issue of law enforcement, not acts of war. Bill Clinton did the same after the first World Trade Center bombing in 1993 that killed six people, the bombing of U.S. embassies in Dar Es Salaam, Tanzania and Nairobi, Kenya in 1998 that killed hundreds of people and the attack on the USS Cole in Yemen in 2000 that killed 17 American sailors. We failed to recognize the true nature and intentions of our enemies then and the results of that approach to terrorism were disastrous.

The first case, where a detainee was transferred from Guantanamo to stand trial in civilian federal court, was a disaster of major proportions! Ahmed Ghailani was accused of participating in the1998 al-Qaida attacks on the U.S. embassies in Kenya and Tanzania. Liberal judge Lewis Kaplan of the Federal District Court in Manhattan, a Bill Clinton appointee, had barred prosecutors from using an important witness against Ghailani. In November 2010 the jury acquitted Ghallani of 284 out of 285 counts. He was not convicted in the deaths of 223 people, but only on one count of conspiracy to destroy government buildings and property! [35] That's what you get for treating terrorism as a law enforcement matter, not a war on America and freedom. Juries are notoriously ill-suited to render judgments in truly civil cases like "ordinary" murder, theft, etc., as the O.J. Simpson trial so painfully demonstrated; in cases of terrorism, juries are straight-out disastrous.

In April of 2011 Attorney General Eric Holder announced reluctantly, that his department was reversing the November 2009 decision to try KSM and his four co-conspirators in civilian court in New York; they would face justice before a U.S. military tribunal at Guantanamo. [36] This was a major reversal for both Obama and Holder, especially since Obama initially promised to close Guantanamo within a year from his inauguration in January of 2009. Holder and other administration officials blamed the policy reversal on interference by Congress in a matter of executive counterterrorism efforts and drumming-up of "'needless' political battles" [37] During his announcement of the reversal at a press conference, Holder said: "I know this case in a way that members of Congress do not. I've looked at the files, I've spoken to the prosecutors, I know the tactical concerns that have to go into this decision. So do I know better than them? Yes. " [38]

Instead of manning up and admitting a serious misjudgment in the War on Terror, you can always claim you know better and blame others. But then again, what can you expect from an administration that can't even bring itself to utter the words "War on Terror" or "Islamic terrorists"?

The Fort Hood Shooter
Early November 2009 Army psychiatrist Maj. Nidal Malik Hasan killed 13 people at Fort Hood, Texas. [39] Obama's knee-jerk reaction was to caution against jumping to conclusion. [40]

Hasan turned out to be a radical Muslim, who had extolled the virtues of holy jihad to military colleagues. Even when all the facts about this Muslim terrorist became evident, the Obama Regime did not treat this person as an enemy combatant, but treated him as a common criminal, reading him his Miranda Rights and provided him with tax-payer-paid lawyers. A January 2010 86-page army report on the Fort Hood massacre did not once refer to the over-abundantly clear linkage to Islamic terrorism. [41] Whitewash our enemy's atrocities and appease the radical Muslim thugs! Political correctness and disdain for America brought to a whole new level!

The Underwear Bomber

On Christmas Day, 2009 a Nigerian set off a bomb aboard a Northwest jet heading for Detroit from Amsterdam with nearly 300 people on board.

This man, Umar Farouk Abdulmutallab, had been re-cruited by "al-Qaida in the Arabian Peninsula" and trained in Yemen (the two top leaders of this arm of al-Qaida, by the way, are previous Guantanamo detainees; yet another example of how people we release from Guantanamo con-tinue to fight us). Abdulmutallab had been linked in the past to the same radical imam that Nidal Malik Hasan, the Fort Hood terrorist, had been linked to, which landed him a spot on our terrorist watch-list. And his father, a banker, had contacted the U.S. embassy in Nigeria and told them that he was very concerned about his son's text message from Yemen about his pro-jihad "conversion" and that he would not see his son ever again. And he traveled without luggage; who needs luggage when you go to heaven and get 62 Muslim virgins, or is the exchange rate now higher than 62? And he paid with cash for his ticket. Yet he was not signaled as needing immediate attention. And England had barred him from entering the country. And the death of nearly 300 people was averted by sheer luck, when the de-tonator of his bomb malfunctioned. And Abdulmutallab was subdued by passengers not by safety personnel. Clearly our safety systems had failed miserably.

Yet, the incredibly incompetent Homeland Security Secretary Janet Napolitano commented that "*the system worked*." [42] The next day she had to backtrack: "Our systems did not work in this instance." [43] This woman heads Homeland Security and *she has no clue!* She should be removed from her position immediately, but I don't think that's going to happen anytime soon!

After three days of his underlings bungling the case, Obama had to avert further political fall-out - our safety being less important than the Chosen One's political standing - and talk about the case. Trying to pretend it never really happened hadn't worked too well! He called Abdulmutallab an "isolated extremist", but *also* said: "We will not rest until we find all who were involved and hold them accountable." [44] What is it, Waffle Meister? Is this an extremist acting alone or is this an al-Qaida terrorist attack in American airspace? Most reasonable people know what this is, but not our Commander-in-Chief!

Yet again, this Muslim terrorist was not treated as an enemy combatant and handed over to the military. Instead, he was interrogated for only 50 minutes during which he disclosed that other attacks had been planned and he knew about those plans, but before he could disclose more details he was read his Miranda rights and provided with taxpayer-paid lawyers. Instead of being subjected to harsh interrogation by the military, he was advised by his lawyers to stop talking, which he promptly did. Again, Obama was more concerned about the rights of terrorists than the safety of Americans.

After many weeks of withering criticism from both the Right and the Left on how this case was botched, the Obama Regime suddenly claimed that Abdulmutallab was cooperating with investigators and was divulging valuable information about al-Qaida. [45] Oh sure, we believe that in a heartbeat, don't we? And even if this had been true, it certainly would have been extremely stupid to tip off al-Qaida on what we might have been learning.

The Bali Bomber
Umar Patek, an Indonesian terrorist and member of the al-Qaida linked Jemaah Islamiyah Islamic terrorist organization in South-East Asia, was wanted in the U.S., Australia and Indonesia for the 2002 bombings in Bali, Indonesia, which killed 202 people, including seven Americans. He was captured by Pakistani security officials in March 2011 with the help of CIA tips, yet Obama refused to seek to interrogate Patek. [46]

Pandering to Muslims

NASA Redefined
NASA Administrator Charles Bolden's "foremost" mission has apparently been re-defined by Obama as improving relations with the Muslim world. "...and perhaps foremost, he wanted me to find a way to reach out to the Muslim world and engage much more with dominantly Muslim nations to help them feel good about their historic contribution to science ...and math and engineering," Bolden said in an interview. He also said that "...better interaction with the Muslim world would ultimately advance space travel." [47] Silly me; I thought that NASA's foremost mission was space exploration, but no, it's pandering to the Muslim world.

The Ground Zero Mosque Scandal
Imam Feisal Abdul Rauf, CEO of the "Cordoba Initiative" and his largely unknown backers want to build "Cordoba

House", a 13-story, $100 million mosque and Muslim community center *near Ground Zero* in New York City. This is not an issue of freedom of speech, freedom of religion or whether they can do this legally. Nobody denies Muslims the right to practice their religion in America and build places of worship. This is an issue of common decency and respect for grieving Americans. This imam's claim of wanting to build a bridge between America and the Muslim world is not credible, given the place where he wants to build the mosque and the Muslim's habit of building mosques at Muslim victory sites.

More than likely, the imam named his organization and planned mosque after the Great Mosque of Cordoba, Spain, built by Muslims on the site of a Christian church after their conquest of a large part of Spain around 600AD.

Neither the city of New York nor Obama raised objections. Instead of using his power of persuasion as president and pointing out the need for peace-loving Muslims to respect the feelings of Americans, Obama spoke - at a Muslim Ramadan dinner of all places - [48] and as much as endorsed building the mosque there, talking only about the rights of Muslims. Fact was that Americans opposed the plans 68 to 29%, [49] but who cares about what Americans think? Certainly not Obama!

The next day he tried to spin the issue by saying that he had not and would not comment on the wisdom of building the mosque at that location. [50] We don't need Obama as the country's top legal analyst; we have the Supreme Court for that. We need a leader, who can speak out for common courtesy and decency!

It is also unclear where the money for this mosque would come from. The developer for the mosque so far has not been willing to say where the money would be coming from, but would not rule out contributions from Saudi Arabia or Iran! [51]

The imam in question has blamed America for being an accessory to the 9/11 attacks, has called Osama Bin Laden *"made in the USA"*, refused to condemn Hamas as a terrorist organization, has said that the U.S. has more blood on its hands than al-Qaida and has called for America to be more sharia-law-compliant. [52] [53]

Sharia law is barbaric, brutal and oppressive, particularly to women, gays and lesbians. Among its many horrors are stoning as punishment for "offenses" like adultery and an-eye-for-an-eye "justice". Let's all remember that Islam is "the religion of peace" and if we repeat it often enough, we'll believe it too!

Yet, in their infinite wisdom, the State Department sent this imam on three missions - two during Bush's presidency - to the Middle East to represent America vis-à-vis the Muslim world, paid for by the taxpayer! [54] Unbelievable! They were sending Rauf on yet another taxpayer funded trip to the Middle East at a cost of $ 16,000. And to top it all off, they also sent Rauf's wife, Cordoba Initiative fellow director Daisy Khan, on her own "public diplomacy" tour to the United Arab Emirates at a taxpayer cost of $12,000. [55] She called people who objected to the mosque **beyond Islamophobic** and **Muslim haters**. [56]

To add insult to injury, the developer for the mosque had the nerve to submit several grant requests totaling more than **$5 million** to the Lower Manhattan Development Corporation, a New York state agency, established to help Lower Manhattan recover from the 9/11 attacks. [57]

Pelosi just couldn't help herself and opined: "There is no question that there is a concerted effort to make this a political issue by some, and I join those who have called for looking into how is this opposition to the mosque being funded? How is this being ginned up?" [58] Intimidate, attack, vilify, demonize and destroy those who don't agree with your political agenda! I guess Nancy Pelosi, Democrat, Speaker of the House of Representatives, is going to investigate Harry Reid, Democrat, Senate Majority Leader and other Democrats who oppose the location of the new mosque as well!

And then there was the issue of rebuilding the St. Nicholas Church, a tiny Greek Orthodox Church that was completely destroyed on 9/11. The same Port Authority that approved the building of the Cordoba House mosque in August of 2010, thwarted the plans to rebuild the St. Nicholas church The Port Authority refused to meet with church officials and withdrew their promise to rebuild the church! [59]

Muslim Teacher Appeasement
In December 2010 Attorney General Eric Holder's Assistant Attorney General for Civil Rights Thomas Perez announce to sue, at taxpayer's expense, a suburban Chicago school district on behalf of a Muslim middle school teacher and its only math lab instructor, for discrimination by denying the teacher unpaid leave for a pilgrimage to Mecca. The request for 19 days of leave after being on the job for only nine months was denied, as it was unrelated to the teacher's professional duties and not covered by the teacher's union contract. Perez explained that he took the case in part to combat "a real head wind of intolerance against Muslim communities." [60] Apparently a Muslim teacher's desire to

take time off was more important than the children's right to education during weeks leading up to final exams.

Mismanaging the War in Afghanistan

During his campaign and as president, Obama claimed that Afghanistan was a greater security threat than Iraq, and that he would fight the war in Afghanistan vigorously.

In December of 2008 Defense Secretary Robert Gates got Bush's go-ahead to send 20,000 to 30,000 more troops to Afghanistan in 2009. [61] In February of 2009 Obama reduced that number to 17,000. "This increase is necessary to stabilize a deteriorating situation in Afghanistan, which has not received the strategic attention, direction and resources it urgently requires," Obama said. [62] What do you mean, Mr. Obama? You claim that the war in Afghanistan has not received the resources needed and you *reduce* the number of previously committed, additional troops from 20,000-30,000 to 17,000? Isn't it amazing how this man can spin the facts for his own political purposes?

In March of 2009 Obama announced to have conducted an in-depth review of the Afghanistan conflict and developed what he called a "stronger, smarter and comprehensive" Afghan war strategy and re-confirmed his so-called commitment to the war. [63] To lead this new strategy, Obama put General McChrystal in command in Afghanistan in May of 2009..

In August of 2009 McChrystal asked for additional troops to avert defeat in Afghanistan. He proposed three options: a low-risk option of 80,000 more troops, a medium-risk option of 40,000 to 45,000 more troops and a high-risk option of 20,000 more troops. [64] Obama responded by delaying a decision to yet again "review our strategy";

what happened to the March "stronger, smarter and comprehensive" strategy? Obama kept putting off a decision. He should grow a spine, stop dithering and either supply his generals with what they need to win this war or withdraw all troops and take responsibility for the consequences.

Finally, in December of 2009 Obama announced that he would send 30,000-33,000 additional troops to Afghanistan over a six-month period. [65] So it appeared that Obama, after much dithering and navel-gazing, had chosen for a worse than medium-risk scenario for the war in Afghanistan!

In June of 2010 Obama fired McChrystal over some disparaging remarks about Obama and civilians in the Obama Regime involved in Afghanistan, as reported in a Rolling Stone magazine article. He replaced him with general Petraeus, the general he had criticized in the past for his successful surge efforts in Iraq!

Ridiculous Rules of Engagement in Afghanistan

Just like Bill Clinton before him, Obama treated terrorism mainly as a law enforcement matter. He dictated new and ridiculous rules of engagement for our troops in Afghanistan. The Washington Times compiled an informal list of the new rules from interviews with U.S. forces. [66] Among them:

- No night or surprise searches
- Villagers have to be warned prior to searches
- Afghan military or police personnel must accompany U.S. units on searches
- U.S. soldiers may not fire at the enemy, unless the enemy is preparing to fire first
- U.S. forces cannot engage the enemy if civilians are present

- Only women can search women
- Troops can fire at an insurgent if they catch him placing an IED, but not if insurgents are walking away from an area where explosives have been laid

Instead of fighting a war, they want our men and women in uniform to play detective and collect evidence for the lawyers to get their hands on, so liberal peaceniks can feel good about themselves for being so sensitive and considerate to those who would kill them in a heartbeat if they got the chance.

11. Foreign Policy

The foreign policy of the Obama Administration, if it even deserves that title, appears weak, confused and splintered; not a domain of thoughtful diplomacy, born out of clear visions, but a sad state of affairs. We appease dictators and radical Islam and treat our allies with contempt. We no longer lead and stand up for freedom and human rights.

What Is Obama's Foreign Policy?

Foreign policy of the Obama Administration appears weak, incoherent and confused. Secretary of State Hillary Clinton has been overshadowed by Obama himself, George Mitchell, special envoy to the Middle East, and Richard Holbrook, special representative for Afghanistan and Pakistan. If Obama didn't want Hillary Clinton to perform her function as the head of the State Department and key figure in foreign policy, he shouldn't have appointed her.

If there are any key characteristics of Obama foreign policy, it appears to be appeasement of our adversaries like Russia, the Muslim world, Iran, North Korea and Latin American dictators and contempt for our allies like England and Israel.

Just as Jimmy Carter did before him, Obama displays hostility toward Israel. Its prime minister is snubbed and left to wait while Mr. Obama has dinner with his family. Construction of homes in Jerusalem is criticized. Israel is told to retreat to the borders before the 1967 war, making defending the country practically impossible.

A bronze bust of Sir Winston Churchill was removed from the Oval Office shortly before Obama's inauguration and returned to the British. The bust had been given on loan after 9/11 as a symbol of an enduring special relationship between England and the U.S. [1]

Endorsement of Dictator in Syria

In March of 2011 Secretary of State Hillary Clinton commented that the U.S. would not intervene in Syria's uprising against dictator Bashar al-Assad. She referred to him as a "reformer" despite his atrocious human rights record and the regime's violent and bloody crackdown on pro-democracy demonstrators. Clinton said: "There is a different leader in Syria now. Many of the members in Congress of both parties who have gone to Syria in recent months have said they believe he's a reformer." [2] The message to Assad was clear: rest easy now, you can gun down peaceful protesters with impunity and the U.S. won't do a thing about it. Never mind that Assad terrorized his own people and sponsored the Islamic terrorist organizations Hezbollah and Hamas, determined to kill all Jews and destroy Israel.

Clinton tried to undo the damage this blunder of major proportions had caused by saying the next day that she referenced opinions of others, and was not speaking either for herself or for the Obama administration! [3]

Did our Secretary of State not know about the four decades of the Assad family dictatorship and her own State Department's terrorism reports? Of course she knew! But Obama's deep sympathies for all things Islamic and his disdain for Israel required the white-washing of Assad's atrocities.

In early June of 2011 it was reported that more than 1,200 people had died in the Syrian uprising and more than 10,000 had been detained since March of 2011. [4] And what did Obama do? He announced toothless sanctions against three Syrian officials - but not Assad himself – and the Qud's Force, a special unit of the Syrian Revolutionary Guard, accused by the White House of advising the Assad Regime on crowd suppression. Obama conveniently failed to mention that the targets of the sanctions weren't believed to have any U.S. assets! [5]

Pakistan Our Ally?

After Osama bin Laden was killed on May 1, 2011, Secretary of State Hillary Clinton mimicked her handler, Obama, and praised Pakistan's co-operation with hunting down bin Laden, giving the impression that all was well between the U.S. and Pakistan and nothing could be farther from the truth. [6]

We provide Pakistan with billions of dollars of military and civilian aid, but U.S. relations with them have deteriorated significantly. They are increasingly hostile to the U.S. We know that Pakistan has tipped of the Taliban and al-Qaida repeatedly about planned U.S. attacks on them, so there is no way we can trust them. They harbor and protect Taliban and al-Qaida terrorists, including, as it turned out, Osama bin Laden. The Pakistanis must have known that bin Laden lived in that compound, so they clearly double-crossed us. Portraying Pakistan as a close ally is yet another example of the Obama Regime's sickening intellectual dishonesty.

Foreign Aid

In 2009 we gave Foreign Aid to more than 180 countries to the tune of $45 billion. Foreign Aid is supposed to go toward economic development, poverty reduction, democracy promotion and efforts to deter radicalism. [7] One would assume that we give only to those countries that are our allies, but that is not the case! A Heritage Foundation study [8] found that 95% of U.N. member countries that receive aid from us, vote more often than not *against* our diplomatic initiatives in the U.N. during the period of 2000 through 2009. We should rethink our Foreign Aid strategy and drastically cut aid to countries that don't support us in the U.N., particularly to those countries hostile to the U.S., like Pakistan. Pakistan received $4.5 billion in military and economic aid in 2010 alone. [9] And $20 million of your taxpayer money will go towards remaking "Sesame Street" for Pakistani children. [10]

The Egypt Crisis

Demonstrations and riots in Tunisia in December 2010 and January 2011 led to the ousting of the 23 year Tunisian president Zine El Abidine Ben Ali, and a caretaker coalition government was created. These developments triggered unrest in Egypt as well and demonstrations there against President Hosni Mubarak got very serious, bloody and deadly in January 2011. Demonstrators demanded the immediate resignation of Mubarak and political reforms.

In spite of the wonders of its ancient civilization, Egypt today is a dismal place with wide-spread poverty, high unemployment and very little freedom. Mubarak has ruled

Egypt as a dictator for 29 years, suppressing his people. However, he honored the peace treaty with Israel, helped to keep Iran in check and participated in the War on Terror.

The Obama Regime reacted to these developments in Egypt with a stupendous lack of coordination and common sense. Vice President Biden claimed that Mubarak wasn't a dictator. [11] Obama, however, outdid everybody by repeatedly calling for Mubarak to resign immediately, for elections to be held as soon as possible and for ensuring that all opposition parties would be represented in an interim government. That sounded reasonable enough, right? Well, maybe not. On closer examination, these words clearly showed either how ***incredibly stupid*** Obama was or how he ***appeased radical Islam.*** And I don't believe he's incredibly stupid.

While Mubarak basically was a despicable person and didn't represent our values, he was far better for Egypt, Israel, the U.S. and the rest of the world than the very likely alternative, if he left immediately and all opposition parties participated in an interim government, as Obama was stressing openly and often.

The only real opposition in Egypt was the Muslim Brotherhood and they had an overall approval rating of 75% among Egyptians. [12] Furthermore, in Egypt 95% of Muslims said that it was good that Islam played a large role in politics, 59% identify with Islamic fundamentalists, 54% favor gender segregation in the workplace, 82% favor stoning people who commit adultery, 77% favor whippings or cutting off of hands for theft and robbery and 84% favor the death penalty for people who leave the Muslim religion. [13] Given these radical views of large parts of the Egyptian population, it was very likely that the radical Muslim Brotherhood would seize power in Egypt.

This would be more or less a replay of what happened in Iran in 1979, when Democrat President Jimmy Carter refused to support the Shah and radical ayatollahs seized power after the Shah was ousted, or what happened when the Muslim terrorist organization Hamas took over the Gaza Strip after elections there.

So what does the Muslim Brotherhood stand for? It's a radical Muslim terrorist organization. Their goal is to turn the world into an Islamist empire. Founded in Egypt in 1928, it is a revolutionary fundamentalist movement to restore the caliphate and strict sharia (Islamist) law in Muslim lands and, ultimately, the world. They and associated organizations assassinated Egyptian Prime Minister Pasha in 1948 and Egyptian President Sadat in 1981. [14] Today groups in over 80 countries trace their ideology to the Muslim Brotherhood. The terrorist organization Hamas, for instance, was spawned by the Brotherhood. [15]

Their motto speaks for itself: "Allah is our objective. The Prophet is our leader. Qur'an is our law. Jihad is our way. Dying in the way of Allah is our highest hope." [16] Its founder Hassan al-Banna, said: "It is in the nature of Islam to dominate, not to be dominated, to impose its law on all nations and to extend its power to the entire planet." [17]

The American leadership of the Brotherhood described its mission as follows: "a kind of grand jihad in eliminating and destroying the Western civilization from within and 'sabotaging' its miserable house by their hands and the hands of the believers so that it is eliminated and God's religion is made victorious over all other religions." [18]

The Brotherhood wants America's demise. Muslim Brotherhood Supreme Guide Muhammed Badi told its followers as recently as September 2010 "to be 'patient' because America 'is heading towards its demise.' The U.S. is an infidel that 'does not champion moral and human values and cannot lead humanity.'" [19]

The Muslim Brotherhood said in January 2011 during the demonstrations that Egypt needed to prepare for war with Israel and the closing of the Suez Canal. [20]

So, did Obama strongly condemn the Muslim Brotherhood? No, he didn't! Did he caution against radical Islam playing a role, any role, in Egypt's future government? No, he didn't. As he had done repeatedly, he sympathized with radical Islam. By insisting that all opposition parties in Egypt - of which the Muslim Brotherhood is the biggest - be part of government reform, he basically legitimized the Muslim Brotherhood. He threw an ally, warts and all, under the bus, instead of seeking ways to help with a transition to a more democratic Egypt without handing it over to radical Islam. Obama will leave a legacy of losing Egypt to the radicals, just as Jimmy Carter did with Iran.

Obama even went so far as to *invite* members of the Muslim Brotherhood to attend his speech in Cairo in June of 2009, [21] during which he invoked the Quran and his rarely used middle name, Hussein. [22] To add insult to injury he said during that speech: "America and Islam are not exclusive, and need not be in competition. Instead, they overlap, and share common principles of justice and progress, tolerance and the dignity of all human beings." [23] *Common principle of justice and progress, tolerance and the dignity of all human beings?* Was he addressing decent, moderate Muslims, few of which have spoken out forcefully and repeatedly against radical Islam, or was he addressing the members of the Muslim Brotherhood in his audience, there on Obama's specific invitation?

Obama's support for Egyptian demonstrators wanting to overthrow an ally in the War on Terror, who helped keep radical Islam in check, is in stark contrast with his lack of any support for Iranian demonstrators when they wanted to overthrow their oppressive regime, one of the biggest threats to Israel, the U.S. and world peace.

Then, to top it all, Obama's Director of National Intelligence James Clapper had the nerve to say: "The term 'Muslim Brotherhood'...is an umbrella term for a variety of movements, in the case of Egypt, a very heterogeneous group, largely secular, which has eschewed violence and has decried Al Qaeda as a perversion of Islam." [24] *Largely secular? Eschewed violence?* This man is part of Obama's so-called "security team"? Unbelievable!

So, what's up with Obama, Biden, Clinton and Clapper ignoring or whitewashing the radical, violent nature of the Muslim Brotherhood? Are their actions and pronouncements driven by ignorance and wishful thinking? Are they foolishly hoping for pacifying the Brotherhood and radical Islam in general with their incredibly harebrained posturing? Or are there more sinister motives, like legitimizing radical Islam?

Obama's Illegal Libyan War

Dictator Moammar Gadhafi of Libya is believed to personally have ordered the bombing of Pan Am flight 103 over Lockerbie, Scotland in 1988, [25] killing all 259 people on board, including 189 Americans, and 11 people on the ground. He is also believed to have ordered the 1986 bombing of a Berlin, Germany disco club frequented by U.S. servicemen, killing 2 of them and a Turkish woman and injuring 200. After the U.S. went after Osama Bin Laden in Afghanistan and Saddam Hussein in Iraq, Gadhafi got scared and voluntarily disclosed his weapons of mass destruction programs to us and dismantled them. In a questionable move, President Bush then reestablished relations, Foreign Aid and limited military assistance.

In February 2011 Libyans rose up against Moammar Gadhafi's brutal, terrorism-supporting regime and the death toll quickly rose to hundreds and possibly thousands. Obama didn't speak up for **nine** days [26] and when he finally did, he made some wimpy remarks about considering "a full range of options" and "the entire world is watching". That's not behavior worthy of what is supposed to be the leader of the world's most powerful, freedom-loving nation. Could it be that our "leader" hesitated about speak out on Gadhafi's terror and bloodshed, because of the buddy-buddy relations between Gadhafi, Obama's long-time spiritual mentor Reverend Jeremiah Wright and Nation of Islam leader Louis Farrakhan? [27]

When Gadhafi ordered his air force to attack his own people, many countries, including England and France and the Arab League and U.S. senators Lieberman and McCain urged to enforce a no-fly zone over Libya. Obama stalled. His mouthpiece, Hillary Clinton, said that any no-fly zone over Libya needed international backing and not be a U.S.-led effort: "…we think it's important that the United Nations make this decision, not the United States. So far the United Nations has not done that." [28]

The United Nations Security Council finally did issue a resolution calling for a cease fire and establishing a no-fly zone to protect the Libyans. Obama, pushed by Hillary Clinton and others, [29] acted without consulting Congress and without their approval and decided to attack Libya. A first wave of U.S. and U.K. cruise missiles was launched against Gadhafi's air defenses and command and control network on March 19, 2011. The action was supposed to take "*days, not weeks*". [30] Approval by the U.N. and the Arab League were apparently more important to Obama than approval by the U.S. Congress, notwithstanding U.S. law!

Details about the illegality of starting this war without the approval of Congress and the subsequent failure to seek approval within 60 days can be found in Chapter 2, The Obama Culture, Obama the Dictator and Outlaw.

The initial lead of the U.S. would be replaced by yet-to-be-agreed-upon control, possibly by NATO or others. [31] After much deliberation NATO finally agreed to take so-called full command of the military action against Libya, more than 10 days after the initial attacks. [32] Maybe, just maybe, Mr. Obama, you should have defined goals and exit strategies, figured out the command structure and gotten buy-in and approval from American citizens, the U.S. Congress and coalition partners before starting another hostile, military operation, also known as war.

To any reasonable person, launching cruise missiles, using B52's to drop bombs on airfields, shooting airplanes out of the sky and firing missiles at tanks are acts of war. But when asked if the fighting in Libya was a war, military officers, White House spokespersons and Obama himself said no. So, what is it? National security adviser Ben Rhodes had the answer: "I think what we are doing is enforcing a resolution that has a very clear set of goals, which is protecting the Libyan people, averting a humanitarian crisis, and setting up a no-fly zone. Obviously that involves kinetic military action, particularly on the front end." [33] Ah, clarity at last! It's *not war* but *kinetic military action!*

We were told that the U.S. would not put boots on the ground in Libya, but then we learned that military special ops and intelligence people were on the ground right from the beginning. [34] Obama had stated that Gadhafi had to go. [35] At the same time, it was stated that Gadhafi was not a target of the military action and that it was not about regime change! [36] There was absolutely no agreed-upon strategy, no clearly defined objectives, no definition of victory or success, no exit strategy. Nobody knew what our mission really was or who was really in charge. Charles Krauthammer summed it up very well: "The Professor's War, America is led by a man determined that it should not lead." [37]

So, who were those Libyan so-called "freedom fighters" and "democratic forces" Obama wanted to protect so badly that he committed our troops and resources without consulting with Congress and without a clear plan? Fact was that a large part of foreign fighters attacking our troops in Iraq were Libyans and that the Libyan "rebels" we were now protecting had ties to al-Qaida. [38] Fact was that the powerful radical faction Libyan Islamic Fighting Group (LIFG) waged Jihad against Gadhafi and had been affiliated with al-Qaida. [39] Fact was that one of the Libyan "rebel" commanders, Abdul-Hakim al-Hasidi, was a member of LIFG, fought American troops in Afghanistan and recruited Libyans to fight American troops in Iraq. [40] Fact was that the Libyan faction of the Muslim Brotherhood, the Libyan Muslim Brotherhood, had been operating in Libya for decades and was the most organized bloc inside the "rebel" political structure. [41]

Obama even went so far as to sign a secret order for covert support of the Libyan "rebels" and seriously considered providing arms to them in the future. [42] Never mind that the U.N. resolution on Libya also included an embargo on weapon shipments to Libya. [43] In typical Obama doublespeak fashion "Secretary of State Hillary Clinton has suggested that the embargo on weapons likely applies only to those sold to the government." [44] Suuuure. Let's arm "rebels" with ties to - if not controlled by - al-Qaida and the Muslim Brotherhood. A similar strategy worked so well in Afghanistan, when we armed "freedom fighters" to drive the Russians out of Afghanistan, "freedom fighters" who later transformed into the radical Muslim terrorist organization, the Taliban. Yeah, that worked really well!

Oh, but wait, a couple of days later, Obama still hadn't made up his mind whether or not to arm the "rebels" and a couple of days after that he said he preferred that other nations, not the U.S., supply weapons to the "rebels" and train them. [45] Don't you love this guy? Can't decide on arming so-called rebels, but would like others to do that. Should we ask Iran, Syria, Hamas or Hezbollah to supply weapons and training to the Libyan "rebels"? How about al-Qaida or the Muslim Brotherhood? After all, they may want to help "build" the Libyan nation to their liking and Obama would be very glad to hand over anything related to what he started in Libya, but couldn't stomach to finish or even properly define.

After the initial phase of knocking out Gadafi's air defenses and command and control network, the U.S. and its allies shifted to ferocious airstrikes on Libyan ground forces, tanks and artillery in efforts to prevent Gadhafi's troops to overrun the so-called rebels. Secretary of Defense Robert Gates "admitted that there was no clearly defined end to the military action in Libya and suggested it might drag on for an undetermined period." [46] What happened to "days, not weeks"?

What had been sold to the American people as an action of days, had predictably turned into a stalemate, with the upper hand in fighting switching on a daily basis between ill-equipped "rebels" and Gadhafi's troops, attacked on occasion, but not persistently, by NATO forces, with the U.S. still in the lead role, in spite of claims that the lead role officially was NATO's.

On April 21, 2011 Obama authorized the use of armed Predator drones for ground attacks on Gadhafi's forces. [47] Previously, unarmed Predators had been used for surveillance missions only. France, Italy and the U.K. announced that they would send military advisors to Libya. [48] And so the conflict escalated.

Around the same time Republican Senator McCain from Arizona travelled to Libya to meet with rebel leaders and pleaded for more U.S. support for them, in the form of arms and money frozen in Gadhafi accounts. Did McCain really want to escalate this war even more? He also said: "I have met these brave fighters, and they are not Al Qaeda." [49] How ignorant could this man be to believe that, if radical Islamists or al-Qaida were part of the so-called rebel leadership, they wouldn't have made sure that they were invisible? Did McCain expect them to be paraded before him and identified? It was time for McCain to retire and leave the job of senator to less gullible, less so-called moderate people.

Could there have been motives for Obama to wage war on Libya, other than the claimed humanitarian concerns? Who knows? Transparency had been in short supply ever since

Obama appeared on the national scene. It certainly couldn't have been to protect the supply of Libyan oil to the U.S. According to the Energy Information Administration 28% of Libya's oil went to Italy, 15% to France, 11% to China, 10% to Germany, 10% to Spain, 5% to Greece, 4% to the U.K. and only 3% to the U.S. [50]

And what about the cost to American taxpayers of Obama's illegal war? In May of 2011, Defense Secretary Robert Gates estimated the cost for the Libyan war through September of 2011 at $750 million, but one month later Defense officials stated that it could be as high as $850 million! [51] Hold it right there! Obama was planning to wage this illegal, days-not-weeks war through at least September of 2011, Congress didn't act and American taxpayers had to cough up close to $1 billion just through September of 2011 to finance Obama's reckless and illegal activities? Maybe Congress should have gotten their heads out of the sand and started impeachment proceedings!

As with other foreign affairs, Obama showed a total lack of purpose and leadership concerning the Libyan crisis. There was no clearly defined strategy, approved by Congress. His actions, inactions and pronouncements were incoherent and confused. He clearly failed to a) do everything in his power to ensure Gadhafi 's removal from the world scene and b) speak out forcefully about defending freedom and human rights and c) strengthening pro-democracy, pro-Western, pro-USA elements in the Libyan population to prevent Libya from being overtaken by radical elements, Islamic or otherwise.

Professor Obama should have taken a "peace through strength" course from Reagan, who defeated the "evil empire", the Soviet Union, without firing a single shot. Obama should never have committed our military to wage war in Libya. He should have pressured Gadhafi to drastically reform his rule over Libya or resign. Gadhafi had shown to respond to U.S. pressure in the past. But then again, because of his methodical destruction of our power and influence in the world, Obama had become inconsequential on the world stage.

Hostility towards Israel

Obama follows in the footsteps of Jimmy Carter to displays contempt and sometimes straightforward hostility toward Israel, one of the few allies we have in the Middle East.

The Gaza Strip is controlled by the Palestinian Hamas terrorist organization, largely financed by Iran and Syria. Israel's blockade of the Gaza Strip - in conjunction with Egypt's closing their border with the Gaza strip - has been very successful in significantly reducing attacks on Israel from the Gaza Strip. Instead of supporting Israel's efforts to quell violence, the Obama Regime chose for appeasement of Hamas and opined that the blockade was too harsh. [52]

When Israeli soldiers boarded ships that were trying to break through the blockade instead of off-loading their cargo under Israeli supervision, to ensure no weapons were smuggled into Gaza, pro-Hamas activists on board attacked them. In the ensuing fight 11 activists were killed. Instead of speaking out for Israel's right to defend itself against terrorism and sending a clear signal to terrorists around the world, Obama weaseled out and said he supported an investigation of the incident by the U.N. [53]

Obama did additional, massive damage to the U.S.-Israel relationship and endanger Israel's security in May of 2011, when he called for reverting to the prevailing borders before the 1967 Arab-Israeli war, adjusted to some degree to account for Israeli settlements in the West Bank. He threw this curve ball just one day before Israeli Prime Minister Benjamin Netanyahu arrived in Washington for a meeting with Obama. You don't treat your friends and allies that way. The Israelis promptly protested against Obama's pronouncement, saying that return to the pre-1967 borders, with or without some adjustments, would leave Israel indefensible. Netanyahu had an angry phone exchange with Hillary Clinton before his arrival in Washington and this may have caused Obama to make changes to his planned speech the next morning, although Obama did not remove the proposal about the borders. [54]

Upon arrival Netanyahu rebuffed Obama and rejected the compromise Obama had outlined. Netanyahu warned against "a peace based on illusions" and said that Israel would not accept a return to the old boundaries. Obama did not back away from his proposal. [55]

Israel officially withdrew from the Gaza Strip in 2005 in the false hope of appeasing the Palestinians. The terror organization Hamas took control after the Israelis left and they launched thousands of rockets from Gaza into Israel. Was Obama really thinking that if Israel would give up more territory - this time the Golan Height and the West Bank - the Palestinians and Muslims in general would stop hating the Israelis and a true peace deal could be brokered? Apparently Obama hasn't listened to Netanyahu and others who have warned that the Arab world sees Israel as "Little Satan" and their goal is to first annihilate "Little Satan" and then "Big Satan", the U.S.

Obama is competing with, if not outdoing, Jimmy Carter in terms of hostility towards the tiny nation of Israel. His actions will no doubt fuel more anti-Israel sentiment in the Arab world and gravely endanger the safety of one of the few allies we have in the Middle East.

Freedom and Human Rights

It used to be that America stood for defending freedom and human rights. In the first and second world wars, we liberated hundreds of millions of people in Europe, Africa, Asia and the Pacific from the clutches of Nazi Germany, Italy and Imperial Japan. We won the Cold War and liberated millions and millions in Eastern Europe from brutal Soviet Union oppression. We spoke out against Apartheid and other dictatorial regimes and the human rights abuses in communist China and other countries.

With Obama however, that's all changed. He does not lead and stand up for freedom and human rights. Dictators and enemies of America – Iran, radical Islam, Venezuela - are pandered to. Our allies are chastised, in particular Israel. To add insult to injury, Obama goes on a world-tour, apologizing profusely for America's supposed shortcomings, without speaking about America's greatness and exceptionalism. He bends over backwards to appease our enemies in the Arab world, in particular Iran, without obtaining any concessions or change in their hostile attitudes whatsoever. Under pressure from Moscow he compromises the defense of Western Europe.

Germany's Chancellor Angela Merkel invited Obama to attend the ceremony in Berlin in November 2009 to commemorate the fall of the Berlin Wall 20 years earlier. He offended her, her country and freedom-loving people all over the world by declining the invitation to attend in person and speak out, standing at the Brandenburg Gate like Reagan had done many years before, against tyranny and for freedom and represent the U.S. as the force behind the liberation of hundreds of millions of Europeans from Soviet oppression. Instead he sent his mouthpiece Hillary Clinton and spoke via a surprise video address from Washington. [56]

In Iran, applying barbaric sharia law, people are stoned to death for "offenses" like adultery. Their death sentence is commuted if they can break free, after first being buried to their waste for men and to their neck for women!

An Iranian court couldn't prove allegations of adultery by a mother of two, but she was sentenced to 99 lashes anyway. She "confessed" after the lashing and was sentence to death by stoning. [57] You would think that the U.S. would strongly protest such barbarism. Did President Obama speak out? No! Did Secretary of State Hillary Clinton speak out? No! Assistant Secretary of State J.P. Crowley said: "We have grave concerns that the punishment does not fit the alleged crime." [58] Wonderful! Maybe Obama, Clinton or Crowley should explain what alleged crimes would justify stoning people, after burying a woman to the neck or a man only to the waste!

In August of 2010 the Obama administration's State Department under Hillary Clinton, in its first report to the U.N. Human Rights Council, stated that America's human rights record is less than perfect, that some Americans, notably minorities, are still victims of discrimination, that large segments of American society suffer from unfair policies and practices and that considerable progress is needed! To add insult to injury, the State Department report included the Justice Department's lawsuit against Arizona's immigration law to show to the world how the U.S. protects human rights! [59] With this government, who needs enemies to disparage and destroy our country? And why for heaven's sake are we still lending any credibility to the U.N., by being a member and paying billions of dollars each year to this corrupt group of mostly enemies of America, freedom and human rights?

Epilogue

So there you have it. When you take it all in, an ominous picture of President Obama and his Regime emerges. A nightmarish picture of relentless, dictatorial pursuit of destructive, socialist ideology at all cost, ever-increasing reach and power of an out-of-control government, widespread corruption and economic collapse. Obama's "fundamental transformation of America" is a deliberate plan to destroy our country, collapse the system, take full control and reshape our society in the socialist image.

All this is forced upon us under the false pretense of fairness, justice, saving the planet and protecting us from evil, greedy businesses. It's all in the name of the "common good", we are told. And if you don't agree, you are a racist, a bigot, a hypocrite. In Obama's socialist Utopia, there is no room for independent thinkers.

The collective damage, brought upon this country by Obama, is staggering. His policies have failed in each and every area: jobs; the economy; spending, deficits and debt; energy; health care; administration of justice; national security; containment of our enemies; support for our allies; foreign policy; our standing in the world; illegal immigration; financial reform; corruption; transparency; bipartisanship; race relations; human rights.

But it doesn't have to be this way. We can and we must reverse this path toward the destruction of the greatest country in the history of the world. Our country can once again become the "shining city upon a hill". One term of Obama has been one term too many. We must take back control of our country, our freedom, our well-being, our future. We need to assert our inalienable rights, get involved, vote the radicals out of office and make Washington understand that they work for us, that we don't work and slave for them.

Let us remember Ronald Reagan's words: "Freedom is never more than one generation away from extinction. We didn't pass it to our children in the bloodstream. It must be fought for, protected, and handed on for them to do the same, or one day we will spend our sunset years telling our children and our children's children what it was once like in the United States where men were free."

Index

257

Preventive Services Task Force, 194
primary balance, 94, 101, 109
prime interest rate, 120, 121, 122
progressive, 73, 108
Progressive, 2, 5, 11, 22, 23
Public Broadcasting System, 116
Qom, Iran, 218
Qud's Force, 234
Quran, 238
race, 5, 56, 57, 58, 61, 205, 251
racial, 5, 22, 43, 58, 60, 61
racial profiling, 6, 59, 207
radical Islam, 23, 34, 209, 214, 215, 217, 232, 236, 238, 239, 248
Ramadan, 226
Rangel, Charlie, 33, 34
Rauf, Feisal Abdul, 225, 227
Reagan, Ronald, 97, 123, 142, 204, 245, 249, 252
recession, 14, 15, 54, 63, 74, 83, 109, 111, 120, 121, 122, 123, 127, 131
Reid, Harry, 9, 39, 56, 91, 100, 170, 171, 174, 176, 228
Reklaim Technologies, 149
renewable energy, 6, 137, 138, 139, 147, 148, 149, 150, 151, 152, 156, 157
Republic of Congo, 136
Republican, 8, 9, 10, 11, 12, 13, 14, 15, 16, 17, 36, 39, 47, 51, 56, 57, 58, 61, 72, 75, 76, 78, 90, 94, 95, 96, 97, 98, 99, 100, 101, 102, 103, 104, 105, 106, 112, 113, 122, 124, 132, 139, 140, 160, 163, 164, 167, 168,

170, 173, 174, 175, 176, 177, 178, 181, 196, 202, 205, 217, 244
Resolution Fund, 131, 132
Reuters, 153
Rezko, Antoin, 7, 26
Rhodes, Ben, 241
Richardson, Bill, 32
Rolling Stone, 230
Romanoff, Andrew, 38
Roosevelt, Franklin Delano, 121
Rubio, Marco, 39
Russia, 45, 147, 215, 216, 232, 243
Ryan, Paul, 99, 101, 103, 104, 105, 108
S&P, 81, 82
Sadat, Anwar, 237
Salazar, Ken, 35, 136, 137, 139
San Francisco, 20, 154
sanction, 215, 216, 219, 234
Sanders, Bernie, 174
Saudi Arabia, 45, 137, 147, 227
SBInet, 201
Scotland, 239
Sebelius, Kathleen, 9, 32, 66, 184, 186, 191
SEC, 133
Secure Fence Act of 2006, 201
Securities & Exchange Commission, 133
SEIU, 39
Senate Budget Committee, 80, 176
Sesame Street, 235
Sestak, Joe, 35, 38
Shah, 237
Shakur, Assata, 31
sharia, 227, 237, 249
Shepherds Flat, 149

Notes

Chapter 1: The Battle Between Conservatism and Liberalism

1 Lydia Saad, "'Conservatives' Are Single-Largest Ideological Group", gallup.com, June 15, 2009.

2 "Media Bias Basics, How the Media Vote", mrc.org.

3 Josef Federman, "Fact Check: Netanyahu speech ignores rival claims", hosted.ap.org, May 24, 2011.

4 Jay Rogers, "The Ten Commandments of Obama", forerunner.com, September 4, 2009.

5 Jon Ward, "A transcript of Gibb's 'manufactured anger' line", washingtontimes.com, August 4, 2009.

6 "DNC Ad Calls Health Care Protesters Angry Mob", foxnews.com, August 6, 2009.

7 Jeff Poor, "The Untold Story of Astroturf: Corporate-Sponsored Environmentalism", mrc.org, May 12, 2010.

8 Mark Hemingway, "And the Hits Just Keep On Coming", nationalreview.com, August 13, 2009.

9 Vincent Rossmeier, "On what planet do you spend most of your time?", salon.com, August19, 2009.

10 jbranstetter04,"Rep. Brian Baird accuses protests of driving people to violence like Timothy McVeigh", youtube.com , August 7, 2009.

11 "Fear or Loathing: Democrats Raise Specter of Swastikas to Cancel Town Halls", FOXNews.com, August 6, 2009.

12 Michelle Malkin, "What's the SEIU up to now?; another Democrat calls Obamacare protesters 'political terrorists'", michellemalkin.com, August 12, 2009.

13 "Congresswoman Calls Senate Dems Who Oppose Public Option 'Neanderthals'", breitbart.tv

14 Brian Montopoli, "Alan Grayson 'Die Quickly' Comment Prompts Uproar", cbsnews.com, September 30, 2009

15 Amanda Carpenter, "Liberal actress says tea parties were racist", washingtontimes.com, April 17, 2009.

16 Ed Hornick, "Leahy: 'Seething rhetoric' has gone too far", articles.cnn.com, January 11, 2011.

17 Paul Krugman, "Climate of Hate", nytimes.com, January 9, 2011.

18 Paul Krugman, "Pass the Bill", nytimes.com, December 17, 2009.

19 Deborah White, "Palin's Political Dog Whistle in Arizona Yields Unintended Results", usliberals.about.com, January 9, 2011.

20 Michelle Malkin, "The Hate Speech Inquisition", michellemalkin.com, January 19, 20011.

21 Jonathan Karl, "Say What? Democrat Compares Republicans to Nazis", blogs.abcnews.com, January 19, 2011.

22 "Cavuto Catches Dem Faking Obamacare Repeal 'Victim' Live on Air", nation.foxnews.com, January 19, 2011.

23 "State of the Union: President Obama's Speech", abcnews.go.com, January 27, 2010.

24 Ibid.

25 "Biden: Iraq One of Obama's 'Greatest Achievements'", nation.foxnews.com, February 11, 2010.

26 Howard Fineman, "Obama's Midterm Strategy: Blame the GOP", newsweek.com, May 17, 2010.

27 David Freddoso, "Pelosi: Unemployment benefits create more jobs than any other initiative", washingtonexaminer.com, June 30, 2010.

28 Greg Knapp, "Food Stamps for Prosperity! Welfare for Jackpots!", biggovernment.com.

29 Philip Rucker, "Gingrich promises to slash taxes, calls Obama 'food stamp president'", washingtonpost.com, May 13, 2011.

30 Tim Alberta, "Stark's town hall answer goes viral", politico,com, August 3, 2010.

31 David A. Patten, "Obama, Democrats Declare War on U.S. Chamber", newsmax.com, October 11, 2010.

32 John McCormack, "Obama to Latinos: 'Punish' Your 'Enemies' in the Voting Booth", weeklystandard.com, October 25, 2010.

33 Richard Sisk, "Hillary Clinton says Barack Obama can rebound by taking page from Bill Clinton's playbook", articles.nydailynews.com, November 9, 2010.

34 "Speaker Pelosi Leaves With a Whopper", nation.foxnews.com, January 4, 2011.

35 Lucy Madison, "Muslim Rep. Keith Ellison breaks down in Muslim radicalization hearings", cbsnews.com, March 10, 2011.

36 "Mohammed Salman Hamdani", en.wikipedia.org

37 "Homeland Security chief stresses that 'very, very, very few people' get hands-on treatment at U.S. airports", PolitiFact.com, May 7, 2011.

38 Wyatt Emmerich, "With welfare it makes sense to work less", northsidesun.com, undated, around November 2010.

39 "Enter the salt police", nypost.com, March 15, 2010.

40 Greg Knapp, "Ronald McDonald Is a Murderer and Racist!...Or Something", biggovernment.com.

41 Todd Starnes, "San Francisco Considers Ban on Goldfish as Pets to Prevent Their 'Inhumane Suffering'", foxnews.com, June 16, 2011.

42 Brent Hunsberger, "Oregon measure pitches college savings for newborns", oregonlive.com, February 19, 2011.

43 Darren Murph, "Anaheim school district handing out GPS trackers to chronically absent students", engadget.com, February 21, 2011.

Chapter 2: The Obama Culture

1 "55 Percent of Likely Voters Find 'Socialist' an Accurate Label of Obama?", nationalreview.com, July 9, 2010.

2 Dinitia Smith, "No Regrets for a Love Of Explosives; In a Memoir of Sorts, a War Protester Talks of Life With the Weathermen", nytimes.com, September 11, 2001.

3 Ben Smith, "Ax on Ayers", politico.com, February 26, 2008.

4 Jerome R. Corsi, "The Obama Nation", Threshold Editions, A Division of Simon and Schuster, Inc., 2008.

5 Ibid.

6 Michelle Malkin, "Crooked Carol Browner: Obama's ethically-challenged energy czar", michellemalkin.com, December 12, 2008.

7 Neil King Jr. and Stephen Power, "Times Tough for Energy Overhaul", online.wsj.com, December 12, 2008.

8 Joseph Abrams, "Obama's Science Czar Considered Forced Abortions, Sterilization as Population Growth Solutions", foxnews.com, July 21, 2009.

9 "Glenn Beck: Manufacturing Czar says 'the free market is nonsense'", glennbeck.com, October 20, 2009.

10 "Cass Sunstein has Secret Animal Rights Agenda", opinion by Consumer Freedom at opposingviews.com, January 15, 2009.

11 Kathy Shaidle, "Van Jones, 'Green Jobs Czar', a self-described 'communist' arrested during Rodney King riots", examiner.com, July 17, 2009.

12 Jung Chang and Jon Halliday, "The Unknown Story – Mao", Anchor Books, A Division of Random House, Inc., 2005,2006.

13 Mark Hemingway, "Van Jones, Obama czar forced to resign over being 9/11 'truther,' to teach at Princeton", washingtonexaminer.com, February 24, 2010.

14 Glenn Beck, "The Radical Truth About Anita Dunn", foxnews.com, October 18, 2009.

15 Robert Farley and Angie Drobnic Holan, "Elena Kagan and the military recruiters at Harvard Law School", politifact.com, June 30, 2010.

16 Terence P. Jeffrey, "What Did Kagan Tell Her Deputy About Winning the Health-Care Case? DOJ Won't Say", cnsnews.com, April 26, 2011.

17 Lea Winerman, "Government Regulation Prompts New Look at 'Death Panel' Debate", pbs.org, January 5, 2011.

18 "The Honduran coup d'etat", boston.com, July 3, 2009.

19 "Should Controversial Rapper Common Have Been Invited to White House?", foxnews.com, May 10, 2011.

20 Brian Thompson and Marcus Riley, "NJ State Police 'Outraged Over Rapper Invite to White House", nbcnewyork.com, May 12, 2011.

21 Martin Crutsinger, "Geithner apologizes for not paying taxes", breitbart.com, January 21, 2009.

22 Jeffrey Smith, Cecilia Kang and Joe Stephens, "Old Ways Doomed New Job for Daschle", washingtonpost.com, February 4, 2009.

23 Erica Werner, "Sebelius admits errors, pays $7,000 in back taxes", breirbart.com, March 31, 2009.

24 "Trade Nominee Ron Kirk to Pay $10,000 in Back Taxes", foxnews.com, March 2, 2009.

25 Michelle Malkin, "Adios! Bill Richardson drops out as Commerce Secretary", michellemalkin.com, January 4, 2009.

26 Michael J. Sniffen and Liz Sidoti, "Official: Performance czar withdraws candidacy", breitbart.com, February 3, 2009.

27 "Just the Facts, Ma'am", the editors of nationalreview.com, May 18, 2008.

28 "93 Days to Decide: GOP Leaders Add Rangel Charges to Campaign Arsenal; Focus on Jobs", foxnews.com, August 1, 2010.

29 Sean Lengell, "House colleges find Rangel guilty of 11 ethics violations", washingtontimes.com, Novermber 16, 2010.

30 Michelle Malkin, "How Eric Holder fixed the FALN pardons", michellemalkin.com, January 9, 2009.

31 Andrew C. McCarthy, "AG Eric Holder Refuses to Say 'Radical Islam' Is a Cause of Terrorism Committed by Muslims", nationalreview.com, May 13, 2010.

32 Susan Schmidt, "Waters Helped Bank Whose Stock She Once Owned", online.wsj.com, March 12, 2009.

33 "McCaskill now owes $320,000 in taxes on plane", mcclatchydc.com, April 13, 2011.

34 Jan Crawford, "Judge Slams Administration, Lifts Drilling Moratorium", cbsnews.com, June 22, 2010.

35 Rajesh Rajagopalan, "Harry Reid's 'Senator Ben Nelson 60th Healthcare vote purchase' – The 49 state tax payer funder bribe", examiner.com, December 19, 2009

36 Dana Milbank, "Sweeteners for the South", washingtonpost.com, November 22, 2009.

37 Brian Montopoli, "Tallying the Health Care Bill's Giveaways", cbsnews.com, December 21, 2009.

38 "Sestak confirms WH job offer to get out of Senate race", politico.com, May 23, 2010.

39 Brian Montopoli, "Joe Sestak Was Contacted by Bill Clinton About Dropping Primary Bid", cbsnews.com, May 28, 2010.

40 "Romanoff to Washington: Local Races Not Your Business", foxnews.com, June 4, 2010.

41 Susan Davis, "White House, Romanoff Discussed Jobs", blogs.wsj.com, June 2, 2010.

42 Peter Wallsten, "Clinton Asked Democrat to Quit Florida Senate Race", online.wsj.com, October 29, 2010.

43 Doug Powers, "Attn. Nevada Voters: Carefully Proof-Reid Your Ballot Before Submitting; Update: Voting Machine Techs are SEIU", michellemalkin.com, October 26, 2010.

44 Paul Steinhauser, "CNN poll: 56 percent oppose stimulus program", politicalticker.blogs.cnn.com, January 24, 2010.

45 Dr. Arthur Laffer, Donna Arduin, Dr. Wayne Winegarden, "Diagnosing the Health Care Industry: Strengths", lafferhealthcarereport.org.

46 "Health Care Reform – It's time to Decide, and 54% of Voters Oppose the Health Care Plan", rasmussenreports.com, March 21, 2010.

47 "71% in Arizona Now Support State's New Immigration Law", rasmussenreports.com, May 20, 2010.

48 Quinn Bowman, "Arizona Immigration Law Has Broad Support Across U.S., New Polls Show", pbs.org, May 13, 2010.

49 Nicolas Loris, "EPA Formally Declares CO2 a Dangerous Pollutant", blog.heritage.org, December 7, 2009.

50 Vince Haley, "Stop the EPA Power Grab", americansolutions.com, March 31, 2011.

51 Julia A. Seymour, "Foreign Unrest Raises Energy Worries, but Media Put Down Coal", mrc.org, February 10, 2011.

52 Stephanie Condon, "Donald Berwick's Recess Appointment Draws Ire from Republicans, Support from Democrats", cbsnews.com, July 7, 2010.

53 "Editorial: Obama appointee's prescription for socialism", washingtontimes.com, July 9, 2010.

54 "Breaking News: Obama Appoints Berwick to CMS", healthcareinformatics.com, July 7, 2010.

55 Jason Millman, "White House attempts to quiet revived talk of 'death panels'", thehill.com, December 27, 2010.

56 "Former Justice Department Lawyer Accuses Holder of Dropping New Black Panther Case for Racial Reasons", foxnews.com, June 30, 2010.

57 Angie Drobnic Holan, "Justice Department will no longer defend DOMA against constitutional challenges", politifact.com, February 24, 2011.

58 Fred Lucas, "Obama: 'President Does Not Have Power Under Constitution to Unilaterally Authorize a Military Attack'", cnsnews.com, March 21, 2011.

59 "Obama delivers remarks on Libya", projects.washingtonpost.com, March 19, 2011.

60 David A. Fahrenthold, "Obama fails to get Congress' OK on Libya action", journalgazette.net, May 21, 2011.

61 Donna Cassata, "House scolds Obama on Libya; dozens of Dems join", hosted2.ap.org, June 3, 2011.

62 Donna Cassata, "Senators unveil tough resolution on Libya", hosted.ap.org, June 8, 2011.

63 Ibid.

64 Charlie Savage and Mark Landler, "White House Defends Continuing U.S. Role in Libya Operation", nytimes.com, June 15, 2011.

65 Sam Stein, "Obama Administration Drafts Executive Order On Contractor Donation Transparency", huffingtonpost.com, April 19, 2011.

66 Angelia Phillips, "McConnell Slams Executive Order Requiring Contractors to Disclose Political Contributions", patdollard.com, April 20, 2011.

67 "Joint Press Availability With President Obama and President Gul of Turkey", whitehouse.gov, April 6, 2009.

68 Gary Langer, "Poll: Most Americans Say They're Christian", abcnews.go.com.

69 Brooks Jackson, "Obama: U.S. 'One of the Largest Muslim Countries.' Not!", factcheck.org, June 4, 2009.

70 Jake Tapper, "President Obama Says America Has Shown 'Arrogance'", abcnews.go.com, April 3, 2009.

71 Jill Stanek, "Obama's 10 reasons for supporting infanticide", wnd.com, January 16, 2008.

72 Eric Cantor, "Obama's 32 Czars", washingtonpost.com, July 30, 2009.

73 Declan McCullagh, "EPA May Have Suppressed Report Skeptical Of Global Warming", cbsnews.com, June 26, 2009.

74 Paul Driessen, "Cap and tax hoax", congress.org, October 15, 2009.

75 "White House putting off release of budget update", Associate Press article on the USA Today website, July 20, 2009.

76 Trish Turner, "Sen. Dodd Admits Adding Bonus Provision to Stimulus Package", foxnews.com, March 18, 2009.

77 Mark Mooney, "Obama Aide Concedes 'Dollar Bill' Remark Referred to His Race", abcnews.go.com, August 1, 2008.

78 Pierre Thomas, "Stinging Remarks on Race From Attorney General", abcnews.go.com, February 18, 2009.

79 Amanda Carpenter, "Liberal actress says tea parties were racist", washingtontimes.com, April 17, 2009

80 Charlie Savage, "A Judge's View of Judging is on the Record", nytimes.com, May 14, 2009

81 Jesse Washington, "Tea Party Health Care Protests: N-Word Feud Still Rages After Video Discredited", huffingtonpost.com, April 13, 2010

82 "Former Justice Department Lawyer Accuses Holder of Dropping New Black Panther Case for Racial Reasons", foxnews.com, June 30, 2010.

83 "Video Shows USDA Official Saying She Didn't Give 'Full Force' of Help to White Farmer", foxnews.com, July 20, 2010.

84 Henry J. Reske, "Rep. Moran: GOP Won Midterms Due to Racism", newsmax.com, January 27, 2011.

85 Michael Getler, "The Mailbag: Talk About Race and You Will Be Talked About", pbs.org, April 29, 2011.

86 "Obama attends Easter church services in D.C.", content.usatoday.com, April 24, 2011.

Chapter 3: The Economy

1 "Employment Situation Archived News Releases", bls.gov.
2 Michael Cembalest, "Obama's Business Blind Spot", forbes.com, November 24, 2009.
3 Gary Jason, "The Ethical Case for Boycotting Chrysler and GM", americanthinker.com, June 10, 2009.
4 Frank S. Rosenbloom, M.D., "ObamaCare, Point and Counterpoint", americanthinker.com, October 20, 2009.
5 "Sebelius calls on health insurers to stop misinformation and unjustified rate increases", hhs.gov, September 9, 2010.
6 Michelle Malkin, "Torquemada Waxman is still watching you", michellemalkin.com, April 16, 2010.
7 Newt Gingrich, "Sopranos-style tactics in health care", washingtonexaminer.com, August 21, 2009.
8 Russ Brown and Ivan Osorio, "Unionization by Regulation", spectator.org, March 30, 2011.
9 Mike Ramsey and Kate Linebaugh, "Early Tests Pin Toyota Accidents on Drivers", online.wsj.com, July 13, 2010.
10 Robert Longley, "US Labor Union Membership Declined in 2010", usgovinfo.about.com, January 24, 2011.
11 Mary Lan Tomkins, "Union Jobs Pay Better", financeglobe.com, January 22, 2010.
12 Keith Koffler, "Labor Chief at the White House 2-3 Times a week", February 23, 2011."
13 "About Us", aflcio.org.
14 "Bill O'Reilly says unemployment is lower in 'right-to-work' states", politifact.com. February 28, 2011.
15 Steven Greenhouse, "Labor Board Tells Boeing New Factory Breaks Law", nyt.com, April 20, 2011.
16 "Boeing and the N.L.R.B.", editorial, nytimes.com, April 25, 2011.
17 Greg Knapp, "New Government Programs Cost More Than Predicted", biggovernment.com.
18 "A Consumer Report on Government – from the publisher", citizenreviewonline.org.
19 "Gary Johnson says U.S. has 'the highest corporate income tax in the world right now'", politifact.com, May 6, 2011.

20 "The Top 10 Percent of Earners Paid 70 Percent of Federal Income Taxes", heritage.org.

21 Stephen Ohlemacher, "Nearly half of U.S. households escape federal income tax", usatoday.com, April 8, 2010.

22 "No family making less than $250,000 will see 'any form of tax increase'", politifact.com, April 1, 2009.

23 Edwin Mora, "Value Added Tax Not a Bad Idea, Says Top White House Economic Advisor", cnsnews.com, April 8, 2010.

24 Jackie Calmes, "Study Looks at Tax Cut Lapse for Rich", nytimes.com, August 10, 2010.

25 "Democrats to Vote on Tax Cut Extension for Middle Class Only", newsboxnow.com, November 18, 2010.

26 Jake Tapper and Sunlen Miller, "President Obama's $3.8Trillion Budget", blogs.abcnews.com, February 1, 2010.

27 William R. Bischoff, "What to expect if Bush tax cuts expire", blogs.reuters.com, July 29, 2010.

28 Michelle Malkin, "Deal with the devil: Temporary across-the-board tax relief for more endless jobless benefits", michellemalkin.com, December 6, 2010.

29 Danny Yadron and Patrick O'Connor, "The Number: $858 Billion", blogs.wsj.com, December 10, 2010.

30 "Who We Are", plannedparenthood.org, May 23, 2011.

31 Charmaine Yoest and Anna Franzonello, "Nation's largest abortion provider: Planned Parenthood, washingtontimes.com, April 18, 2011.

Chapter 4: Spending, Deficits, Borrowing and National Debt

1 Terrence P. Jeffrey, "March Madness: U.S. Gov't Spent More Than Eight Times Its Monthly Revenue", cnsnews.com, April 4, 2011.

2 Karen Brettel and Walter Brandimarte, "UPDATE 3-Moody's may shift US rating outlook on tax package", reuters.com, December 13, 2010.

3 Dan Jones, "Moody's warns again on US AAA rating", portfolioadvisor.com, January 28, 2011.

4 Chris Giles and James Politi, "US lacks credibility on debt, says IMF", ft.com, April 12, 2011.

5 Damien Paletta and E.S. Browning, "U.S. Warned on Debt Load", online.wsj.com, April 19, 2011.

6 Yepoka Yeebo, "Obama Officials Privately Asked S&P Not To Lower U.S. Credit Outlook; Report", huffingtonpost.com, April 20, 2011.

7 Scott Wilson, "Obama, Avert move to reduce deficit 'on your backs'", post-gazette.com, April 20, 2011.

8 Sewell Chan and Jackie Calmes, "World Leaders Agree on Time Table for Cutting Deficits", nytimes.com, June 27, 2010.

9 Louise Egan, "Wrapup 1-Canada budget tackles deficit, averts election", reuters.com, March 4, 2010.

10 "U.K. Treasury Chief Announces Massive Cuts", thedailybeast.com, October 20, 2010.

11 "Cuba to cut one million public sector jobs", bbc.co.uk, September 14, 2010.

12 Actuals are calculated from the CBO Monthly Budget Reviews on cbo.gov; 2011 and 2012 numbers are from Obama's 2012 budget proposal and information at usgovernmentspending.com.

13 Ibid.

14 Data from CBO and treasurydirect.gov.

15 Jackie Calmes, "Estimate for 10-year Deficit Raised to 9 Trillion", nytimes.com, August 25, 2009.

16 Richard Vedder and Jordan Templeton, "The Wealth of the United States", centerforcollegeaffordability.org, February 25, 2009.

17 "2011 OASDI Trustees Report", ssa.gov.

18 "Monthly Statistical Snapshot, April 2011", ssa.gov.

19 "A Summary Of The 2011 Annual Reports", ssa.gov.

20 "Obama: GOP Want to Privatize Social Security", cbsnews.com, August 14, 2010.

21 Erica Werner, "Obama: GOP trying to destroy Social Security", msnbs.msn.com, August 14, 2010.

22 "A Summary Of The 2011 Annual Reports", ssa.gov.

23 "Draft - Co-Chairs' Proposal – November 2010 – 11.10.10 Draft Document", fiscalcommission.gov.

24 Marc Goldwein, "Fix the Deficit? We Can Do That", time.com, March 17, 2011.

25 Quinn Bowman, "Debt Commission Fails to Send Plan to Congress", pbs.org, December 3, 2010.

26 Ross Kaminsky, "The Means Testing Temptation", spectator.org, undated.

27 Andrew Taylor, "Obama's budget: $3.7 trillion", dailynews.com, February 14, 2011.

28 "Preliminary Analysis Of The President's Budget For 2012",
cbo.gov, March 2011.

29 Lori Montgomery, "Obama spending plan criticized for avoiding
deficit commission's major proposals", washingtonpost.com, February 14, 2011.

30 Reps. Gohmert, King and Bachmann, "Raising the Debt Ceiling:
Republicans' Last Stand", centralvalleyteaparty.com, May 6, 2011.

31 Kevin Spak, "Dems Offer $33B in Cuts to Revive Budget Talks",
newser.com, March 31, 2011.

32 Devonia Smith, "Bachmann laughs Weiner tells Hannity 'I don't
support taxes for billionaires'", examiner.com, March 17, 2011.

33 Robert Schlesinger, "The Numbers Behind the $38.5 Billion (or
$352 Million) Budget Deal", usnews.com, April 15, 2011.

34 Ibid.

35 Ibid.

36 Ibid.

37 "CBO: Recent spending bill cuts $122 billion over 10 years", webcenter11.com, May 16, 2011.

38 "Democrat: Cutting Spending Will Hurt People With Cancer", nation.foxnews.com, January 25, 2011.

39 "Pelosi Floor Speech Against Republican Continuing Resolution",
pelosi.house.gov, February 15, 2011.

40 Jim Hoft, "Nice. Wasserman Schultz: If We Don't Fund Early
Schooling for Poor Families Their Kids Will Become Criminals
(Video)", gatewaypundit.rightnetwork.com, March 4, 2011.

41 Trish Turner, "Senate Dems Answer House GOP on Spending
Cuts, Reid Predicts Bill Will Fail", foxnews.com, March 4, 2011.

42 J.P. Freire, "Harry Reid calls cuts to 'cowboy poetry festivals' heartless", washingtonexaminer.com, March 8, 2011.

43 Noah Davis, "WATCH: Anthony Weiner's Epic, Sarcastic Rant
Against The House Republicans", businessinsider.com, March 17,
2011.

44 "Pelosi: Republican Budget Will Force Seniors Into Starvation",
nation.foxnews.com, April 5, 2011.

45 Joe Newby, "Nancy Pelosi falsely claims GOP budget will starve
millions of seniors", examiner.com, April 7, 2011.

46 "Fiscal Year 2012 Budget – The Path to Prosperity: Restoring America's Promise", budget.house.gov.

47 Ernest Istook, "Paul Ryan Offers a Budget for Grown-Ups", heritage.org, April 6, 2011.

48 Ibid.

49 Ibid.

50 Ibid.

51 "Ryan's Budget Plan A 'Shameful Attack' On Public Workers, Union Leader Says", afge.org, April 13, 2011.

52 Paul Krugman, "Redo That Voodoo", nytimes.com, July 15, 2010.

53 Paul Krugman, "Who's Serious Now?", nytimes.com, April 14, 2011

54 Paul Krugman, "Ludicrous and Cruel", nytimes.com, April 7, 2011.

55 "House Vote 277 – Passes Ryan Budget Bill", politics.nytimes.com, April 15, 2011.

56 "Remarks by the President on Fiscal Policy", whitehouse.gov, April 13, 2011.

57 Ibid.

58 "Fact Sheet: The President's Framework for Shared Prosperity and Shared Fiscal Responsibility", whitehouse.gov, April 13, 2011.

59 Katrina Trinko, "Obama: Not Always a Fan of Upping Debt Ceiling", nationalreview.com, January 3, 2011.

60 Ibid.

61 Dennis Jacobe, "Americans Oppose Raising Debt Ceiling, 47% to 19%", gallup.com, May 13, 2011.

62 S.A. Miller, "Uncle Sam hit$ ceiling", nypost.com, May 17, 2011.

63 "Interest Expense on the Debt Outstanding", treasurydirect.gov.

64 Felicia Sonmez and Lori Montgomery, "Obama to meet with key law makers on debt reduction", post-gazette.com, June 25, 2011.

65 Ibid.

66 "Remarks by the President on Fiscal Policy", whitehouse.gov, April 13, 2011.

67 "Policy Basics: Where Do Our Federal Tax Dollars Go?", cbpp.org, April 15, 2011.

Chapter 5: Bailout and Stimulus – Choosing Winners and Losers

1 Jeanne Sahadi, "Bailout is law", money.cnn.com, October 4, 2008.

2 "GAO - Report to Congressional Committees – Troubled Asset Relief Program", gao.gove, October 2009.

3 Robert Samuelson, "Give TARP a Break", realclearpolitics.com, March 28, 2011.

4 Glen Kessler, "President Obama's phony accounting on the auto industry bailout", washingtonpost.com, June 4, 2011.

5 Louise Story, "New Aid for Fannie and Freddie", nytimes.com, December 24, 2009.

6 "The Second Presidential Debate", realclearpolitics.com, October 8, 2008.

7 "Employment Situation Archived News Releases", bls.gov.

8 "Consumer Price Index – All Urban Consumers", data.bls.gov.

9 "Gross Domestic Product", bea.gov.

10 "Selected Interest Rates - Bank prime loan", federalreserve.gov; "Prime Rate – Historical Graph", moneycafe.com; "Prime Rate History", wsjprimerate.us.

11 George Will says most recent recession killed more jobs than previous four recessions combined," Politifact.com, April 4, 2011.

12 Ed Morrissey, "Rasmussen: Stimulus bill support drops to 37%", hotair.com, February 4, 2009.

13 David M. Herszenhorn, "Recovery Bill Gets Final Approval", nytimes.com, February 13, 2009.

14 David Goldman, "Stimulus now $75 billion more expensive, money.cnn.com, January 26, 2010.

15 Declan McCullagh, "AIG Bonuses Renew Call for Congress to Read Bills", cbsnews.com, March 25, 2009.

16 Stephen Gandel, "Obama's Stimulus Plan: Failing by Its Own Measure", time.com, July 14, 2009.

17 "Employment Situation Archived News Releases", bls.gov.

18 Ibid.

19 Jake Tapper, "Farewell 'Saved or Created': Obama Administration Changes the Counting of Stimulus Jobs*", blogs.abcnews.com, January 11, 2010.

20 "Renewing America's Infrastructure', whitehouse.gov, March 3, 2009.

21 Stephanie Condon, "Obama: No Such Thing as Shovel-Ready Projects", October 13, 2010.

22 Sheryl Gay Stolberg, "Obama Pushes an Agenda, Despite Political Risks", nytimes.com, July 15, 2010.

23 Laura Tyson, "Why We Need a Second Stimulus", nytimes.com, August 28, 2010.

24 "Employment Situation Archived News Releases", bls.gov.

25 "US House approves $155 billion jobs bill", reuters.com, December 16, 2009.

26 Troy McMullen, "The Senate's $149 Billion Jobs Bill: What Does It Do For You?", abcnews.go.com.

27 Lisa Lambert, "House passes state aid bill", reuters.com, August 11, 2010.

28 Jill Jackson, "Wall Street Reform: A Summary of What's in the Bill", cbsnews.com, June 25, 2010.

29 Senate Committee on Banking, Housing, and Urban Affairs, Chairman Chris Dodd, "Summary: Restoring American Financial Stability", banking.senate.gov.

30 John Carney, "TARP Money May Help Fund Financial Reform Legislation", cnbc.com, June 29, 2010.

31 Kenneth R. Bazinet, "President Obama signs most sweeping Wall Street reform bill since Great Depression", articles.nydailynews.com, July 21, 2010.

32 Brian Montopoli, "Obama Signs Sweeping Financial Reform Into Law", cbsnews.com, July 21, 2010.

33 "The Uncertainty Principle-II", online.wsj.com, July 22, 2010.

34 Dunstan Prial, "SEC Says New Financial Regulation Law Exempts it From Public Disclosure", foxbunisess.com, July 28, 2010.

35 Erik Berte, "The Next Bailout: $165B for Unions", foxbusiness.com, May 24, 2010.

36 Sheryl Gay Stolberg and Mary Williams Walsh, "Obama Offers a Transit Plan to Create Jobs", nytimes.com, September 6, 2010.

Chapter 6: Energy

1 Suzanne Goldenberg, "Barack Obama orders six-month freeze on offshore drilling and expansion", guardian.co.uk, May 28, 2010.

2 "Obama's Drill Ban May Trigger Job Losses, Slow Gains", businessweek.com, June 4, 2010.

3 "Update-1-Factbox-Deepwater rigs moved out of the Gulf of Mexico", af.reuters.com, January 27, 2011.

4 Jonathan Weisman, "BP Softens Political Hit", online.wsj.com, June 21, 2010.

5 David Hammer, "Experts seek to clarify their views on drilling moratorium", nola.com, June 8, 2010.

6 Jan Crawford, "Judge Slams Administration, Lifts Drilling Moratorium", cbsnews.com, June 22, 2010.

7 Larry West, "Government Imposes New Deepwater Offshore Drilling Moratorium", environment.about.com, July 13 2010.

8 Michelle Malkin, "Culture of contempt: Interior Department spanked yet again", michellemalkin.com, February 18, 2011.

9 John M. Broder and Clifford Krauss, "U.S. Halts Plan to Drill in Eastern Gulf", nytimes.com, December 1, 2010.

10 "Obama Underwrites Offshore Drilling – Too bad it's not in U.S. waters", online.wsj.com, August 18, 2009.

11 Steve Everley, "Obama Supports Drilling in Brazil So America Can Import More Oil", americansolutions.com, March 21, 2011.

12 "Barack Obama says U.S. oil production last year was highest since 2003", politifact.com, March 15, 2011.

13 "Barack Obama says Gulf oil production hit record level in 2010", politifact.com, March 15, 2011.

14 Carol Greenberg, "Shocker: 30-40 new permits needed in Gulf per month just to keep up with demand", conservative-outlooks.com, April 8, 2011.

15 Carl Hulse, "Senate Rejects Republican Bill on Exploration for Oil and Gas", nytimes.com, May 18, 2011.

16 "Department of Energy to Release Oil from the Strategic Petroleum Reserve", energy.gov, June 23, 2011.

17 "Short-Term Energy Outlook", eia.gov, June 7, 2011.

18 "Gulf Oil Spill Spin: Was The Obama Administration There On Day One?", huffingtonpost.com, May 4, 2010.

19 Paul Rioux, "Federal government will make BP pay for all 6 berms in Gulf oil spill fight", nola.com, June 2, 2010.

20 Cain Burdeau, "Federal officials halt sand dredging to create Gulf of Mexico oil spill barrier", nola.com, June 22, 2010.

21 "Dutch Offered Oil Spill Help; Obama says 'Thanks, but no thanks'", cniworldnews.com, May 26, 2010.

22 Maya Jackson Randall, "Obama Creates Oil Spill Panel", online.wsj.com, May 23, 2010.

23 Stephen Power, "Dispute on Oil Spill Panel Flares Before First Meeting", online.wsj.com, July 10, 2010.

24 "WH Changes Reason Obama Hasn't Talked to BP CEO", nation.foxnews.com, June 10, 2010.

25 Brian Swint, "BP Dividend 'Off the Table' on Obama Spill Demands (Update-1)", businessweek.com, June 16, 2010.

26 "BP to create $100 million fund for unemployed workers", nola.com, June 16, 2010.

27 Ibid.

28 "Congress Gets Ready to Quadruple Tax on Oil", foxnews.com, May 25, 2010.

29 "Obama Draws Bipartisan Criticism for Using Oil Spill to Push Energy Policy", foxnews.com, June 16, 2010.

30 Peter Fowler, "Obama Says World 'Running out of Oil'", newsroomamerica.com, June 15, 2010.

31 "Energy Myths of the Left", peakoil.com, May 27, 2011.

32 Jim Ostroff, "The U.S.' Untapped Oil Bounty", kiplinger.com, June 30, 2008.

33 "Sliced and diced on Capitol Hill: BP boss treated like Public Enemy No 1 by American politicians", dailymail.co.uk, June 18, 2010.

34 "U.S. Accepts Relief Aid for Gulf Spill From 12 Countries", foxnews.com, June 29, 2010.

35 Colleen Long and Harry R. Weber, "BP, feds clash over uncapping well", heraldsun.com, July 18, 2010.

36 John M. Broder, "Report Slams Administration for Underestimating Gulf Spill", nytimes.com, October 6, 2010.

37 "Key BP spill evidence at risk, rig owner says", msnbc.msn.com, November 10, 2010.

38 "Probe: Pipe piece contributed to Gulf oil spill", cbsnews.com, March 23, 2011.

39 Jim Ostroff, "The U.S.' Untapped Oil Bounty", kiplinger.com, June 30, 2008.

40 "George Allen says U.S. leads world in energy resources", politifact.com, June 17, 2011.

41 "U.S. Energy Consumption by Energy Source", eia.gov, August 2010.

42 Mike Dorning, "For Obama, High Oil Prices Have a Green Lining", businessweek.com, March 17, 2011.

43 Harry Esteve, "How many jobs from Oregon's green energy incentives? No one knows", oregonlive.com, March 13, 2011.

44 Torey Holderith and Todd Wynn, "Renewable Energy Failure – Why Government Mandates Don't Work And What They Will Do To Our Economy", cascadepolicy.org.

45 Charles Abbott, "House Bill Extends Ethanol Tax Breaks To 2016", planetark.org, March 26, 2010.

46 "Reinstated: The Buck is Back", biodieselmagazine.com, January 12, 2011.

47 "Can This Green Stuff End Our Addiction To Oil?", biocominstitute.org, March 8, 2011.

48 Jason Dearen, "Calif. wants third of its power renewable by 2020", scpr.org, September 23, 2010.

49 Patrick McGreevy, "Gov. Brown signs law requiring 33% of energy be renewable by 2010", articles.latimes.com, April 13, 2011.

50 Clive Matthew-Wilson, "The Emperor's New Car", dogandlemon.com, 2010.

51 Iris Kuo, "Is one million electric cars by 2015 too ambitious?", reuters.com, February 10, 2011.

52 Ted Sickinger, "Oregon's electric car charging network is behind schedule", oregonlive.com, May 19, 2011.

53 Kenneth Green, lead author, "Media Release – Green Jobs, The European Experience", fcpp.org, April 26, 2011.

54 Hazel Healy, "Spain slashes solar energy subsidies", dw-world.de, September 9, 2010.

55 "Australia to Reduce Funding for Solar Projects Program", sfgate.com, May 18, 2011.

56 Steve LeBlanc, "Solar company that got $58M leaving Massachusetts", boston.com, January 11, 2011.

57 Molly Young, "SoloPower to announce plans for $340 million North Portland solar power plant", oregonlive.com, May 12, 2011.

58 Richard Read, "After ditching Wilsonville, SoloPower gets a richer deal in Portland", oregonlive.com, May 14, 2011.

59 Timothy P. Carney, "U.S. taxpayers guarantee $2.1b loan to German firms", washingtonexaminer.com, April 20, 2011.

60 Molly Young, "Aurora-area solar farm reaps $20,000 a month from PGE program", oregonlive.com, July 10, 2011.

61 "Schedule 7 – Residential Service", portlandgeneral.com, July 2011.

Chapter 7: Obsession with the Environment

1 Ken Gregory, "Climate Change Science", friendsofscience.org, May 21, 2011.

2 "Long Debate Ended Over Cause, Demise Of Ice Ages – May Also Help Predict Future", oregonstate.edu, August 6, 2009.

3 Christopher C. Horner, "The Politically Incorrect Guide to Global Warming and Environmentalism", 2007.

4 Gordon Fulks, "Climate science: The real reason we need to worry", oregonlive.com, December 27, 2010.

5 Paul Hudson, "Winter 2010-2011: Cold and dry – as forecast!", bbc.co.uk, March 2, 2011.

6 Ibid.

7 Graham Tibbetts, "Scientist sign petition denying man-made global warming", telegraph.co.uk, May 30, 2008.

8 "Obama implores Senate to pass climate bill", msnbc.msn.com, June 27, 2009.

9 Edward Felker, "Rep. Kaptur gets $3.5 billion sweetener in climate bill", washingtontimes.com, July 1, 2009.

10 Chip Knappenberger, "Climate Impacts of Waxman-Markey (the IPCC-based arithmetic of no gain)", masterresource.org, May 6, 2009.

11 William Beach, Karen Campbell, Ph.D., David Kreutzer, Ph.D., Ben Lieberman and Nicolas Loris, "The Economic Consequences of Waxman-Markey: An Analysis of the American Clean Energy and Security Act of 2009", heritage.org, August 6, 2009.

12 Ibid.

13 Ibid.

14 Ibid.

15 Ibid.

16 Christopher Booker, "Climate change: this is the worst scientific scandal of our generation", telegraph.co.uk, November 28, 2009.

17 James Murray, "Senate votes down Australian cap-and-trade bill", businessgreen.com, December 2, 2009.

18 Henry Chu, "British climate researchers had high scientific standards, review finds", articles.latimes.com, July 8, 2010.

19 "U.N.: Himalayan glaciers warning not backed up by evidence", usatoday.com, February 9, 2010.

20 Christi Parsons and Jim Tankersley, "EPA takes reins on climate change", articles.chicagotribune.com.

21 Janet Raloff, "EPA issues greenhouse-gas rules for new factories and more", sciencenews.org, May 13, 2010.

22 Stephanie Condon, "Kerry, Lieberman Unveil Bill to 'Change the Face of American Energy", cbsnews.com, May 12, 2010.

23 John M. Broder, "Graham Pulls Support for Major Senate Climate Bill", nytimes.com, April 24, 2010.

24 Steve Everley, "Senators Unveil New 1,000-Page Gas Tax", americansolutions.com, May 12, 2010.

25 Ibid.

26 "Claims island of plastic waste twice the size of Texas is floating in the Pacific are 'false'", dailymail.co.uk, January 6, 2011.

27 "Oceanic 'Garbage Patch' Not Nearly As Big As Portrayed In Media", oregonstate.edu, January 4, 2011.

28 "Republican Lawmaker Ends Pelosi's House Composting Program", foxnews.com, January 25, 2011.

Chapter 8: Health Care

1 Terence P. Jeffrey, "Congress Votes to Socialize Health Care in United States", cnsnews.com, March 22, 2010.

2 Sally C. Pipes, "Health 'Reformers' Ignore Facts", online.wsj.com, March 6, 2009.

3 "House Democrats unveil $894 billion health care bill", articles.cnn.com, October 29, 2009.

4 Ezra Klein, "The $900 billion mistake", voices.washingtonpost.com, November 11, 2009.

5 "House Democrats unveil $894 billion health care bill", articles.cnn.com, October 29, 2009.

6 Neal Boortz, "Want Some Medicare Cost History?", boortz.com, May 26, 2011.

7 CBO analysis, cbo.gov, October 29, 2009.

8 Janet Adamy, "House Leaders Unveil Health Bill", online.wsj.com, October 30, 2009.

9 "Dems Plotting Health Bill Seek $245B for Doctors", foxnews.com, July 21, 2009.

10 Carrie Budoff Brown, "Harry Reid: Democrats reach 'broad agreement'", politico.com, December 10, 2009.

11 Conn Carroll, "The Mother of All Public Options", blog.heritage.org, December 10, 2009.

12 Glen Enloe, "White House threatens to close of US Strategic Command air base – some dare call it treason", examiner.com, December 17, 2009.

13 Rajesh Rajagopalan, "Harry Reid's 'Senator Ben Nelson 60th Healthcare vote purchase' – The 49 state tax payer funder bribe", examiner.com, December 19, 2009.

14 Kate Pickert, "What if All 50 States Get Ben Nelson's Medicaid Deal?", time.com, January 15, 2010.

15 Dana Milbank, "Sweeteners for the South", washingtonpost.com, November 22, 2009.

16 Brian Montopoli, "Tallying the Health Care Bill's Giveaways", cbsnews.com, December 21, 2009.

17 Carl Campanile, "Unions will dodge O's health tax", nypost.com, January 15, 2010.

18 "Transcript Of Pelosi, House Democratic Leaders' Press Availability Today At Democratic Issues Conference", democraticleader.gov, January 15, 2010.

19 Jordan Fabian, "Sanders withdraws single-payer healthcare bill amendment", thehill.com, December 16, 2009.

20 Jeffrey Young, "Final Senate healthcare bill released by Reid in drive for 60 votes", thehill.com, December 19, 2009.

21 CBO analysis, cbo.gov, March 11, 2010.

22 "Legislative Notice No. 28, H.R. 3590: The Quality, Affordable Health Care for All Americans Act", rpc.senate.gov, December 2, 2009.

23 Paul Krugman, "Do the Right Thing", nytimes.com, January 21, 2010.

24 David Jackson, "Obama unveils health care plan that combines Senate and House bills", content.usatoday.com, February 22, 2010.

25 Chip Reid, "At Health Care Summit, More Pomp Than Pith", cbsnews.com, February 26, 2010.

26 Edwin Mora, "Rep. Sessions: 'Slaughter Rule' to Pass Health Care With No Up-Down Vote on Bill is Unconstitutional", cnsnews.com, March 17, 2010.

27 "Obama: 'Procedural' Spat Over Health Bill Vote Doesn't Worry Me", foxnews.com, March 17, 2010.

28 "CBO's Analysis of the Major Health Care Legislation Enacted in March 2010", cbo.gov, March 30, 2011.

29 Timothy P. Carney, "Student loans get the Obamacare treatment", washingtonexaminer.com, March 19, 2010

30 "Americans Like Their Coverage: High Satisfaction with Quality and Current Coverage", americanhealthsolutions.org, August 3, 2009.

31 Philip Klein, "The Myth of the 46 Million", spectator.org, March 20, 2009.

32 Ibid.

33 Byron York, "Obama: I used to say 47 million uninsured. Now, it's 30 million", washingtonexaminer.com, September 9, 2009.

34 Christina Wijfjes-Smit, "Health care reform to cover illegal immigrant?", examiner.com, August 12, 2009.

35 David Weinberger, "Medicair: Largest Denier Of Health Care Claims", blog.heritage.org, October 6, 2009.

36 "Expanding Medicare Would Punish Health Care Providers, Raise Taxes, Critics Say", foxnews.com, December 11, 2009.

37 Stanley Feld, MD, "Why Physicians Are Going To Stop Accepting Medicare", getbetterhealth.com, January 26, 2010.

38 Christopher Neefus, "Nearly One-Third of Doctors Could Leave Medicine if Health-Care Reform Bill Passes, According to Survey Reported in New England Journal of Medicine", cnsnews.com, March 15, 2010.

39 Karl Rove, "How to Stop Socialized Health Care", online.wsj.com, June 11, 2009.

40 Michael Barone, "Video proof: Obama wants a single-payer system", washingtonexaminer.com, August 9, 2009.

41 "HHS Sec: I'm for Single-Payer System", loudobbs.com, October 20, 2009.

42 Jeffrey H. Anderson, "Insurers' Profits Aren't the Problem", nationalreview.com, February 24, 2010.

43 "Obama challenges GOP critics on health care", msnbc.msn.com, July 20, 2009.

44 Calvin Woodward, "Fact check: Health insurance companies' profits not so fat", washingtonexaminer.com, October 26, 2009.

45 Andrea Fuller, "Show Us The Money; Checking Insurers' Wallets", query.nytimes.com, August 20, 2009.

46 Joshua Dunn, Ph.D. and D. Wilson, "Economics of Play-or-Pay Mandates in Health Care Reform Bills", heritage.org, August 28, 2009.

47 Shubham Singhal, Jeris Stueland and Drew Ungerman, "How US health care reform will effect employee benefits", mckinseyquarterly.com, June 2011.

48 Sally C. Pipes, "The Truth About Obamacare", igs.berkely.edu, November 18, 2010.

49 Scott Atlas, "10 Surprising Facts about American Health Care", ncpa.org, March 24, 2009.

50 Pericles K., "Greek Health System Opts for Amputation as Money-Saver", dailycaller.com, October 11, 2010.

51 Betsy McCaughey, "Obama's Health Rationer-in-Chief", online.wsj.com, August 27, 2009.

52 Nancy Morgan, "Who's minding the store?", examiner.com, August 28, 2009.

53 John Boehner, "SOTU FACT: ObamaCare Will Increase the Deficit, Repeal Will Save Taxpayers Billions", speaker.gov, January 25, 2011.

54 Michelle Andrews, "When Preventive Care Costs More", prescriptions.blogs.nytimes.com, September 3, 2009.

55 Charles Krauthammer, "The Great 'Prevention' Myth", washintonpost.com, August 14, 2009.

56 Pat Wechsler, "States Sue Over Overhaul That Will Bust State Budgets (Update 2)", bloomberg.com, March 23, 2010.

57 Sally C. Pipes, "New Health Care Law Cripples State Budgets", forbes.com, May 9, 2011.

58 Michael Barone, "Gangster Government Stifles Criticism of Obamacare", rasmussenreports.com, September 13, 2010.

59 Joe McKendrick, "Harvard study says computerization costs hospitals more than it saves", smartplanet.com, December 1, 2009.

60 "AT&T Plans $1 Billion Charge for Health Care", nytimes.com, March 26, 2010.

61 David A. Patten, "Obamacare's Prescription for Disaster: $14 Billion Cost to Industry", newsmax.com, March 31, 2010.

62 Robert Pear, "Obama Returns to End-of-Life Plan That Caused Stir", nytimes.com, December 25, 2010.

63 Doug Powers, "Those 'Death Panels'? Bush's Fault", michellemalkin.com, December 27, 2010.

64 "Analysis: Gov't Health Care Already Here", cbsnews.com, February 10, 2010.

65 "Income, Poverty and Health Insurance Coverage in the United States: 2008", census.gov, September 2009.

66 "United States Preventive Services Task Force", topics.nytimes.com, November 20, 2009.

67 Pam Belluck, "As Health Plan Falters, Maine Explores Changes", nytimes.com, April 30, 2007.

68 "Universal coverage? First, look at the disaster in Massachusetts", washingtonexaminer.com, January 11, 2009.

69 Julian Pecquet, "HHS approves 200 more new healthcare reform waivers", thehill.com, May 13, 2011.

70 Kevin Sack, "Battle Over Health Care Law Shifts to Federal Appellate Courts", nytimes.com, May 8, 2011.

71 "House Republicans Vote to Overturn ObamaCare in Symbolic Move", foxnews.com, January 19, 2011.

72 "Senate Votes Down GOP Effort to Repeal Health Care Law", foxnews.com, February 2, 2011

73 Parija B. Kavalanz, "Health care's big money wasters", money.cnn.com, August 10, 2009.

Chapter 9: Illegal Immigration

1 Michael Hoefer, Nancy Rytina and Bryan C. Baker, "Estimates of the Unauthorized Immigrant Population Residing in the United States: January 2009", dhs.gov, January 2010.

2 Jack Martin and Erik A. Ruark, "The Fiscal Burden Of Illegal Immigration On United States Taxpayers", fairus.org, July 2010, Revised February 2011.

3 Dave Gibson, "Janet Napolitano claims border is safe, as families flee cartel violence", examiner.com, February 2, 2011.

4 "Obama says the border fence is 'now basically complete'", politifact.com, May 16, 2011.

5 Barry Leibowitz, "$1.7 Billion Worth of Pot Seized, 100 Arrests, in California Drug Sweep", cbsnews.com, July 30, 2010.

6 Ibid.

7 "Homeland Security chief cancels costly virtual border fence", articles.cnn.com, January 14, 2011.

8 "Border Security, Preliminary Observations on Border Control Measures for the Southwest Border", gao.gov, February 15, 2011.

9 Jake Tapper, "White House: Senator Kyl Not Telling Truth About Immigration Reform Conversation", blogs.abcnews.com, June 21, 2010.

10 Amanda Carey, "McCain defends Kyl in immigration clash with Obama", dailycaller.com, June 22, 2010.

11 "Our Mission", dol.gov, as it read on June 5, 2011.

12 "Obama's Labor Secretary Reaches Out to Illegal Aliens With Paycheck Complaints", cnsnews.com, June 22, 2010.

13 "Yep. Reagan did the A-word", politifact.com, January 6, 2008.

14 http://abcnews.go.com/images/Politics/memo-on-alternatives-to-comprehensive-immigration-reform.pdf

15 "Arizona governor signs immigration enforcement bill", lasvegassun.com, April 23, 2010.

16 Quinn Bowman, "Arizona Immigration Law Has Broad Support Across U.S., New Polls Show", pbs.org, May 13, 2010.

17 Alex Fitzsimmons, "Media Mash: Hannity and Bozell Discuss MRC Study on Anti-Arizona Bias", mrctv.org, August 2, 2010.

18 "Obama 'Poorly Conceived' AZ Law Unfair to Hispanics", foxnews.com, April 28, 2010.

19 "AZ Gov Calls Obama 'Comic-in-Chief'", nation.foxnews.com, May 17, 2010.

20 "Holder Admits to Not Reading Arizona's Immigration Law Despite Criticizing It", foxnews.com, May 14, 2010.

21 "Napolitano Admits She Hasn't Read Arizona Immigration Law in 'Detail'", foxnews.com, May 18, 2010.

22 "White House, Democrats Applaud Mexican President Slamming Arizona Law", foxnews.com, May 20, 2010.

23 "Top Official Says Feds May Not Process Illegals Referred From Arizona", foxnews.com, May 21, 2010.

24 Jeremy Pelofsky and James Vicini, "Obama administration sues Arizona over immigration law", reuters.com, July 6, 2010.

25 "Holder Floats Possibility of Racial Profiling Suit Against Arizona", foxnews.com, July 11, 2010.

26 "Federal Judge Blocks Key Portions of Arizona Illegal Immigration Law", foxnews.com, July 28, 2010

27 "Supreme Court Upholds Arizona's Immigration Employer Sanctions Law", latino.foxnews.com, May 26, 2011.

Chapter 10: National Security

1 Rowan Scarborough, "Navy SEALs Face Assault Charges for Capturing Most-Wanted Terrorist", foxnews.com, November 25, 2009.

2 "Obama budget cuts target military funding", washingtontimes.com, May 8, 2009.

3 Lee Cary, "Obama's Civilian National Security Force", americanthinker.com, July 20, 2008.

4 Phil Stewart and Matt Spetalnick, "Obama limits U.S. use of nuclear arms", reuters.com, April 6, 2010.

5 Lucy Madison, "Rumsfeld: mistake to end enhanced interrogation", cbsnews.com, May 8, 2011.

6 Vanessa Buschschluter, "The Obama approach to interrogation", news.bbc.co.uk, January 29, 2009.

7 "Eric Holder Vows to Close Guantanamo", newsmax.com, May 9, 2011.

8 Jon Ward, "Obama releases memos detailing interrogations", washingtontimes.com, April 17, 2009.

9 Dana Chivvis, "Bush Admin. Official Criticizes CIA Probe", cbsnews.com, August 25, 2009.

10 "Holder Okays Criminal Probe of CIA", nation.foxnews.com, June 30, 2011.

11 "CIA chief: Waterboarding aided bin Laden raid", to-day.msnbc.msn.com, May 3, 2011.

12 "Remarks By The President On Osama Bin Laden", m.whitehouse.gov, May 2, 2011.

13 Ibid.

14 Huma Khan and Matthew Jaffe, "After Osama bin Laden's Death, Billions in U.S. Aid to Pakistan Questioned", abcnews.go.com, May 5, 2011.

15 Matthey Cole, Jim Sciutto, Lee Ferran and Brian Ross, "Osama Bin Laden Raid: Pakistan Hints China Wants a Peek at Secret Helicopter", abcnews.go.com, May 10, 2011.

16 "Obama's Missile Offense", online.wsj.com, September 18, 2009.

17 Ibid.

18 "Tentative Inspection Program Would Allow Russia to Visit U.S. Nuclear Sites", foxnews.com, October 13, 2009.

19 Steven Pifer, "Aspen Institute Congressional Program, Managing the U.S.-Russian Nuclear Relationship", brookings.edu, April 2011.

20 Ibid.

21 Baker Spring, "Sixteen Steps to Comprehensive Missile Defense: What the FY 2012 Budget Should Fund", heritage.org, May 3, 2011.

22 Desmond Butler and Donna Cassata, "Senate ratifies New START nuclear pact", washintontimes.com, December 22, 2010.

23 Louis Charbonneau, "Obama to chair historic UN council nuclear meeting", reuters.com, September 24, 2009.

24 "Iran: Nuclear plant is sited to thwart attack", msnbc.msn.com, September 29, 2009.

25 Siobhan Gorman, "U.S. Knew About Site for Years", online.wsj.com, September 26, 2009

26 Christopher Ruddy, "Gordon Brown vs. Obama on Iran", newsmax.com, September 20, 2009.

27 Con Coughlin, "Barack Obama is giving Iran the time it needs to build a nuclear bomb", telegraph.co.uk, May 21, 2009.

28 David E. Sanger and Thom Shanker, "Gates Says U.S. Lacks a Policy to Thwart Iran", nytimes.com, April 17, 2010.

29 "IAEA report on Iran likely to boost West's opposition to Tehran's fuel swap offer", foxnews.com, May 31, 2010.

30 "UN votes for new sanctions on Iran over nuclear issue", bbc.co.uk, June 9, 2010.

31 Thomas Erdbrink, 'Iran's Ahmadinejad faults sanctions, delays nuclear talk till late August", washingtonpost.com, June 29, 2010.

32 Rich Lowry, "The Great Iran Charade", nationalreview.com, April 6, 2010.

33 James Gordon Meek, "9/11 plotter Khalid Sheikh Mohammed, 4 other Gitmo detainees will stand trial in NY", articles.nydailynews.com, November 13, 2009.

34 Sean Hannity, "KSM Trial to Cost $200 million Per Year?", foxnews.com, January 8, 2010.

35 Doug Mataconis, "Terrorism Show Trial Ends With Near-Complete Acquittal", outsidethebeltway.com, November 18, 2010.

36 Jordy Yager, "In about-face, 9/11 mastermind to have Gitmo military trial", thehill.com, April 4, 2011.

37 Ibid.

38 Ibid.

39 Ana Campoy, Peter Sanders and Russell Gold, "Hash Browns, Then 4 Minutes of Chaos", online.wsj.com, November 9, 2009.

40 "Obama: 'Don't Jump to Conclusions' on Fort Hood Shooting", foxnews.com, November 6, 2009.

41 Mark Thompson, "The Fort Hood Report: Why No Mention of Islam?", time.com, January 20, 2010.

42 Michelle Malkin, "Clown alert: Janet Napolitano says 'the system worked;' Update: And now...J-No's about-(clown)face", michellemalkin.com, December 27, 2009.

43 "Napolitano concedes security system failed", usatoday.com, December 28, 2009.

44 Claudia Rosett, "Not So Isolated, And More Than Extremist", forbes.com, January 1, 2010.

45 "U.S. says airline terror suspect cooperating", msnbc.msn.com, February 2, 2010.

46 Thomas Joscelyn, "U.S. Won't Interrogate Top Al Qaeda Terrorist", weeklystandard.com, April 11, 2011.

47 "NASA Chief: Next Frontier Better Relations With Muslim World", foxnews.com, July 5, 2010.

48 Richard Adams, "Obama's mixed message on New York mosque helps no-one", guardian.co.uk.

49 "CNN Opinion Research Poll", i2.cdn.turner.com, August 6-10, 2010.

50 Richard Adams, "Obama's mixed message on New York mosque helps no-one", guardian.co.uk.

51 Russell Goldman, "Islamic Center Backers Won't Rule Out Taking Funds from Saudi Arabia, Iran", abcnews.go.com, August 18, 2010.

52 "Haunting Words From Imam Behind Ground Zero Mosque", foxnews.com, August 5, 2010.

53 "Ground Zero Mosque Imam: America Killed More Innocents Than Al Qaeda", foxnews.com, August 24, 2010.

54 Robert Farley, "Fact-Checking the 'Ground Zero mosque' debate", politifact.com, August 20, 2010.

55 Claudia Rosett, "Cashing in On Ground Zero", forbes.com, August 24, 2010.

56 Joshua Miller, "Moving Islamic Center 'Not' On the Table for Now, Backer Says", abcnews.go.com, August 22, 2010.

57 Kareem Fahim, "Islamic Center Seeks 9/11 Recovery Grants for Lower Manhattan", nytimes.com, November 22, 2010.

58 "Pelosi: Trace Mosque Opponents' Money Trail", newsmax.com, August 18, 2010.

59 Judson Berger, "What About the Ground Zero Church? Archdiocese Says Officials Abandoned Project", foxnews.com, August 17, 2010.

60 Jerry Markon, "Justice Department sues on behalf of Muslim teacher, triggering debate", washingtonpost.com, March 22, 2011.

61 Tim Shipman, "US to send up to 30,000 extra troops to Afghanistan next year", telegraph.co.uk, December 20, 2008.

62 Tim Reid and Tom Coghlan, "Barack Obama will send 17,000 extra troops to fight in Afghanistan", timesonline.co.uk, February 18, 2009.

63 "Remarks By The President On A New Strategy For Afghanistan And Pakistan", whitehouse.gov, March 27, 2009.

64 Jonathan S. Landay, John Walcott and Nancy A. Youssef, "Obama leaning toward 34,000 troops for Afghanistan", mcclatchydc.com, November 7, 2009.

65 Karen DeYoung, "Obama to let Pentagon deploy even more troops, but numbers remain murky", washingtonpost.com, December 3, 2009.

66 "U.S. troops battle both Taliban and their own rules", washingtontimes.com, November 16, 2009.

Chapter 11: Foreign Policy

1 Tom Baldwin, "Churchill bust casts shadow over special relationship with the US", timesonline.co.uk, January 31, 2009.

2 Claudia Rosett, "America and Syria", nationalreview.com, March 30, 2011.

3 James Taranto, "The Heat Is On", online.wsj.com, March 31, 2011.

4 Nidaa Hassan, "Syria death toll rises amid violent government crackdown on protests", guardian.co.uk, June 5, 2011.

5 Mark Landler, "U.S. Moves Cautiously Against Syrian Leaders", nytimes.com, April 29, 2011.

6 "Clinton: Bin Laden raid a watershed for Pakistan", cbsnews.com, May 27, 2011.

7 "U.S. Rep. Ron Paul Says 'the Arab and the Muslim nations' get twice as much foreign aid as Israel", politifact.com, May 21, 2011.

8 Josh Rogin, "Pakistan military aid safer than the economic aid", thecable.foreignpolicy.com, May 11, 2011.

9 Brett Schaeffer and Anthony Kim, "U.S. Foreign Aid Recipients and Voting at the United Nations", heritage.org, April 6, 2010.

10 Doug Powers, "The Spending Cut That Got Away: $20 Million for Sesame Street… in Pakistan?", michellemalkin.com, April 9, 2011.

11 Jake Tapper, "VP Biden Calls Egyptian President Mubarak an 'Ally' – and Would not Call Him a Dictator", blogs.abcnews.com, January 27, 2011.

12 Rick Baker, "Middle East Policy in Shambles", examiner.com, April 25, 2011.

13 "Muslim Publics Divided on Hamas and Hezbollah", pewresearch.org, December 2, 2010.

14 Victor Sharpe, "Obama Well Knows What Chaos He Has Unleashed", americanthinker.com, February 5, 2011.

15 Lorenzo Vidino, "Five myths about the Muslim Brotherhood", washingtonpost.com, March 6, 2011.

16 Daveed Gartenstein-Ross, "MAS's Muslim Brotherhood Problem", weeklystandard.com, May 25, 2005.

17 Clifford D. May, "The Taboo of the intellectuals", nationalreview.com, August 12, 2010.

18 Ibid.

19 "Why is Obama promoting the Muslim Brotherhood?", cfns.org, February 7, 2011.

20 John Ellis and Grace Wyler, "Today's Politics Headlines in 60 Seconds", businessinsider.com, February 2, 2011.

21 "Muslim Brotherhood Members to Attend Obama's Cairo Speech", foxnews.com, June 3, 2009.

22 "Obama seeks 'new beginning' in Muslim world", msnbc.msn.com, June 4, 2009.

23 Ibid.

24 "Obama's Intel Chief: Muslim Brotherhood Non-Violent, 'Secular' Group", foxnews.com, February 11, 2011.

25 "Report: Ex-Minister Says Gadhafi Ordered Lockerbie Bombing", blogs.wsj.com, February 23, 2011.

26 Glenn Beck, "President Obama Breaks His Silence on Libya", foxnews.com, February 23, 2011.

27 Doug Powers, "Gaddafi Was Jeremiah Wright Before Jeremiah Wright Was Cool", michellemalkin.com, February 24, 2011.

28 Olesya Dmitracova, Adrian Croft and Janet Lawrence, "Clinton says Libya no-fly zone should not be U.S.-led", us.mobile.reuters.com, March 8, 2011.

29 Helene Cooper and Steven Lee Meyers, "Obama Takes Hard Line With Libya After Shift by Clinton", nytimes.com, March 18, 2011.

30 Ibid.

31 "U.S. intends to step back in Libya mission, but timing uncertain", articles.cnn.com, March 21, 2011.

32 "NATO takes full command of Libya air operations", cbsnews.com, March 30, 2011.

33 "White House: Libya Fight is Not War, It's 'Kinetic Military Action'", nation.foxnews.com, March 23, 2011.

34 Paul Harris, "Robert Gates: no US 'boots on ground' in Libya", guardian.co.uk, March 31, 2011.

35 Stephanie Condon, "Obama: Qaddafi must go, but current Libya mission focused on humanitarian efforts", cbsnews.com, March 21, 2011.

36 "U.S.: Gaddafi not target of allied military action", reuters.com, March 21, 2011.

37 Charles Krauthammer, "The Professor's War", nationalreview.com, March 25, 2011.

38 Amanda Marshall, "'Flickers' of Al Qaeda in Libya Aren't New", foxnews.com, March 30, 2011.

39 Nic Robertson and Paul Cruickshank, "New jihad code threatens al Qaeda", edition.cnn.com, November 10, 2009.

40 Praveen Swami, Nick Squires and Duncan Gardham, "Lybian rebel commander admits his fighters have al-Qaeda links", tele-graph.co.uk, March 25, 2011.

41 Paul Cruickshank and Tim Lister, "Energized Muslim Brotherhood in Libya eyes a prize", articles.cnn.com, March 25, 2011.

42 Mark Hosenball, "Exclusive: Obama authorizes secret help for Libya rebels", reuters.com, March 30, 2011.

43 "Security Council imposes sanctions on Libyan authorities in bid to stem violent repression", un.org, February 26, 2011.

44 Jake Tapper, Jon Karl and Russell Goldman, "President Obama Authorizes Covert Help for Libyan Rebels", abcnews.go.com, March 30, 2011.

45 Jonathan S. Landay, "U.S. wants others to arm, train Libyan rebels", mcclatchydc.com, March 31, 2011.

46 Charles S. Faddis, "Lesson for Libya fight: You go to war to win", articles.cnn.com, March 27, 2011.

47 "Obama OKs use of armed drone aircraft in Libya", cbsnews.com, April 21, 2011.

48 "Britain, France, Italy Sending Military Advisers to Libay; Wildfires Hit Texas", pbs.org, April 20, 2011.

49 Rod Nordland and Steven Lee Meyers, "Libya Could Become Sta-lemate, Top U.S. Military Officer Says", nytimes.com, April 22, 2011.

50 "Libya sells most of its oil to Europe, not China", politifact.com, April 11, 2011.

51 Justin Fishel, "As Cost of Libyan War Rises, Gates Scolds NATO for Not Pulling its Weight", foxnews.com, June 10, 2011.

52 "Obama: Mideast Standoff 'Unsustainable'", msnbc.msn.com, June 9, 2010.

53 "Obama Administration Welcomes U.N. Flotilla Probe, Downplays Panel's Authority", foxnews.com, August 2, 2010.

54 Mark Landler and Steven Lee Myers, "Obama Sees '67 Borders as Starting Point for Peace Deal", nytimes.com, May 19, 2011.

55 Steve Lee Meyers, "Divisions Are Clear as Obama and Netanyahu Discuss Peace", nytimes.com, May 20, 2011.

56 "Berlin remembers fall of the Wall", news.bbc.co.uk, November 9, 2009.

57 "NOT free: Iran dashes hope that woman sentenced to be stoned to death for adultery has been released", dailymail.co.uk, December 11, 2010.

58 "Philip J. Crowley/Assistant Secretary/Daily Press Brief-
ing/Washington, DC /July 1, 2010", state.gov.
59 "Report of the United States of America, Submitted to the U.N.
High Commissioner for Human Rights, In Conjunction with the
Universal Periodic Review", aka "A more perfect union, a more
perfect world", state.gov.